THE DINNER PARTY COOK BOOK

BY THE SUNSET EDITORIAL STAFF

Annabel Post, *Home Economics Editor, Sunset Magazine* *Staff Home Economists:* Shirley Sarvis

Edited by Dorothy Krell © 1962 by Lane Book Company. Library of Congress Number 62-17766. First Edition.

Designed and illustrated by William S. Shields

LANE BOOK COMPANY, MENLO PARK, CALIFORNIA

THE DINNER PARTY COOK BOOK

A *Sunset* BOOK

Jerry DiVecchio, Carol Flood

First Printing October 1962.

CONTENTS

The Art of the Dinner Party

A SUCCESSFUL DINNER PARTY has flair. From the moment guests enter the door, they sense the festive mood that has been created by an imaginative hostess who has skillfully blended many small elements of design into one exciting, harmonious whole. The decorations, the service, the table setting, every item on the menu—all have been thoughtfully combined to produce a dinner party that has all of the balance and color and impact of a masterpiece on canvas ⚘ This kind of dinner party does not just happen. Although the dinner party of today is far less formal than the one of the past, its very informality calls for a pleasant, relaxed atmosphere that can be attained only if the hostess has given careful thought to every detail long before the first guest arrives ⚘ The modern hostess, with a busy daily schedule, generally does not have the time to devote many days to planning and staging an original dinner party. Yet today's entertaining needs demand menus to suit many situations—from the very elegant sit-down dinner to the opposite extreme of casual outdoor dining; and the perfect hostess wants to make each of these occasions different and memorable ⚘ We believe that this book will open new vistas for both beginning and experienced hostesses. These are new menus that can be tried with confidence. Each dinner was carefully planned and prepared by *Sunset* home economists and served to a discriminating panel of invited guests. No matter which dinner you choose to serve, you can be certain that the complete design is a proven success and that each individual recipe is perfect ⚘ The young hostess, entertaining at her first dinner party, can use any one of these dinners to impress her first dinner party guests with her talents as cook and hostess. The experienced hostess is certain to find inspiration for unusual dinner parties that will bring new excitement to her entertaining.

A Springtime Buffet

OFFER YOUR GUESTS a cup of hot soup to sip as a prelude to this meal. They might like to inspect spring's arrival in your garden while you add the final touches to the buffet ⚘ You can combine the soup ingredients ahead of time and then heat the soup just before serving. Start cooking the lamb an hour before you plan to serve dinner. (Although lamb riblets aren't usually considered company fare, they make tempting crisp morsels when broiled and then baked as directed here.) ⚘ The stuffed cabbage rolls can be prepared ahead and then simmered for 20 minutes just before serving. Make the salad dressing ahead and prepare the salad fruits and greens; arrange and dress the salad at the last minute ⚘ The Imperial Mousse can be made the night before or the morning of the party. Chill it in the refrigerator; unmold and add the topping at serving time.

SPRING POTATO SOUP

GRILLED LAMB RIBLETS

STUFFED CABBAGE ROLLS

MINTED CITRUS SALAD

DARK RYE BREAD

IMPERIAL MOUSSE

9

SPRING POTATO SOUP

    1 can (10¼ oz.) frozen potato soup
    1 can (1 pt. 4 oz.) chicken broth
    1 cup milk
       Green onions

Combine potato soup, chicken broth, and milk. Whirl in blender and heat (or just combine ingredients and heat). Sprinkle each serving with thin rings of green onion tops. Makes 6 servings.

GRILLED LAMB RIBLETS

    4 to 5 pounds lamb riblets (about ¾ pound
       or 4 to 5 ribs per serving)
    ¾ teaspoon each seasoned salt, garlic salt,
       salt, and pepper
    2 tablespoons Worcestershire

Cut lamb riblets between each rib. Arrange on a broiler rack. Combine remaining ingredients; brush on lamb. Place lamb about 6 inches below heat source, and broil 20 to 30 minutes, turning to brown, on all sides. Place in moderately hot oven (375°), and bake for 30 minutes. Serve to eat as finger food. Makes 6 servings.

STUFFED CABBAGE ROLLS

    12 medium-sized cabbage leaves
        Boiling water
     3 cups finely chopped cabbage
     ¼ cup minced onion
     4 tablespoons butter or margarine
    1½ cups cooked rice
     6 tablespoons grated Romano or
        Parmesan cheese
    1½ teaspoons salt
     ½ teaspoon freshly ground pepper
    1¼ cups tomato juice

Immerse cabbage leaves in boiling water for about 3 minutes. Set aside to drain. Sauté chopped cabbage and minced onion in butter until tender. Add rice, cheese, salt, and pepper. Divide this mixture among the cabbage leaves. Fold in sides and roll to enclose filling; fasten with toothpicks. To heat and serve, place rolls in a single layer in a shallow saucepan, add tomato juice, and simmer for 20 minutes. Makes 6 servings.

Cabbage leaves are stuffed with filling of chopped cabbage, minced onion, rice, cheese, salt, and pepper. Leaves are tightly rolled, then secured with toothpicks and heated in tomato juice.

MINTED CITRUS SALAD

- 2 cups fresh grapefruit sections
- 2 or 3 large oranges, peeled and thinly sliced
  Salad greens (leaf lettuce, butter lettuce, or romaine tips)
  Mint leaves
- 3 tablespoons mint jelly
- 1 tablespoon honey
  Grated peel and juice of 1 lime
  Juice of 1 lemon

Arrange grapefruit sections and orange slices on a bed of salad greens on individual serving plates or in a large salad bowl. Garnish with mint leaves. Blend together mint jelly, honey, grated lime peel, lime juice, and lemon juice. Ladle some of the dressing on each serving. Makes 6 servings.

IMPERIAL MOUSSE

- 1 envelope (1 tablespoon) unflavored gelatin
- ½ cup cold water
- ½ cup boiling water
- 2 cups (1 pint) commercial sour cream
- ½ cup sugar
- ½ teaspoon almond extract
- 1 teaspoon vanilla
  Pineapple ice cream sauce, fresh crushed berries, or jelly or jam

Soften gelatin in cold water. Add boiling water and stir until gelatin is dissolved. Blend in sour cream, sugar, almond extract, and vanilla. Pour into a 1-quart mold. Chill until firm, about 3 hours. Unmold and serve with pineapple ice cream sauce, fresh crushed berries, or jelly or jam of your choice. Makes 6 servings.

Candlelight Dinner

THIS DINNER PARTY combines a buffet with a sit-down dinner. Guests serve themselves from a candlelit sideboard, then move along to a set table. Coffee service and dessert are arranged on a separate side table The main-dish casserole is easy to serve and can be made the day before the party. Rounding out the menu are two salads (one a make-ahead gelatin mold), and an overnight refrigerator dessert. Rolls are from the bakery. Almost the entire dinner can be prepared a day ahead.

TOMATO ASPIC RING WITH AVOCADO

SOUR CREAM HERB DRESSING

TOSSED GREEN SALAD

CHICKEN DIVAN   BUTTERFLAKE ROLLS

ORANGE REFRIGERATOR CAKE

TOMATO ASPIC RING WITH AVOCADO

Avocado half circles, arranged in a scalloped design, make this basic tomato aspic very decorative. The tangy sour cream dressing is a good complement.

> 3 envelopes (3 tablespoons)
>   unflavored gelatin
> ½ cup cold water
> 5 cups tomato juice
>   Few celery leaves
> 1 bay leaf
> 8 peppercorns
> 6 whole cloves
> 1 small onion, sliced
> 1 tablespoon sugar
> 1 teaspoon salt
> ¾ teaspoon Worcestershire
> 1½ tablespoons each lemon juice
>   and vinegar
> 1 large or 2 small avocados
>   Lemon juice for dipping avocado slices

Soften gelatin in cold water. Put tomato juice in a saucepan with celery leaves, bay leaf, peppercorns, cloves, onion, sugar, salt, Worcestershire, lemon juice and vinegar. Bring to a boil and simmer for 10 minutes; strain. Add softened gelatin and stir until dissolved. Chill until thick, but not set.

Peel and halve avocado, then slice crosswise into thin slices, and dip each one in lemon juice. Arrange half the avocado slices in a scalloped pattern in the bottom of a 9-inch ring mold. Gently pour in half the thickened aspic; chill until set. Arrange remaining avocado slices in a layer over the molded aspic; and pour in the remaining syrupy aspic mixture. Chill until set. Serve with sour cream dressing (recipe follows). Makes 8 to 10 servings.

Sour Cream Herb Dressing:

> 1 cup (½ pint) commercial sour cream
> 2 tablespoons red wine vinegar
> 1 teaspoon sugar
> ½ teaspoon each salt and celery seed
>   Dash of pepper
> ¼ teaspoon crumbled dried thyme

Blend together the sour cream, vinegar, sugar, salt, celery seed, pepper, and thyme. Turn into a sauce bowl and chill. Makes 1 cup.

CHICKEN DIVAN

To simplify the preparation of this rather complicated, well-known casserole, cook the chicken, broccoli, and sauces a day ahead and refrigerate them separately. Just before the party, assemble the casserole and whip and fold the cream into the sauce.

> 3 packages (1 lb. each) chicken breasts
> 2 cups water
> 1 tablespoon salt
>   Celery leaves
> 1 medium-sized onion, quartered
> 2 pounds fresh broccoli, or 2 packages
>   (12 oz. each) frozen broccoli
> 2 cups medium white sauce (made with
>   half milk and half chicken stock)
> ½ cup hollandaise sauce
> ¾ teaspoon salt
> 3 tablespoons sherry
> 1 teaspoon Worcestershire
> 1 cup (¼ lb.) grated Parmesan cheese
> ½ cup whipping cream

Simmer chicken in water with the 1 tablespoon salt, celery leaves, and onion until tender, about 25 minutes. Let cool. Remove skin and bones and slice the chicken meat. Separate broccoli into flowerets, and cook in boiling salted water until tender, about 15 minutes.

Combine the white sauce, hollandaise sauce, the ¾ teaspoon salt, sherry, and Worcestershire. Butter a large, shallow casserole, and arrange broccoli spears, spoke-fashion, around the edge; place the remainder in the center of the dish. Sprinkle with half the grated cheese. Arrange sliced chicken on top. Whip cream and fold into the combined sauces; spoon over the chicken. Sprinkle with the remaining cheese.

Bake in a hot oven (400°) for 20 minutes (be careful not to overcook). Then place about 5 inches under the broiler and broil until lightly browned and bubbly. Makes 6 to 8 servings.

ORANGE REFRIGERATOR CAKE

This four-layer refrigerator cake is almost delicate enough to be classed as a pudding—each bite melts in your mouth. Be sure the sauce is hot when you fill the cake so the layers will soak it all up.

>   2 *eight-inch sponge cake layers*
>   3 *eggs, separated*
>   ½ *cup sugar*
>   1 *tablespoon cornstarch*
>   *Dash of salt*
>   1 *cup orange juice*
>   5 *teaspoons lemon juice*
>   1 *cup whipping cream*
>   *Preserved orange slices or fresh orange*
>   *sections for garnish*

Slice each cake layer in half horizontally, making 4 layers in all. Beat egg whites until stiff, but not dry. In the top part of the double boiler, mix together the sugar, cornstarch, and salt; stir in orange juice, lemon juice, and slightly beaten egg yolks. Cook over hot water, stirring constantly, until thickened; remove sauce from heat.

Fold beaten egg whites into the orange sauce while it is still hot. Spread filling between the cake layers (use a spatula to spread excess filling onto sides of cake until all has been absorbed into the cake). Refrigerate overnight. Several hours before serving time, whip cream and sweeten to taste. Frost top and sides of cake. Refrigerate until time to serve. Then garnish top of cake with preserved orange slices or orange segments. Makes 8 to 10 servings.

Coffee service and dessert of layered sponge cake with orange filling and whipped cream frosting are arranged on side table. Nosegay of petunias and geraniums adds festive note.

Buffet dinner is set up on a candlelit sideboard so guests can help themselves to Chicken Divan, avocado-tomato aspic, mixed green salad, buttery rolls.

A South American Soup Party

IF YOU FAVOR small informal dinners with your guests actively participating, then you may find a South American soup party an interesting new idea. The idea is simple, but unique. You cook the various ingredients for the soup meal in one pot, in the same stock, but not all at the same time. When it is time to serve, the clear stock is brought to the table in a tureen. Meat, vegetables, fruit, sauce, whatever the soup is to contain, are in serving bowls or plates. After the hostess has ladled broth into each guest's large soup bowl, the guest puts some of each of the other ingredients into his bowl as these are passed ⥼ In South America, soup is almost always a separate course at noon and evening—either meal likely to be a five- or six-course affair. (A vegetable-filled soup actually takes the place of vegetables served with the

CRISP GREENS SALAD

CHICKEN SOUP

BREAD STICKS

DULCE DE LECHE

17

entrée in a typical meal.) But even when the complete soup is brought to you, as it would be in South America, the various components keep their identity in the bowl of broth.

One of these hearty soups is just right to serve as a main dish here, where we are accustomed to lighter meals than some of our neighbors south of the border. You might start the meal with a very simple first-course salad. Serve bread sticks to accompany the main soup course, and conclude with dessert and coffee.

Wine with the meal would be a pleasant addition, and in keeping with the South Americans' customs. They would always have on the table a hot red pepper sauce called *ahi*. You might provide Tabasco for guests who enjoy plenty of "heat" in their foods; but without this addition, the soup is not very highly seasoned.

CRISP GREENS SALAD

Break 1 or 2 kinds of crisp greens into a chilled salad bowl. Toss with dressing made of 3 parts salad oil mixed with 1 part vinegar and salt and pepper.

CHICKEN SOUP

    1 stewing hen, 4 or 5 pounds
    3 quarts water
    3 stalks celery
    1 medium-sized onion
   10 whole black peppercorns
    1 tablespoon salt
    2 bay leaves
    2 carrots
    2 cups each green peas and French-cut
         green beans (fresh, frozen, or canned)
    4 green onions, finely chopped
    ½ teaspoon oregano
    1 small jar (2 oz.) pimientos, chopped
    1 small head iceberg lettuce, finely chopped
    1 whole orange, thinly sliced
       Onion sauce

Put whole chicken into a Dutch oven or other large pan. Add water, whole stalks of celery, whole onion, peppercorns, salt, bay leaves, and whole carrots. Cover and bring to a boil. Remove scum that comes to the top. Reduce heat and simmer for 1½ to 2 hours or until chicken is tender. Remove chicken and strain stock. Put stock back into pan. (Discard vegetables cooked with chicken.) Add peas, beans, green onions, oregano, pimientos, and lettuce. Cover and simmer for 15 to 20 minutes. Meanwhile, remove chicken from bones and cut into thin strips. Place chicken on warm platter and garnish with orange slices. Keep warm until ready to serve. Prepare the Onion Sauce (see below).

To serve, remove vegetables from soup, drain, and put into serving dish. Pour soup stock into tureen or bowl. At the table, after this broth is served in individual bowls, pass the vegetables, then the chicken (each person takes an orange slice, too), and last the Onion Sauce. Makes 6 generous servings.

Onion Sauce:

    2 tablespoons olive oil or salad oil
    2 medium-sized red or yellow onions,
         thinly sliced
       Dash Tabasco
    2 tablespoons chopped parsley
    ½ teaspoon salt

Heat oil in a small pan. Separate onion slices into rings, and add to oil with Tabasco, parsley, and salt. Cook over low heat for about 5 minutes until onions are limp but not browned. Bring to the table in a bowl.

DULCE DE LECHE

This deliciously smooth, almost candy-like sweet is a popular South American dessert. Its name, *Dulce de Leche*, means "sweet of milk." It's an easy dessert to make if you can be close to the kitchen for a few hours. Just two ingredients, milk and sugar, are cooked at low heat until thickened to the creamy consistency of fondant. A bit of patient tending is the only other requirement.

In a heavy pan over high heat, bring 1 quart milk and 2 cups sugar to a full boil. (For a richer version, use light cream instead of milk; for a darker, caramel-like dulce, substitute ¼ cup brown sugar for an equal amount of white sugar.) Immediately reduce heat, and cook, reducing heat as necessary during the cooking to keep the mixture just simmering gently (do not boil). When mixtures takes on a caramel color and thickens to the consistency of a caramel topping or light pudding, remove from heat and cool. Cooking will take 5 to 6 hours, probably a little less if you use cream instead of milk. If desired, flavor with 1 teaspoon vanilla or a drop of almond extract when you remove it from the heat. Set in the freezer or refrigerate to chill (it becomes a little firmer in the freezer). Makes 6 generous servings (about 3 tablespoons are sufficient for one serving; use tiny containers such as cordial glasses, nut cups, or Japanese sake cups. Top with chopped nuts if you wish. Dulce de leche keeps a week in the refrigerator or freezer.

Four-Course Steak Dinner

THIS STEAK DINNER is served in four courses. A miniature barbecue or hibachi would be fine for cooking the bacon-wrapped tidbits that accompany the before-dinner beverages. The curried chicken soup and sesame toast strips are served at the table, followed by the main course of pan-broiled steak with bean sprouts and toasted buns. Warm deep-dish peach pie, topped with thick sweet or sour cream, tops off the meal The soup can be made early in the day and chilled. Other preparations are simple and you'll probably want to do them just before dinner time. If you want to make the dessert ahead, cover it with foil and warm it for about 10 minutes in a moderate oven (350°) before serving.

BACON APPETIZERS

COLD CREAM OF CURRIED CHICKEN SOUP

SESAME TOAST

PAN-BROILED STEAK WITH BEAN SPROUTS

TOASTED BUNS

DEEP-DISH PEACH PIE WITH ALMONDS

BACON APPETIZERS

Cubes of lobster, scallops, shrimp, stuffed olives, water chestnuts, and chicken livers are all good to use for these appetizers. Wrap them in bacon, fasten with toothpicks, and broil over charcoal until the bacon is crisp.

COLD CREAM OF CURRIED CHICKEN SOUP

¼ *cup minced onion*
2 *tablespoons butter*
1 *tablespoon curry powder*
2 *cups rich chicken stock*
2 *cups whipping cream*
3 *egg yolks*
  Salt and pepper to taste
1 *large apple, finely diced*
  Juice of ½ lemon

Cook onion in butter until wilted; stir in curry powder and then chicken stock. Simmer for 5 minutes, add cream, and bring just to a boil. Beat the egg yolks slightly and beat ½ cup of the hot stock into them slowly. Combine mixtures and cook gently until thickened, but do not boil. Season with salt and pepper and chill. Serve garnished with the diced apple that has been soaked in lemon juice. Makes 6 servings.

SESAME TOAST

Heat sesame seeds in a heavy skillet, stirring, until brown. Sprinkle them generously on buttered toast strips. Serve with hot soup.

PAN-BROILED STEAK WITH BEAN SPROUTS

Have a large steak of your choice cut about 1½ inches thick. Heat a heavy skillet well, and grease it lightly with a little of the fat cut from the steak. Add steak and press down with a spatula. Cook until one side is very well browned; turn and cook other side. When almost done (it may be cooked rare, medium, or well done), put 4 tablespoons butter on top of the meat. When butter melts, remove steak to a warm platter.

Stir into the pan juices 1 cup finely slivered green onions, 2 cups fresh bean sprouts, and 2 tablespoons soy. Heat vegetables well but do not cook. Serve sprouts with steak to 6 persons, along with toasted split buttered buns or English muffins.

DEEP-DISH PEACH PIE WITH ALMONDS

  About 8 peaches, sliced
1 *cup chopped toasted almonds*
½ *cup (¼ pound) melted butter*
2 *tablespoons tapioca*
½ *to 1 cup sugar*
  Few drops almond extract or
    2 tablespoons rum (optional)
  Rich pastry based on 1 cup flour
  Thick sweet cream or sour cream

Slice enough ripe peaches to fill an 8-inch-square deep baking dish or a deep, round 2-quart casserole. Mix together almonds, melted butter, tapioca, and sugar (from ½ to 1 cup depending on sweetness of fruit). If desired, add a few drops of almond extract or rum to flavor. Top with rich pastry, pressing edges firmly to side of baking dish.

Bake in a very hot oven (450°) for 10 minutes; reduce heat to moderate (350°) and bake for 30 to 40 minutes longer, or until pastry is nicely browned. Serve warm with thick sweet cream or sour cream. Makes 6 servings.

Casserole Dinner for a Crowd

THIS DINNER may be almost completely prepared a day in advance. Wash the salad greens and put in plastic bags in the refrigerator to crisp. Make your favorite dressing. Assemble the casserole and the Noodles Romanoff and refrigerate. Bake the festive cherry dessert. Before the party, you need only bake the chicken casserole and noodles and toss the salad.

TOSSED GREEN SALAD

CHICKEN AND MUSHROOM CASSEROLE

NOODLES ROMANOFF   FRENCH BREAD

CHERRY TORTE

CHICKEN AND MUSHROOM CASSEROLE

36 pieces chicken (breasts, thighs, or drumsticks)
   Salt, pepper, and paprika
¾ cup butter or margarine
¾ pound fresh mushrooms, sliced
4 tablespoons (¼ cup) flour
1½ cups chicken broth
6 tablespoons sherry
3 sprigs fresh rosemary or ½ teaspoon crumbled dried rosemary

Sprinkle chicken pieces with salt, pepper, and paprika. Brown in half the butter, and remove to a casserole or shallow baking pan. Add remaining butter to drippings, and sauté sliced mushrooms until tender. Sprinkle flour over mushrooms, and stir in chicken broth, sherry, and rosemary. Cook until thickened, then pour over chicken. Cover and bake in a moderate oven (350°) for 45 minutes (if refrigerated, 1 hour). Makes 18 servings.

NOODLES ROMANOFF

2 packages (8 oz. each) egg noodles
3 cups large curd cottage cheese
2 cloves garlic, minced or mashed
2 teaspoons Worcestershire
1 pint (2 cups) commercial sour cream
1 bunch green onions, finely chopped
½ teaspoon Tabasco
1 cup grated or shredded Parmesan cheese

Cook noodles in boiling salted water until tender; drain. Combine cooked noodles, cottage cheese, garlic, Worcestershire, sour cream, onions, and Tabasco. Turn into a greased casserole; sprinkle cheese over the top. Bake in a moderate oven (350°) for 25 minutes. (If you have refrigerated the casserole unbaked, increase cooking time 5 to 10 minutes.) Makes 18 servings.

CHERRY TORTE

1¼ cups flour
⅛ teaspoon salt
½ teaspoon baking powder
2 teaspoons sugar
6 tablespoons each butter and shortening
1 egg yolk
2 tablespoons water
2 cups canned pitted sour cherries
½ cup juice from cherries
½ cup sugar
2 tablespoons cornstarch
2 egg whites
⅛ teaspoon cream of tartar
4 tablespoons sugar

Sift flour, measure, then sift with salt, baking powder, and the 2 teaspoons sugar into a bowl. Cut in butter and shortening with pastry blender or 2 knives. Mix egg yolk with the 2 tablespoons water, and stir into mixture to make a very stiff dough. With the back of a spoon, spread dough evenly in a 9-inch pie pan. Heat cherries and juice; stir in mixture of the ½ cup sugar and the cornstarch, and cook until thick; cool.

When cherries are cold, pour into torte shell. Bake in a hot oven (425°) for 25 minutes. Meanwhile, beat egg whites with cream of tartar until foamy; gradually beat in the 4 tablespoons sugar; beat until stiff but not dry. Remove torte from oven, spread with meringue, and return to a moderate oven (350°). Bake 15 minutes longer, or until meringue is lightly browned. Makes 6 to 8 servings. To serve 18, make 3 tortes.

A Roman Dinner

MELON WITH ITALIAN PROSCIUTTO

BREAD STICKS (OPTIONAL)

LASAGNE (OPTIONAL)

SCALOPPINE DI TACCHINO (TURKEY SCALOPPINE)

ASPARACI (ASPARAGUS WITH HOLLANDAISE)

PATATE FRITTI (POTATO PUFFS)

SWEET FRENCH ROLLS   BUTTER

INSALATA ROMANA (ROMAINE SALAD)

CASSATA DI FRAGOLE (STRAWBERRY MERINGUE CAKE)

ASSORTED FRESH FRUITS (OPTIONAL)

THE ELEGANT FOOD OF ROME makes an excellent choice for a meeting of a gourmet dinner group or any special-occasion dinner party You handle this dinner in various degrees of elaborateness—from three courses to six. If you make use of a serving cart and buffet table (and invite guests who are not reluctant to spend a leisurely evening at dinner), two people, host and hostess, can manage even the six-course menu smoothly and without extra help. You can simplify the dinner to three courses by eliminating the lasagne and the fresh fruit dessert and serving the salad along with the main course of turkey, asparagus, potatoes, and rolls Here are some serving notes for the full production: If you are serving wine, start the wine service with the pasta course and continue with the same wine throughout the main course. Have the melon on the table when your guests sit down. Serve the lasagne onto individual warm plates in the kitchen. For the main course, bring serving dishes filled with turkey, asparagus, and potatoes to the table along with warm dinner plates. The salad course follows the main course according to European tradition; serve it onto chilled plates at the table. At dessert time, bring the cake to the table to cut and serve. For the fruit course, provide each guest with a fruit plate, a fruit knife, and perhaps a finger bowl; pass the platter of fruits.

Keep in mind this timing as you plan the last-minute preparations: The lasagne should go into a moderate oven (350°) to bake 40 minutes before serving time. Just before you serve the main course, heat the potato puffs for 20 minutes in a moderate oven (350°); meanwhile, cook the asparagus, prepare the hollandaise, and finish the turkey. Dress the washed and chilled salad greens just before you serve them.

MELON WITH PROSCIUTTO

Imported prosciutto (Italian ham), sliced paper thin, is available at Italian delicatessens. You will need about ¼ pound for 6 servings.

Cut a ripe cantaloupe into 6 wedges. Remove seeds; cut melon as shown in photographs. Drape a strip of prosciutto over top of melon wedge. Garnish each plate with one or two black olives and a lemon wedge. Offer black pepper in a mill for each person to grind over his fruit.

LASAGNE

Only homemade pasta and freshly grated, aged Parmesan will make this lasagne as good as it can be. If making pasta seems too much of a chore, you can substitute fresh lasagne noodles from an Italian pasta maker.

Braised beef juices, simmering for hours into fresh tomato sauce, give the sauce its rich flavor. After you make the sauce, put the beef roast to another use. (You might slice it cold for sandwiches or slice it and cook it into a stroganoff.)

To make fresh lasagne dough, gradually work egg yolks, olive oil, and salt into well of flour, using as much flour as you need to form a firm ball.

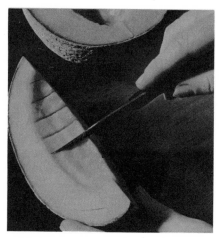

Cut melon from rind except at the ends, then cut into bites from one side, leaving the opposite side uncut.

Melon wedges, draped with paper-thin slices of prosciutto ham, can be seasoned with lemon juice and freshly ground black pepper if desired.

Noodles:

Put about 2 cups flour on board. Make a well in center; place in well 6 egg yolks, 1 teaspoon olive oil, and ⅛ teaspoon salt. With your hands, lightly beat egg yolks, then gradually work flour into eggs from edge. Add as much flour as eggs will absorb to form a firm ball; knead ball thoroughly on board until very smooth (surface should spring back when touched lightly with a finger). Cover the dough with a bowl and let stand for 5 minutes.

Lightly coat ball with flour. Pinch off a small portion and roll out as thin as possible on floured board. (If you use pasta-making machine to roll dough, lightly flour noodles and roll through several times, adjusting machine to make noodles thinner with each rolling.) Cut rolled dough into 8 strips about 4½ inches wide and 13 inches long (so that 2 strips can be arranged side by side in 9- by 13-inch baking dish).

Just before assembling casserole, bring to a boil a large flat pan of salted water with a little olive oil added. Cook noodles, two at a time, for about 30 seconds (to *al dente* stage; don't cook until noodles are soft). With slotted spatula, lift noodles from boiling water and lay flat on damp towels.

Tomato Sauce:

  5-pound beef roast (chuck, rump, or
      heel of round)
  Salt and pepper
  Olive oil
2 medium-sized onions, finely chopped
3 tablespoons minced parsley
  5-inch celery stalk, finely chopped
  4-inch piece carrot, shredded
  Pinch dry sage
1½ cups dry red table wine
6 large tomatoes (or 2 cans, 1 lb. 12 oz. each,
      solid-pack tomatoes, well drained)
2 cans (8 oz. each) tomato sauce
  Pinch dried thyme
¾ cup heavy cream

Rub beef roast with salt and pepper. In a large kettle, brown meat on all sides in olive oil. Add onions and sauté until limp. Add parsley, celery, carrot, sage, and wine; simmer (do not boil), stirring occasionally, until all wine is reduced. Skim off fat. Add fresh tomatoes (peeled, seeded, and cut in pieces) *or* drained canned tomatoes. Stir in tomato sauce. Bring to a boil, reduce heat, and add thyme. Simmer very slowly, stirring occasionally, until thick and even in consistency (at least 2½ hours). Remove meat and set aside for later use. Add cream to sauce; just heat through.

To assemble, spoon tomato sauce into 9- by 13-inch casserole to cover bottom. Arrange 2 strips cooked noodles side by side over sauce. Cover noodles with more sauce, then with about ⅓ cup crumbled Ricotta cheese (Italian cottage cheese) and about ⅓ cup grated Parmesan cheese. Repeat layers three times, omitting Ricotta cheese the third time. (Refrigerate or freeze casserole at this point.) Before baking, dot surface with 2 tablespoons *each* butter and heavy cream. Bake in a moderate oven (350°) for 25 minutes or until heated through. (If casserole has been refrigerated or frozen and thawed, increase baking time to 40 minutes.) Makes 12 servings.

SCALOPPINE DI TACCHINO

Tender pieces of boned turkey breast are cooked here in flavorful Marsala wine sauce, then finished with a satiny egg and cream glaze. A whole breast for a 13-pound hen will make 12 servings, but you can usually purchase a split turkey breast to serve only 6. (You might ask your poultry man to bone it for you).

    1 *split turkey breast (about 3 pounds)*
      Flour, salt, and pepper
    ½ *cup olive oil*
    4 *tablespoons (¼ cup) butter*
    1 *cup Marsala wine*
      Pinch powdered oregano
    ½ *pound fresh mushrooms, sliced*
    4 *tablespoons (¼ cup) butter*
    ½ *can (10½ oz. size) beef consommé*
    1 *egg yolk*
    1 *tablespoon heavy cream*

You can do this much preparation ahead of time: Skin and bone turkey; slice meat across grain, as thin as possible. Coat slices in flour seasoned with salt and pepper. In a large frying pan, heat together olive oil and ¼ cup butter. Lightly brown turkey slices on both sides, a few at a time; pour off excess fat and return meat to frying pan with Marsala wine and oregano. Cook over medium heat until almost dry (about 8 minutes), turning meat gently as it cooks to coat all sides. Sauté mushrooms in ¼ cup butter; drain off liquid and add mushrooms to turkey. Add beef consommé.

Just before serving, cook turkey mixture over low heat until almost dry, about 10 minutes. Beat egg yolk with cream; remove turkey from heat. Pour the cream mixture over meat; turn meat gently to glaze all sides. Serve immediately. Makes 6 servings.

ASPARACI

Prepare hollandaise just before serving (or use canned hollandaise, if you wish). Cook 2½ pounds asparagus in boiling salted water just until tender. Drain, and arrange in serving dish. Pass hollandaise (about 1½ cups in all) for each person to ladle over asparagus. Makes 6 servings.

PATATE FRITTI

These may be the most fragile, moist potatoes you've ever eaten. They're made of a combination of *pâté à choux* (cream puff paste) and soft mashed potatoes. They can be eaten immediately after frying, or wrapped in foil and reheated in the oven.

    ½ *cup hot water*
    4 *tablespoons (¼ cup) butter*
    ⅛ *teaspoon salt*
    ½ *cup sifted flour*
    2 *eggs*
    1½ *cups mashed potatoes*
    3 *tablespoons grated Parmesan cheese*
      Salt and pepper to taste
      Flour
      Salad oil

To make *pâté à choux*, bring water, butter, and salt to a boil; add flour all at once, and beat over low heat until mixture leaves sides of pan and forms a compact ball. Remove from heat; continue beating to cool mixture slightly, about 2 minutes. Add eggs, one at a time, beating well after each addition; continue beating until mixture has a satin-like sheen.

Combine mashed potatoes (these should be soft and fluffy, whipped with butter and milk) with the *pâté à choux* and Parmesan cheese; season to taste. Cool. Roll spoonfuls of dough on a lightly floured board (use as little flour as possible) to shape cylinders or cones about 1 by 2½ inches. In a heavy frying pan heat salad oil (about ¾ inch deep) to 370°. Lightly brown potatoes on all sides; drain on paper towels.

To reheat before serving, wrap in foil and heat in moderate oven (350°) for about 25 minutes. If you wish, garnish with paper frills. Makes 12 puffs.

INSALATA ROMANA

This is a simple but very refreshing salad. Taste the dressing as you make it, to adjust oil-vinegar proportions to suit the strength of your vinegar.

In a salad bowl rubbed with a cut clove of garlic, toss broken romaine leaves with dressing made of about 3 parts olive oil to 1 part wine vinegar. Season with salt and freshly ground black pepper.

CASSATA DI FRAGOLE

The cake's meringue shell is made with whites of eggs left after the yolks were used for lasagne. Any sliced, sweetened fresh fruits in season can be used in place of the strawberries.

> 6 egg whites
> 1½ cups sugar
> 1 teaspoon vinegar

In large bowl of electric mixer, beat egg whites until foamy. Gradually add sugar (a tablespoon at a time), beating until sugar is completely dissolved and soft peaks form. Beat in vinegar. Turn into a well-greased 9-inch spring-form pan; spread smooth on top. Bake in moderately slow oven (325°) for 1 hour. Place on wire rack to cool thoroughly. (Center of meringue will drop.) When meringue is thoroughly cool, gently loosen around outside edge. Remove sides of pan. Fill center of meringue with Strawberry Cream Filling (recipe follows). (If edges of meringue break off, replace, securing with filling.) Serve immediately or chill in refrigerator overnight. Before serving, decorate cake top with a few whole strawberries with stems. Cut into wedges to serve. Makes 10 to 12 servings.

Strawberry Cream Filling:

> 1 box strawberries
> ⅓ cup sugar
> 1 pint heavy cream
> 1 teaspoon vanilla

Hull and slice strawberries (save a few whole berries for garnish). Mix gently with sugar. Whip cream with vanilla. Fold in sliced strawberries.

Striking meringue cake, topped with whole fresh strawberries, climaxes Roman dinner. Soft, delicate filling is sliced strawberries combined with whipped cream.

A Salmon Dinner

ICED CUCUMBER SOUP

GRILLED SALMON STEAKS

ASPARAGUS WITH HOLLANDAISE

RING OF ROLLS

LEMON CREAM CHEESE TARTS

THE CHILLED CUCUMBER SOUP that starts this dinner is a perfect prelude to the grilled salmon that follows. Accompaniments are simple: fresh asparagus with hollandaise sauce, and an oven-fresh ring of rolls. Creamy lemon tarts top off the meal. The soup and the pie filling can be made the day before, and both the rolls and the pastry tart shells freeze nicely. The salmon, asparagus, and hollandaise sauce require last-minute cooking.

ICED CUCUMBER SOUP

    3 large cucumbers
    1 small white onion
    3 tablespoons butter or margarine
    3 tablespoons flour
    2½ cups chicken stock (chicken stock base or
        chicken bouillon cubes may be used)
    1 teaspoon dill weed
    2 teaspoons lemon juice
    2 cups thin cream
      Salt and pepper to taste
      Sour cream

Peel and split cucumbers, remove and discard seeds, and chop. Chop onion, combine with cucumber, and sauté in butter until soft. Stir in flour, then chicken stock, dill weed, and lemon juice.

Cook until thickened, then whirl in blender or press through a sieve. Combine with cream, and season to taste with salt and pepper. Chill. Serve very cold, topped with a spoonful of sour cream. Makes 6 to 8 servings.

GRILLED SALMON STEAKS

Brush 6 salmon steaks (about ¾ inch thick) with lemon juice, dot with butter, and sprinkle with salt and pepper. Place fish under a heated broiler for about 12 minutes, or until browned and the fish flakes with a fork. Remove to a hot platter and serve at once. Makes 6 servings.

ASPARAGUS WITH HOLLANDAISE

Clean 3 pounds asparagus well, breaking off tough ends and scraping off leaves if sandy. Cook in boiling salted water until tender-crisp, about 6 to 8 minutes. (The exact time depends on the thickness and tenderness of the stalks, so test them with a fork.) Drain asparagus the minute it is done—it should still be bright green. Serve asparagus with heated canned hollandaise or with the homemade hollandaise sauce described below.

Hollandaise Sauce:

    3 egg yolks
    1 tablespoon lemon juice
    ¼ teaspoon salt
      Cayenne
    ½ cup (¼ pound) melted butter

Have ready the egg yolks in a round-bottomed bowl, a French whip, a pan of hot water over which the bowl will fit, and the lemon juice to which the salt and a few grains of cayenne have been added. Have melted butter ready in a small saucepan.

When you are ready to make the hollandaise, remove pan of hot water from heat and place over it the egg yolks. Add the lemon juice and seasonings to the egg yolks and mix well, then very slowly pour in the melted butter, whisking the mixture constantly as you pour. (It will begin to thicken almost at once.)

Keep sauce warm (not hot) until serving time. Serve over cooked asparagus. Makes 6 servings.

RING OF ROLLS

    2 packages yeast, active dry or compressed
    1 cup warm (not hot) water
    1 cup milk, scalded then cooled
    ½ cup (¼ pound) butter or margarine, melted
    6 cups flour
    2 tablespoons sugar
    1 tablespoon salt

Soften yeast in ½ cup of the water. In a mixing bowl, combine the remaining ½ cup water and the cooled milk. Add softened yeast, and stir until dissolved. Add 2 tablespoons of the butter. Sift flour, measure, then sift with sugar and salt into the liquid. Mix well and allow to rise until almost double in bulk.

Turn out on a floured board and divide dough in half. Roll 1 piece about ¼ inch thick, and cut into rounds with a 2- to 2½-inch cutter. Butter a 1-quart, 8-inch ring mold. Brush each circle of dough on both sides with some of the melted butter; overlap about 14 of the circles evenly around the bottom of the mold. Stand about 10 more circles (also brushed with butter) around the sides of the ring, with edges touching.

Fill another ring with the other half of the dough, following the same procedure, or shape into regular rolls. Allow to rise in a warm place until light, about 45 minutes. Bake in a moderately hot (375°) oven until nicely browned, 35 to 40 minutes. Turn out while still hot into a round, napkin-lined basket. Let each guest break off his own rolls. Makes enough rolls for 16 to 18 servings.

LEMON CREAM CHEESE TARTS

3 eggs
¾ cup sugar
2 teaspoons grated lemon peel
½ cup lemon juice
1 large package (8 oz.) cream cheese, softened
6 large baked tart shells

Beat the eggs until light in top of double boiler; then beat in sugar gradually. Stir in lemon peel and juice and place over hot water. Cook until thick, stirring constantly. Gradually add cream cheese, blending in thoroughly. Spoon into baked tart shells. Do not refrigerate. Makes 6 servings.

Fold half circle of dough slightly as you place it around the sides of ring mold to make the ring of rolls.

Patio Dinner Party

HERE'S A DINNER that might be be served in a protected corner of the garden or patio if the weather permits. It can easily be served inside if necessary Arrangements of spring blossoms suggest the season and brighten the table. The food can be garnished with flowers and leaves, or you can decorate cold dishes with radishes, green peppers, olives, almonds, pimiento, and mushrooms, cut and arranged to resemble flowers The chicken is served chilled, so it can be made well ahead of time. You can make the almond sticks several hours before party time and chill them. Prepare the tomatoes the morning of the party; make the avocado mixture and fill tomatoes as close to serving time as possible. Prepare pineapple and line shells with sherbet several hours ahead so the sherbet will freeze very firm. You can prepare the fruits at the same time, then arrange them in the shells just before serving. Make the pound cake a day ahead (it's better with a day of aging), or purchase it, if you prefer.

HOT BOUILLON WITH PAPAYA

ALMOND STICKS

INDIVIDUAL CHAUD-FROID OF CHICKEN

CROISSANTS   GREEN BEANS WITH CHEESE

TOMATOES WITH AVOCADO

PINEAPPLE WITH SHERBET AND STRAWBERRIES

POUND CAKE

HOT BOUILLON WITH PAPAYA

3 cans (10½ oz. each) beef bouillon
¾ cup water
2 tablespoons lime or lemon juice
½ ripe papaya, peeled and cut into
   small cubes

Combine bouillon, water, and lime or lemon juice. Heat and pour into cups. Garnish each serving with small cubes of papaya. Makes 6 servings.

ALMOND STICKS

3 slices fresh white bread (about
   ½ inch thick)
1 small package (3 oz.) cream cheese
1 tablespoon milk
½ teaspoon curry powder
½ teaspoon lemon juice
½ can (about 7 oz.) salted almonds, chopped

Remove crusts from bread. Cut each slice in thirds. Cream the cheese with milk, curry powder, and lemon juice. Spread cheese mixture on all sides of bread sticks. Roll in chopped salted almonds, and chill until time to serve with the hot bouillon. Makes 9 almond sticks.

INDIVIDUAL CHAUD-FROID OF CHICKEN

Chaud-froid gets its name from a combination of warm sauce and a cold glaze, used to coat cold fowl or meat.

After simmering a large whole chicken in well-seasoned water (herb bouquet, onion, carrot, and salt), quickly cool the chicken in the broth, so the meat will be juicy. Remove from broth, carefully pull off skin, and carve meat off bone in as large pieces as possible. Arrange meat in 6 individual servings on a large platter or on plates, covering the boned dark meat with the sliced breast meat. Chill thoroughly.

Strain the broth and reserve 1 cup for the sauce. In the remaining broth, cook 12 to 16 peeled boiling onions until tender; drain, reserving broth, and chill.

Chaud-froid Sauce:

4 tablespoons each flour and melted butter
1 cup reserved chicken stock
1 cup whipping cream
1 tablespoon lemon juice
   Salt and white pepper to taste
3 envelopes (3 tablespoons)
   unflavored gelatin
½ cup cold water

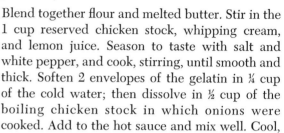

Blend together flour and melted butter. Stir in the 1 cup reserved chicken stock, whipping cream, and lemon juice. Season to taste with salt and white pepper, and cook, stirring, until smooth and thick. Soften 2 envelopes of the gelatin in ¼ cup of the cold water; then dissolve in ½ cup of the boiling chicken stock in which onions were cooked. Add to the hot sauce and mix well. Cool, stirring occasionally, but do not allow to set.

Pour all but ½ cup of the Chaud-froid Sauce over the chicken, and arrange desired decorations on top; chill. Soften the remaining envelope of unflavored gelatin in the remaining ¼ cup cold water, dissolve in 1 cup boiling chicken stock, and refrigerate until it is cool and slightly syrupy; pour carefully over the decorations to hold them in place, and chill until ready to serve.

Spoon about 1 tablespoon of the Chaud-froid Sauce on each onion, and sprinkle with minced parsley or paprika. Arrange these onions around the individual chicken servings. Makes 6 servings.

CROISSANTS

Make up 1 package (about 14 oz.) of hot roll mix according to directions, and allow to rise. When dough is almost doubled in bulk, knead down and roll into a rectangle about ½ inch thick, with the long side parallel to the table in front of you. Spread with ½ pound softened butter, completely to the edges. Fold in thirds lengthwise. Roll until the rectangle is the same width it was before, fold into thirds again, and chill overnight.

Next morning, roll out and fold twice more, making sure to retain the rectangular shape after each rolling. Now divide in half and roll out each half into a circle about ¼ inch thick. Cut each circle into 12 pie-shaped wedges. Starting at the wide end of the wedge, roll up each one and then bend the ends toward each other a little way to form into the shape of a crescent. Put on greased cooky sheets and allow to rise until almost doubled in bulk. Brush with beaten egg yolk mixed with a little water.

Bake in a hot oven (400°) for 6 minutes; reduce temperature to moderately slow (325°), and bake 15 minutes longer, or until nicely browned. Makes 2 dozen croissants.

GREEN BEANS WITH CHEESE

> 1½ pounds fresh green beans, washed and trimmed
> Boiling water
> 1 clove garlic
> 1 teaspoon salt
> ¼ cup melted butter
> Pinch crushed dry basil
> 3 tablespoons grated Parmesan cheese
> ¼ cup toast crumbs
> 1 tablespoon melted butter

Cook beans in water with garlic and salt until tender but still crisp and green; drain well; discard garlic. Mix beans with the ¼ cup melted butter, basil, and cheese. Sprinkle with toast crumbs which you have mixed with the 1 tablespoon melted butter. Serve at once. Makes 6 servings.

TOMATOES WITH AVOCADO

> 6 medium-sized tomatoes
> Salt
> 1 large or 2 small avocados
> 2 tablespoons minced canned green chili peppers
> 2 tablespoons mayonnaise
> 1 teaspoon lemon juice
> 2 teaspoons grated onion
> Salt to taste
> Finely minced celery (optional)
> Lettuce
> Additional mayonnaise or sour cream

Peel tomatoes and scoop out centers. Sprinkle inside with salt, and turn upside down to drain. Mash avocados, and mix with chili peppers, the 2 tablespoons mayonnaise, lemon juice, grated onion, salt, and celery. Fill tomatoes with this mixture, arrange on a nest of lettuce leaves, and top each tomato with a little mayonnaise or sour cream. Makes 6 servings.

PINEAPPLE WITH SHERBET AND STRAWBERRIES

> 1 large ripe pineapple
> 1 quart lemon, pineapple, raspberry, or boysenberry sherbet
> 2 baskets strawberries (or other berries in season)
> Sugar
> Mint sprigs

Cut pineapple in half lengthwise, through the crown. Scoop out the core and part of the fruit, leaving a shell with about ½ inch of fruit on it. Line the shells with the sherbet and put at once into the freezer. Cut the pineapple you have scooped from the shell into small pieces. Wash, hull, and mix berries with sugar to taste. At serving time fill the sherbet-lined shells with the berries and pineapple. Garnish with sprigs of mint, and arrange on a silver platter. Garnish with spring blossoms. Scoop fruits and sherbet out of pineapple shell to serve. Makes 6 servings.

Guest Participation Dinner

AN INFORMAL DINNER, cooked by the guests themselves, and served in an Oriental manner, is fun for everyone. The hostess has little to do except cut and arrange meat and vegetables ahead of party time. The guests enjoy the whole process—attractive raw ingredients, delightful cooking aromas, a delicious finished dish ⟫⟫ Several of the ingredients used in the recipes may not be familiar to you, but they are available in Oriental food stores. *Miso* is a fermented rice and soy bean paste that is sold in a carton, like cottage cheese. It keeps for several months in the refrigerator. (Any consommé may be served in place of Miso Soup, but top it with a garnish of chives or green onion rings; or cut a vegetable, such as carrot or turnip, in the shape of a flower to set in the bottom of each bowl.) *Tofu* is soy bean curd, sold in standard blocks (about 1 pound) ⟫⟫ In China, where the recipe for Peking Lamb originated, a special grill is used to provide the characteristic smoky wood fire for cooking the meat and vegetables. The cooking surface of the Chinese grill is oval and consists of broad strips of metal with very narrow spaces between, so the thinly sliced meat and vegetables will not fall through. A portable brazier, or a small barbecue or *hibachi*, works just as well, but you will need to place a sheet of expanded metal, or welded (not galvanized) hardware cloth, over the grill so the meat and vegetables will not fall through. Or use a hinged broiler or toaster rack. Build a wood fire, using partly green wood to increase the smoke; or use

MISO SOUP

PEKING LAMB

SESAME SEED HAMBURGER BUNS

CHINESE CABBAGE

TOFU SALAD

GINGERED CUCUMBERS

MANDARIN ORANGE DESSERT

charcoal instead, and add liquid smoke seasoning to the dipping sauce for the meat and vegetables.

With the exception of the Miso Soup, which is served hot, the other traditional Oriental side dishes are like vegetable, relish, and salad combined and are served cold. All of them can be prepared well ahead. They may be served in bowls on a buffet, or passed at the table, or arranged in individual portions on a Japanese tray. The soup is generally served first, but not as a separate course, and it may be sipped all through the meal. If you have Oriental lacquer soup bowls, the lids will keep the soup warm.

It seems only right that green tea or jasmine tea be served with an Oriental dinner. For convenience you can buy green tea in bags. Keep a pot of hot tea on the table during the meal.

After such a dinner, a light fruit dessert or sherbet is the best choice. You could serve chilled melon, either in wedges or cut into balls, in place of the mandarin orange dessert. Or you might serve fresh fruit cups, perhaps adding a little sherry or orange-based liqueur. In addition, you might like to pass a plate of Chinese fortune cookies.

MISO SOUP

1 quart soup stock (chicken or beef)
¼ cup miso (bean paste)
¼ teaspoon salt
1 egg, beaten
2 teaspoons sherry (optional)
Orange or lemon peel
Chopped chives or green onion rings

Bring to a boil soup stock mixed with miso and salt. While swirling the soup in the pan, gradually trickle in the beaten egg. Add sherry, if you wish. Place a twist of orange or lemon peel in each bowl before adding soup. Top with chopped chives or green onion rings. Makes 4 to 6 servings.

PEKING LAMB

A leg of lamb is the best choice for this dish. One small leg (about 4½ pounds) will make 6 to 8 generous servings. The meat should be very thinly sliced into long, narrow strips, about the way you cut beef for sukiyaki.

For the vegetables, green onions and Chinese parsley are traditional. Chinese parsley somewhat resembles our parsley, but it has an interesting sharp, spicy flavor. It is usually available only in Oriental grocery stores. For 8 people, you will need 3 bunches green onions and 2 bunches Chinese parsley. Cut the green onions and parsley into 1½- to 2-inch strips. Other vegetables can be substituted in this dish, such as fingers of eggplant, parboiled green beans, thin strips of green pepper, or thin slices of zucchini squash.

The dipping sauce is primarily soy. To ¾ cup soy add 1 tablespoon sugar and ¼ cup sherry (optional). If you use a charcoal fire instead of a wood fire, you may wish to add 1 teaspoon of liquid smoke seasoning.

Provide inexpensive wooden chopsticks (have cooking forks or tongs handy, too, for guests who are not proficient with chopsticks). Let your guests cook their own meat and vegetables, using chopsticks or forks to dunk the pieces in the sauce and set them on the hot grill. The broiling takes only about 2 minutes. The sauce drips into the fire and makes it spark and smoke. A slight char on the food seems to make it taste even better.

When each person finishes cooking several slices of meat and vegetables, he can put them in a bun and go to the table to eat, then return to cook some more.

CHINESE CABBAGE

- 3 *dried hot red chili peppers*
- ½ *cup salad oil*
- ¼ *cup vinegar*
- ¾ *teaspoon salt*
- 1 *head Chinese cabbage*

Sauté red peppers in ¼ cup of the salad oil until the oil tastes quite sharp; cool. Remove peppers. In a salad bowl, combine the ¼ cup sharp oil with the remaining ¼ cup salad oil, vinegar, and salt. Cut Chinese cabbage into thin slices, and add to bowl just before serving so it will retain its crispness; toss. Makes 8 servings.

TOFU SALAD

- 1 *block tofu (bean curd)*
- ¼ *cup sesame seed oil or other salad oil*
- ½ *cup soy*
- 1 *teaspoon monosodium glutamate*
- 1 *large bunch chives*
     Water cress or parsley

Crush the tofu together with sesame seed oil, soy, and monosodium glutamate. Chop chives and mix in; chill. To serve, garnish with water cress or parsley. Makes 8 small servings.

GINGERED CUCUMBERS

- 5 *medium-sized cucumbers*
- ½ *cup salad oil (not olive oil)*
- 2 *teaspoons salt*
- 4 *teaspoons lemon juice*
- 1 *teaspoon grated lemon peel*
     1-inch piece fresh ginger, grated
     *Very thin lemon slices or thin slivers
        of fresh ginger*

Using a vegetable peeler, remove alternate strips of cucumber peel lengthwise; slice cucumbers very thinly. Sauté cucumber slices very quickly in salad oil. Add salt, lemon juice, lemon peel, and grated ginger. Pour the cooking liquid into a bowl with the slices; serve cold. Garnish with very thin lemon slices or thin slivers of fresh ginger. Makes 8 servings.

MANDARIN ORANGE DESSERT

This dessert combines several fruits and is very slightly thickened with cornstarch. It may be served warm for guests to help themselves from a large bowl, or served in individual bowls, either warm or chilled.

- 3 *cans (11 oz. each) mandarin oranges*
- 1 *can (1 lb. 13 oz.) pineapple chunks*
- ¼ *cup seedless raisins*
- 2 *teaspoons cornstarch*

Heat oranges in their own syrup. Drain pineapple chunks, reserving syrup. Add raisins and pineapple chunks to oranges. Thicken slightly with cornstarch mixed smooth with a little of the pineapple syrup. Makes 8 servings.

St. Valentine's Day Dinner

THIS IS A DISTINGUISHED St. Valentine's Day dinner. It is rather elegant, but most of the preparation can be done ahead of time. You can prepare the salad except for arranging on crisp greens. Prepare the chicken breasts in their foil wrap. Cut potato balls and keep in water until it is time to cook them. Make the Fried Cream mixture and chill until you are ready for the final cooking.

PIMIENTO CUPS WITH ARTICHOKE HEARTS

CHICKEN BREASTS EN PAPILOTTE

POTATO BALLS   GREEN BEANS

BUTTER ROLLS

FRIED CREAM, FLAMBÉ

PIMIENTO CUPS WITH ARTICHOKE HEARTS

6 *whole canned pimientos*
1½ *cups finely minced celery*
3 *anchovies, chopped*
2 *tablespoons finely minced onion*
  Mayonnaise (about ⅓ cup)
½ *teaspoon salt*
⅛ *teaspoon pepper*
6 *cooked artichoke hearts or bottoms*
  Garlic-flavored French dressing
  Crisp greens

Drain pimientos. Combine celery, anchovies, onion, and enough mayonnaise to bind the other ingredients. Season with salt and pepper. Fill pimiento cups with the celery-anchovy mixture, and top with an artichoke heart or bottom that has been marinated in the garlic-flavored French dressing. Arrange on individual plates garnished with crisp greens. Makes 6 servings.

CHICKEN BREASTS EN PAPILOTTE

2 *tablespoons chopped green onions*
4 *tablespoons (¼ cup) butter*
3 *tablespoons flour*
1¼ *cups light cream*
¼ *cup white wine*
  Salt and pepper to taste
  Pinch of thyme
6 *large, whole, boned chicken breasts*
12 *to 18 cleaned mushroom caps*

Tear off six 10-inch lengths of 12-inch-wide heavy foil. Fold each piece down the middle and cut a large heart from it.

Make a sauce by cooking green onions in butter until wilted. Stir in flour, cook a minute, then add cream and wine (or all cream if you prefer), salt, pepper, and thyme. Cook, stirring, until thick; cool.

Open up each folded foil heart and lightly butter the inside. Then put a breast of chicken on one half, top each with 2 or 3 cleaned mushroom caps, divide the sauce among the six, and fold the other half over. Carefully turn the edges in, making a double fold, and press tightly. When ready to cook, heat oven to 400°, and arrange foil packages on cooky sheets. Cook for 35 to 45 minutes, depending upon how cold the chicken was when put in the oven. Arrange the packets on a platter in pairs, with two straightsides together, to make three large silver hearts. Serve in the foil. Makes 6 servings.

POTATO BALLS

Cut about 5 pounds of large potatoes into balls, using a French cutter. (Keep in water until time to cook.) Cook, covered, in boiling salted water just until tender, 10 to 15 minutes—don't let them get mushy. Drain and serve with melted butter and a dusting of paprika. Makes 6 servings.

GREEN BEANS

Wash and trim 2½ pounds green beans, and cut into 2-inch lengths. Cook, covered, in a small amount of boiling salted water until just tender, about 15 minutes. Drain and dress with melted butter and a sprinkling of minced fresh parsley. Makes 6 servings.

FRIED CREAM, FLAMBÉ

2 *cups whipping cream*
¼ *teaspoon salt*
  1-inch piece vanilla bean, split open,
    or ½ teaspoon vanilla extract
⅓ *cup sugar*
4 *egg yolks*
¼ *cup cornstarch*
¼ *cup milk*
  Finely minced almonds
2 *eggs, slightly beaten*
  Fine dry bread crumbs
¼ *cup warmed brandy*

In the top of a double boiler, scald cream with salt, vanilla bean, and sugar. Beat egg yolks. Stir cornstarch into milk, and add to egg yolks. Add to cream, put over hot water, and cook, stirring constantly, until thick and smooth.

Remove vanilla bean and pour mixture into a lightly greased 8-inch-square pan; chill. Cut into squares or oblongs, and roll in finely minced almonds. Dip into slightly beaten egg; then roll in bread crumbs, and fry in deep fat (370°) until brown. Put on a fireproof dish and keep warm. To serve, pour on warmed brandy and light. Makes 6 servings.

Corned Beef Dinner, Company Style

THE CORNED BEEF for this main dish may be cooked as much as two days in advance; let it cool and chill in its broth so it will retain its juiciness after oven browning. Finish cooking it just in time to serve. A day ahead or the morning of the party, make the cheesecake, cool, and chill (let it warm to room temperature before serving). You can assemble the lima bean casserole in the morning and chill.

FRUITED CORNED BEEF

BROILED WHOLE APRICOTS

LIMA BEAN CASSEROLE   HOT ROLLS

CHEESE CAKE WITH SOUR CREAM TOPPING

FRUITED CORNED BEEF

9 pounds corned beef round (2 pieces, 4 to 5 pounds each)
Water
Whole cloves
1 cup brown sugar, firmly packed
½ cup fine dry bread crumbs
1 teaspoon dry mustard
Grated peel and juice of 2 oranges
Grated peel and juice of 2 lemons
2 cups cider

Cover meat with cold water, bring to a boil, and remove scum. (If beef seems very salty, pour off water and add fresh.) Simmer slowly for 3 hours, or until just tender. Cool. Place drained corned beef in baking pan; score fat and stud with cloves. Combine brown sugar, crumbs, mustard, and grated orange and lemon peels. Pat meat with crumb mixture. Place in a moderate oven (350°) until slightly browned, basting frequently with a mixture of the orange and lemon juices and cider. After browning, continue baking for 30 minutes or until heated through. Slice. Makes 18 servings.

BROILED WHOLE APRICOTS

Drain 3 large cans (1 lb. 13 oz. each) whole peeled apricots and place fruit in a shallow pan. Spoon over some of the basting juices from the meat, and heat in a moderate oven (350°) for 10 minutes, or slip under the broiler just until lightly browned. Use to garnish the meat platter.

LIMA BEAN CASSEROLE

8 medium-sized onions, sliced
4 tablespoons (¼ cup) butter or margarine
3 cans (4 oz. each) sliced mushrooms, drained
2 cans (10½ oz. each) cream of mushroom soup
6 packages (10 oz. each) frozen baby lima beans
1 teaspoon salt
¼ teaspoon pepper
2 teaspoons dill seed
1 pint (2 cups) whipping cream
2 cups grated or shredded Parmesan cheese

Sauté sliced onions in butter until limp. Stir in drained mushrooms and soup. Cook limas in boiling water, with salt, pepper, and dill seed added, for 5 minutes; drain. Turn the parboiled limas and the mushrooms and onion mixture into a greased large, shallow baking pan; mix lightly. Pour over the cream, and sprinkle the top with cheese. Bake in a slow oven (300°) for 30 minutes; increase temperature to 350° (when you put in meat), and bake 20 to 30 minutes longer. Makes 18 servings. (Do not overheat or the cream will separate.)

CHEESE CAKE WITH SOUR CREAM TOPPING

6 large packages (8 oz. each) cream cheese
8 egg whites
2 cups sugar
2 teaspoons vanilla
1⅓ cups rolled zwieback crumbs
2 pints (4 cups) commercial sour cream
¼ cup sugar
1 teaspoon vanilla
⅔ cup toasted, slivered blanched almonds

Cream cheese until soft. Beat egg whites until foamy, and gradually add the 2 cups sugar, beating until stiff but not dry; mix in creamed cheese and the 2 teaspoons vanilla, stirring until blended. Generously butter two deep, 8-inch spring form pans and dust with the crumbs. Pour in cheese mixture. Bake in a moderate oven (350°) for 25 minutes. Mix together the sour cream, the ¼ cup sugar, and the 1 teaspoon vanilla, and spread over hot cheese filling. Sprinkle with almonds and return to a very hot oven (475°) for 5 minutes. Cool, then chill thoroughly. Makes 18 servings.

A Soup and Salad Dinner

A SOUP AND SALAD SUPPER is a perfect way to entertain informally. In Sweden, this yellow pea soup *(arter med flask)* is a favorite Thursday supper dish. In the supper party menu that follows, it is accompanied by slices of meat which are cooked in the soup, whole wheat biscuits, an eye-appealing fruit tray, and a choice of salad dressings The soup timing isn't precise; you start it ahead, simmer it until the meat and peas are tender, and then reheat it thoroughly just before serving. Prepare the fruits and greens for the salad ahead of time, but arrange the salad just before you serve it. The biscuits should be freshly baked.

SWEDISH PEA SOUP

SLICED MEAT

FRUIT SALAD BAR

ASSORTED SALAD DRESSINGS

WHOLE WHEAT BISCUITS

SWEDISH PEA SOUP

- 2 cups (1 pound) dried yellow peas
- 2½ quarts water
- 1-pound piece salt pork or ham
- 1 leek or onion, chopped
  Salt
- ½ teaspoon ground ginger, or more to taste

Wash peas and soak them overnight in the water. Next morning, in the same water, bring quickly to a boil and skim. Add salt pork or ham and chopped leek or onion.

Cover and simmer slowly until the meat and peas are tender. Taste, and season with salt (about 2 teaspoons unless the meat is very salty) and ground ginger. Add a little water if too thick. Remove meat and slice. Serve the meat separately, with mustard. Makes 6 generous servings.

WESTERN FRUIT SALAD

Use any fruits in season. These might include apples, pears, grapefruit, casabas, pineapples, grapes, tangerines, bananas, papayas, strawberries. Cover a large tray with shredded lettuce and arrange the sliced or cubed fruit in symmetrical rows. Let each guest make his own selection. Have two or three salad dressings available, too. Mayonnaise, French dressing, sour cream dressing, and a sweet fruit salad dressing, such as the one below, are good choices.

Fruit Salad Dressing:

- ½ cup orange juice
- 2 tablespoons lemon juice
- 2 eggs
- ¼ cup honey
- 1 cup (½ pint) heavy cream, whipped until thick but not stiff
- ⅛ teaspoon salt
- ½ teaspoon ground cardamom

Mix juices, slightly beaten eggs, and honey. Cook in a double boiler, whipping constantly, for 3 minutes. Cool; add whipped cream. Add seasonings and continue beating until blended. Makes 2½ cups.

WHOLE WHEAT DROP BISCUITS

- 2 cups whole wheat flour
- ¾ teaspoon salt
- ½ cup non-fat dry milk
- 3 teaspoons baking powder
- 4 tablespoons (¼ cup) butter or margarine
- ¾ cup water

Combine flour, salt, dry milk, and baking powder; cut in butter with a pastry blender; add water, and stir just enough to mix. Drop by the spoonful on buttered cooky sheets. Bake in a hot oven (450°) for 12 to 15 minutes. Serve wrapped in a napkin, or in a roll warmer, so that they will keep very hot. Makes 16 biscuits.

Economical Party Dinner

THIS FESTIVE MENU, built around meat-filled crêpes, is actually very low in cost per person. All preparation, except cooking the asparagus, can be done in advance. The tender pancakes can be rolled around the ground meat and spinach filling a day in advance; cover, and refrigerate, and then spoon the tomato sauce and cheese over the pancakes just before you bake them. The Nippy Sauce for the asparagus can be made in advance, and you can make the Apple Bars as much as a day ahead.

PANCAKES POLPETTE

ASPARAGUS SPEARS, NIPPY SAUCE

HOT BUTTERED ROLLS

GLAZED APPLE BARS

PANCAKES POLPETTE

  2 *pounds ground beef*
  1 *pound ground sausage*
  2 *medium-sized onions, finely chopped*
  3 *cloves garlic, minced or mashed*
  4 *packages frozen chopped spinach, cooked
     and well drained*
    Salt to taste
  6 *eggs*
  ¾ *teaspoon salt*
  3 *cups milk*
  2 *cups flour*
    Butter or margarine
  6 *cans (8 oz. each) tomato sauce*
  2 *cups shredded sharp Cheddar cheese*

Brown meats with onion and garlic until crumbly. Add spinach, salt to taste, and mix well. In a mixing bowl, beat eggs with the ¾ teaspoon salt, and stir in milk. Sift flour, measure, and beat into egg mixture until smooth. Pour about 1 tablespoon of the batter into a buttered 7-inch frying pan; tilt pan so batter covers the entire surface. When golden brown underneath, remove from the pan; lay flat on a clean tea towel. Continue until all batter is used, adding more butter to the pan each time. (Should have 36 pancakes.)

Spoon filling onto the center of each pancake, roll up, and place in a shallow baking dish. Pour over tomato sauce and sprinkle with shredded cheese. Bake in a moderate oven (350°) for 30 minutes; if refrigerated, bake 40 to 45 minutes. Makes 18 servings.

ASPARAGUS WITH NIPPY SAUCE

For 18 servings, buy 6 pounds asparagus, figuring 3 servings to 1 pound. (Or use 6 packages frozen asparagus.) Cook asparagus in boiling salted water until tender; drain. Arrange in a shallow serving pan or on a platter, and spoon over cold Nippy Sauce. To prepare sauce, mix together 1 cup cooked salad dressing (not mayonnaise), 2 tablespoons prepared mustard, and 2 tablespoons lemon juice.

GLAZED APPLE BARS

 12 *medium-sized cooking apples*
  ¾ *cup coarsely chopped walnuts*
  2 *cups sugar*
  2 *teaspoons cinnamon*
  ⅛ *teaspoon nutmeg*
  2 *teaspoons lemon juice*
    Double recipe of pastry (4 cups flour)
  4 *tablespoons butter*
  3 *tablespoons lemon juice*
 1½ *cups powdered sugar*
  ¾ *cup finely chopped walnuts*

Peel and slice apples; add the ¾ cup coarsely chopped walnuts, 2 cups sugar, cinnamon, nutmeg, and the 2 teaspoons lemon juice. Stir lightly until well mixed.

Roll out half of the pastry to line bottom and sides of a shallow 11 by 15-inch jelly roll pan. Spread apple mixture over pastry and dot with the butter. Cover with remaining pastry and pinch edges to seal; prick top. Bake in a moderate oven (350°) for 1 hour.

Mix together the 3 tablespoons lemon juice and 1½ cups powdered sugar; spread over the top of the pastry when it comes from the oven. Sprinkle with the ¾ cup finely chopped walnuts. Cool, then cut into bars to serve. Makes 18 bars.

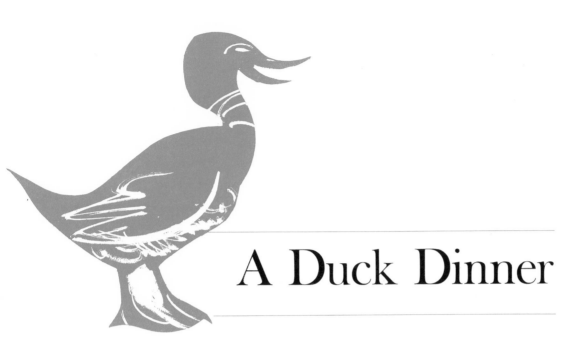

A Duck Dinner

THIS IS DEFINITELY A PARTY MEAL—one that will appeal to the hostess who enjoys cooking and serving memorable dinners. Much of it, however, can be prepared in advance 🌸🌸 The Crème Brûlée may be made the day before except for the brown sugar crust which is added two hours before serving. You can make the rolls early in the day and reheat them in foil in a moderate oven (350°) for 10 minutes. Make the duck sauce and prepare the peas after the duck comes out of the oven. Add oranges to crisp chicory and toss together with French dressing just before serving.

PAPAYA WITH PROSCIUTTO

ROAST DUCK WITH TARRAGON AND LIVER STUFFING

GREEN PEAS, BASQUAIS   PUFF ROLLS

ORANGE AND CHICORY SALAD WITH
FRENCH DRESSING

CRÈME BRÛLÉE, AMANDINE

PAPAYA WITH PROSCIUTTO

Have 3 ounces of prosciutto sliced as thin as possible, allowing 2 or 3 slices for each serving. Cut 1 large papaya in quarters, remove seeds and peel, and cut each quarter into 4 diagonal slices. Arrange the prosciutto on a plate, slices overlapping, and top with the papaya. Garnish the plate with a wedge of lemon. Makes 4 servings.

ROAST DUCK WITH LIVER AND TARRAGON STUFFING ·

      Duck liver
    4 or 5 chicken livers
    3 tablespoons butter or margarine
    1 teaspoon dried tarragon
    1 small can (3 or 4 oz.) liver paste or
        pâté de foie gras
    ½ cup dry white table wine or light cream
    3 cups dry bread cubes
      Salt to taste
    4- or 5-pound duckling (eviscerated weight)
    2 tablespoons flour
    1 cup stock (made from cooking the
        duck neck)
    ½ cup dry white table wine
      Salt to taste
    1 cup seedless grapes

Prepare stuffing as follows: Cook the duck liver and chicken livers in butter for 6 or 7 minutes; coarsely chop. Mix tarragon with liver paste and the ½ cup wine. Combine with the chopped livers and stir in bread cubes. Season with salt to taste, and if the dressing seems dry, add more wine or cream.

Stuff duck, close with a needle and thread or with dressing nails, and lace opening with twine. Place breast-side-up on a rack in a shallow pan, and roast in a moderately slow (325°) oven for 2 to 2½ hours, or until a meat thermometer reads 165° when inserted in the middle of the stuffing. For a crispy, brown skin, place the duck under the broiler for about 10 minutes before serving. Remove to a warm platter and cover with foil. Save drippings in pan.

Spoon off fat from the drippings and reserve to use with the peas. To the drippings add 2 tablespoons flour and cook, stirring, until smooth. Add stock and the ½ cup wine. Cook until smooth, salt to taste, and add grapes. Heat and serve with the duck. Makes 4 servings.

GREEN PEAS, BASQUAIS

    2 pounds fresh peas
    2 tablespoons duck fat
    1 medium-sized tomato, peeled, seeded,
        and diced
    1 canned pimiento, diced
    1 tablespoon chopped ham (optional)
      Salt to taste

Shell peas and put in a heavy saucepan with duck fat. Add tomato, pimiento, and ham to the peas. Cover and simmer slowly until peas are tender, about 10 mintues if the peas are young. Add salt to taste—more will be needed if ham is omitted. Makes 4 servings.

PUFF ROLLS

    1 package hot roll mix
    ½ cup (¼ pound) softened butter
    1 egg, beaten slightly with 1 tablespoon
        water

Prepare roll mix according to directions on box. Allow to rise, punch down, and roll into a 9 by

12-inch rectangle. Spread softened butter evenly over entire surface of the dough; fold in thirds, making sure that the edges meet; press edges; chill. Roll again into a 9 by 12-inch rectangle, and again fold in thirds; chill. Repeat twice more, making four times in all. Now roll again into a 9 by 12-inch rectangle and, using a ruler and a sharp knife, cut in 12 strips 1 inch wide. Cut each strip in thirds.

Arrange on greased baking sheets; brush with egg. Let rise until almost doubled in bulk, and bake in a hot oven (400°) for 5 minutes. Reduce heat to moderate (350°) and bake for another 15 minutes, or until nicely browned. Cool and freeze those not needed. Makes 36 rolls.

CRÈME BRÛLÉE, AMANDINE

    1 pint (2 cups) whipping cream
    7 egg yolks
    1 teaspoon vanilla
    ⅓ cup brown sugar, firmly packed
    ⅛ teaspoon salt
    ½ cup toasted blanched almonds
    ¾ cup brown sugar, firmly packed

Scald cream in top of double boiler. Beat egg yolks until light colored and thick; add vanilla, the ⅓ cup brown sugar, and salt. Add the scalded cream. Return to double boiler and cook over hot water until smooth and about the consistency of thin mayonnaise. Stir constantly so that it will be smooth, and do not overcook or it may curdle.

Chop the toasted almonds very fine. (One easy way is to use a rotary grater; another is to chop in an electric blender.) Stir almonds into the custard and pour into an 8-inch round (1-quart) baking dish. Chill thoroughly.

Two hours before serving, sift the remaining brown sugar in an even layer over the entire top of the custard. (Or, using a rubber spatula, press it through a strainer.) You should have an even layer of brown sugar about ¼ inch thick.

Put under a preheated broiler and watch carefully until the sugar melts in an even glaze. It takes just a few seconds. (You can also use an electric charcoal starter for melting the sugar. Heat the lighter and hold it 3 or 4 inches from the topping, moving it as the sugar melts. In this way you have complete control of the situation and are less apt to overbrown the sugar.) Again chill the dessert.

Serve by breaking the hard top crust with a spoon and giving each person some of this as well as the custard underneath. Makes 4 to 6 servings. Serve with cookies.

Labor Day Dinner

THE HOSTESS can relax and enjoy this Labor Day barbecue. Everything can be done ahead except broiling the turkey and making the pilaff. Make the dressing for the seafood hors d'oeuvre several hours ahead, cover, and chill in the refrigerator; it takes just a few minutes to arrange the hors d'oeuvre at serving time. If you plan to serve the soup cold, allow several hours for it to chill thoroughly; to serve hot, make it ahead and reheat just before serving. Prepare the watermelon bowl at least 1 hour ahead so it will chill thoroughly (you can prepare it as much as 12 hours before serving, if you wish).

SEAFOOD HORS D'OEUVRE, LOUIS DRESSING

MINTED PEA SOUP, HOT OR COLD

BROILED BABY TURKEY

PILAFF MOGHUL

FRESH FRUITS IN WATERMELON BOWL

SEAFOOD HORS D'OEUVRE

Fill a large bowl or tray with cracked ice. On it arrange several different kinds of seafood—cooked shrimps, chunks of lobster meat, clams and oysters in their shells, raw scallops, smoked oysters, squares of smoked sturgeon, rolls of smoked salmon, and chunks of cooked finnan haddie. Have the fish, except those in shells, impaled on picks.

Louis Dressing:

- *1 cup mayonnaise*
- *¼ cup cream, whipped*
- *¼ cup each chili sauce, chopped green pepper, and chopped green onion*
- *Salt*
- *Lemon juice*

Combine mayonnaise, whipped cream, chili sauce, green pepper, and green onion. Season with salt and lemon juice. Serve in a bowl as a dip for the seafood. Makes enough dip to serve 6 people.

MINTED PEA SOUP

- *1 cup chicken stock*
- *1 package frozen peas*
- *1 cup cream*
- *1 teaspoon salt*
- *2 teaspoons finely chopped mint*

Put chicken stock and peas in blender, and whirl until smooth. Add cream, salt, and mint, and bring to a boil. Strain through a fine strainer, and serve hot or chilled. Makes 6 servings.

BROILED BABY TURKEY

Split turkey (about 8 or 9 pounds); broil over medium coals for 45 to 60 minutes, depending on size. Baste frequently with a sauce made of ½ cup butter, 1 tablespoon curry powder, and ½ cup apple cider. Makes 6 servings.

PILAFF MOGHUL

- *2 cups brown or white rice*
- *1 cup seedless raisins*
- *½ cup melted butter*
- *½ cup chopped salted almonds*
  - *Additional chopped almonds and crisp French-fried onions for garnish*

Boil or steam rice until tender. Plump raisins by allowing to stand in warm water or in room temperature wine for about 15 minutes; drain well. Mix rice with raisins, butter, and almonds. Press into a bowl, unmold on a round platter, and sprinkle with a few more chopped almonds. Surround with crisp French-fried onions. Makes 6 generous servings.

FRESH FRUITS IN WATERMELON BOWL

Cut a slice from the top of a ripe watermelon and scoop out the meat, using a French ball cutter. Combine the melon balls with any other fruit—pineapple cubes, strawberries, grapes, peaches, pears, and cantaloupe or other melon balls. Flavor the fruit with rum, brandy, or sherry. Smooth out the inside of the watermelon, cut the edges in scallops or notches, fill with the fruit, and garnish with sprigs of mint. Serve very cold.

Veal Dinner for Eighteen

YOU CAN COOK the Veal Sauté a day ahead; cover and chill, then reheat before serving. Bake the nut bread the day before and wrap in foil (it slices better if allowed to stand a day).

VEAL SAUTÉ   GREEN BEANS AMANDINE

SWISS FRIED NOODLES   APRICOT NUT BREAD

APPLE BRITTLE SUNDAE

VEAL SAUTÉ

8 *pounds veal stew meat, cut in 1 to 1½-inch cubes*
4 *teaspoons salt*
½ *teaspoon pepper*
½ *cup salad oil*
2 *cans (4 oz. each) sliced mushrooms, drained, or ½ pound fresh mushrooms, sliced*
2 *cloves garlic, minced or mashed*
1½ *cups coarsely chopped onion (2 large onions)*
1 *cup diagonally sliced celery*
2 *medium-sized green peppers, seeded and cut in strips*
2 *cans (1 lb. 13 oz. each) solid pack tomatoes*
1 *cup dry red table wine*
4 *tablespoons cornstarch or 8 tablespoons flour*

Season meat with salt and pepper, and brown in oil; remove. Sauté mushrooms and garlic in drippings for 5 minutes; add onion and celery and sauté until onion is clear. Stir in green pepper, tomatoes, wine, and browned meat. Cover and simmer until meat is tender, about 1½ hours. Mix cornstarch with enough cold water to make a paste; stir in; cook until thickened. Makes 18 servings.

GREEN BEANS AMANDINE

Cook 5 packages (10 oz. each) frozen green beans according to package directions; drain. Or cook 4½ pounds fresh green beans in a small amount of boiling salted water for 20 minutes or until tender; drain. Turn into a heated serving dish. Spoon over 1 cup coarsely slivered blanched almonds that you have browned in 4 tablespoons butter or margarine. Makes 18 servings.

SWISS FRIED NOODLES

2 *packages (8 oz. each) egg noodles*
   Salted water
10 *tablespoons butter or margarine*
½ *cup grated sapsago cheese*

Cook noodles in boiling salted water until tender; drain. Use 2 large frying pans, and melt 4 tablespoons butter in each. Divide the cooked noodles between the pans, spreading evenly, and brown on one side. Turn upside down onto a plate. Melt the remaining butter in each pan and return noodles to brown the other side. With a spatula slide noodles onto a chop plate and sprinkle with cheese. Cut in wedges to serve. Makes 18 servings.

APRICOT NUT BREAD

¾ *cup brown sugar, firmly packed*
¾ *cup chopped nut meats (pecans, preferably)*
1 *cup cut-up soft dried apricots*
1 *egg, slightly beaten*
1¼ *cups orange juice*
3 *cups packaged biscuit mix*

Combine sugar, nut meats, and apricots. Stir in egg and orange juice. Add biscuit mix, and beat with a wooden spoon about half a minute. Turn into a buttered loaf pan (9 by 5 inches), or for attractive small slices, make in 2 small 5 by 7-inch loaf pans. Bake in a moderate oven (350°) for 45 minutes, or until a toothpick inserted in the center comes out clean. Serve bread thinly sliced and very lightly buttered. Makes 18 servings.

APPLE BRITTLE SUNDAE

3 *quarts vanilla ice cream*
1 *can (1 lb.) applesauce, chilled*
½ *pound crushed peanut brittle*
   Cinnamon

Scoop ice cream into balls, and top each serving with a spoonful of applesauce and a sprinkling of crushed brittle. Dust with cinnamon. Makes 18 generous servings. (For small servings, ½ gallon of ice cream is sufficient.)

A Dinner for Important Guests

HERE IS A MEAL you will be proud to serve to the most distinguished guests. After an opening course of avocado halves filled with red (or black) caviar comes roast lamb, turnip balls, spinach with cream cheese, and butterfly rolls. The dessert is a special delight—seven rounds of crisp pastry with alternating cream and fruit fillings ⟡ Make the torte early in the day and chill until dinner time. The turnip balls can be prepared ahead and parboiled; brown them in butter just before serving. Cook the spinach at the last minute. If you make yeast rolls ahead, wrap them in foil and reheat them during the last 10 minutes of roasting the lamb. It's best to cut the first-course avocados and fill them just before serving; if you do wish to prepare them ahead, sprinkle the cut surface with lemon juice.

AVOCADO WITH CAVIAR

ROAST LEG OF SPRING LAMB

SPINACH WITH CREAM CHEESE

TURNIP BALLS   BUTTERFLY ROLLS

SEVEN-LAYER TORTE

AVOCADO WITH CAVIAR

Select small ripe avocados, allowing a half for each serving. Put a spoonful of caviar—black or red—in each cavity, place on individual plates, and garnish with fat wedges of lemon. (Or fill the avocados with crab legs or shrimp.)

ROAST LEG OF LAMB

Select a small leg of lamb, about 5 pounds. Contrary to the usual method, prick it all over with a long-tined fork. For this particular recipe, you want to release the meat juices so that they will mix with the wine used for basting. Constant basting is necessary, or the meat will become very dry. If you don't have the time to baste every 10 minutes or so, roast the lamb by the usual method, basting occasionally with the wine and drippings in the pan.

Sprinkle meat with salt. Put it, fat side up, in an open roasting pan with 6 peeled cloves of garlic, slightly crushed, and 2 cups dry white table wine, and baste every 10 or 15 minutes during the cooking. If meat is at room temperature, roast in a moderately slow oven (325°) for 1½ hours, or until the meat thermometer reads 150° if you like your lamb rare; 175° (2 hours) if you prefer it medium; 180° (2½ hours) for well done. Add 30 minutes to roasting time if lamb has been refrigerated.

The sauce, formed by the juices from the meat and the wine, will be slightly thick and richly seasoned. Serve lamb slices with meat juices. Makes 6 servings.

SPINACH WITH CREAM CHEESE

> 3 pounds fresh spinach or 2 packages
> (12 oz. each) frozen chopped spinach
> 1 small package (3 oz.) cream cheese
> Salt and pepper to taste

Steam spinach just until wilted but still bright green, drain well, and chop (if fresh spinach is used). Dice cream cheese and add to spinach along with salt and pepper. Stir until cheese melts. Makes 6 servings.

TURNIP BALLS

Pare 1 bunch large white turnips and, using a French scoop, cut into balls. (You should be able to cut 18 to 24 balls from 1 bunch of turnips.) Cook in boiling salted water until almost tender— this takes a very few minutes—and drain. In a frying pan, brown balls on all sides in about ¼ cup melted butter, and sprinkle with salt and pepper before serving. Serves 6, with 3 to 4 turnip balls per serving.

BUTTERFLY ROLLS

Use packaged hot roll mix and follow directions on package. After the first rising, divide dough in 2 equal parts and roll each into a rectangle about 8 by 12 inches. Spread each piece with 1½ tablespoons soft butter, and roll from the long edge like a jelly roll. Stretch roll evenly to 18 inches in length by rolling under the palms of the hands. Cut in 2-inch-wide pieces and, using wooden spoon handle and holding it parallel to the cut edges, press deeply into the center of each roll until the handle almost cuts it in half.

Place rolls on greased cooky sheets, bending cut ends toward the center as you do so; allow to rise until almost double in bulk, and bake in a hot oven (400°) until brown, about 12 to 15 minutes. Makes 18 rolls.

SEVEN-LAYER TORTE

> 1 cup (½ pound) butter
> 1⅔ cups flour
> ¼ cup ice water
> Sugar

Cream butter; sift flour, measure, then mix into butter alternately with ice water; mix until smooth. Chill for 1 hour. Divide dough into 6 equal portions and form into balls. Return all but 1 of the balls to the refrigerator.

On a piece of waxed paper, dusted lightly with flour, roll pastry ball into a very thin circle. Place a 9-inch plate on the dough and cut carefully around it; remove the trimmings. Turn pastry round onto cooky sheet, and peel off waxed paper; prick pastry all over with a fork, brush with ice water, sprinkle lightly with sugar, and bake in a very hot oven (450°) for 5 to 6 minutes, or until light brown, watching carefully. Make 5 more pastry rounds from the remaining balls of dough, and make the seventh layer from the trimmings cut off the other rounds.

Cream Filling:

- 1½ cups light cream
- 1-inch piece vanilla bean, or
  - 1 teaspoon vanilla
- 3 egg yolks
- ⅛ teaspoon salt
- ⅓ cup sugar
- 2 tablespoons cornstarch or
  - 4 tablespoons flour

In the top of a double boiler, scald cream with the vanilla bean or vanilla; remove bean. Gradually stir milk into slightly beaten egg yolks and return to double boiler. Thoroughly mix the salt, sugar, and cornstarch, and stir into milk and egg. Place over hot water and continue cooking and stirring until cornstarch mixture becomes smooth and thickened. Cool.

Fruit Filling:

- 2 cups applesauce or 1 cup preserves or jelly

Icing:

- 1 cup powdered sugar
- 1 tablespoon lemon juice
- 1 tablespoon water

Garnish:

- 16 blanched almonds, split
  - Angelica or candied orange peel
- 1 cup whipping cream

An hour or two before serving, put the torte together. Spread one pastry layer with one-third of the cool cream filling, top with a second layer, and spread it with one-third of the applesauce or preserves. Continue to stack layers, alternating the fillings. Spread top layer with the powdered sugar icing and garnish with the blanched almonds and the angelica, cut in fancy shapes. Spread the sides with sweetened whipped cream and pipe some whipped cream around the top with a pastry tube. Keep in refrigerator until serving time. Cut in wedges. Serves up to 12 persons.

Spring Lamb Dinner

TOSSED SALAD GREENS
WITH FRESH GRAPEFRUIT SECTIONS

FRENCH DRESSING

CROWN ROAST OF LAMB WITH
FRESH MINT STUFFING

SPICED WHOLE RED CRAB APPLES

SPRING ASPARAGUS WITH BROWNED BUTTER

RUM CUSTARD CREAM PUFF   CHOCOLATE SAUCE

SPRING LAMB takes the central position in this company dinner, accompanied by a fresh mint-and-herb stuffing and tender spears of spring asparagus. A crown roast of spring lamb centered with the mint stuffing makes the most imposing entrée, but you can use the stuffing just as well with other cuts. To serve with a roast leg of lamb and gravy, top a shallow casserole of stuffing with bacon slices and bake it separately. Or arrange 6 thick lamb chops, lightly browned, over a layer of stuffing in a shallow casserole. Bake 2-inch-thick chops, uncovered, in a moderately slow oven (325°) for 1½ hours or until stuffing is browned and lamb is tender. Baste frequently with melted butter.

CROWN ROAST OF LAMB WITH MINT STUFFING

5- to 6-pound crown roast of lamb
¼ cup sliced celery
2 tablespoons chopped onion
6 tablespoons butter
3 cups soft bread crumbs
1 egg
2 tablespoons water
⅓ cup finely chopped fresh mint
½ teaspoon each finely chopped fresh sage, marjoram, and thyme (or ¼ teaspoon of the dried herbs)
Salt and pepper to taste
Spiced whole red crab apples

Place roast on rack in open roasting pan. Prepare stuffing: Sauté celery and onion in butter until soft. Add crumbs, the egg beaten with the water, mint, sage, marjoram, thyme, salt and pepper; mix with a fork. Lightly pack into center of roast. Bake in a moderately slow oven (325°) for about 3½ hours, or figure on about 40 minutes per pound. Top the ends of rib bones with chop frills. Garnish with crab apples. Makes about 6 servings.

SPRING ASPARAGUS WITH BROWNED BUTTER

Cook 3 pounds asparagus, washed and trimmed, just until tender. Drain, season with salt and pepper, and arrange in serving dish. Pour over ⅛ cup butter which has been heated until brown and bubbling.

RUM CUSTARD CREAM PUFF

Make shell and filling from a package (about 15 oz.) of cream puff-eclair mix with vanilla filling and chocolate topping (or make shells, custard filling, and chocolate sauce from your own recipes). Flavor filling with rum or rum flavoring. Add the chocolate topping. Makes 6 desserts.

Seafood Supper

THIS MENU requires just a few finishing touches before dinner. You can assemble the fish dish early in the day and refrigerate until time to bake. Also in the morning, prepare the celery for cooking. Make the dessert ahead and warm it in the oven before serving. Just before serving, cook the celery and the peas. Make the corn muffins from a cornbread mix.

SHRIMP-FILLED SOLE ROLLS

BUTTERED GREEN PEAS   CORN MUFFINS

CELERY HEARTS WITH
SPICED TOMATO SAUCE

DEEP-DISH APPLE PIE

SHRIMP-FILLED SOLE ROLLS

    18 large sole fillets
        Salt, pepper, and paprika to taste
     2 medium-sized onions, finely chopped
     2 cups small cooked shrimp
     3 cans (4 oz. each) mushroom stems and
        pieces, drained
     4 tablespoons (¼ cup) butter or margarine
     3 cans (10½ oz. each) cream of mushroom
        soup
    1½ cups dry white table wine
    1½ cups shredded sharp Cheddar cheese

Sprinkle fish fillets with salt, pepper, paprika, and chopped onion. Chop shrimp and mushrooms and sauté lightly in butter. Spread mixture over each fillet; roll up, and fasten with toothpicks. Place in a large shallow baking pan. Mix together soup and wine and pour over fillets. Sprinkle with cheese. Bake in a hot oven (400°) for 20 minutes, or until fish flakes with a fork. Makes 18 servings.

BUTTERED GREEN PEAS

Cook 12 pounds fresh peas, shelled, in boiling salted water until tender, about 10 minutes. (Or cook 5 packages, 10 ounces each, frozen peas according to package directions.) Drain; season with butter, salt, and pepper. Makes 18 servings.

CELERY HEARTS WITH SPICED TOMATO SAUCE

    18 whole celery hearts
     2 teaspoons salt
    1½ cups water
     2 cloves garlic
    1½ cups catsup
     4 tablespoons (¼ cup) salad oil
     2 tablespoons vinegar
     4 teaspoons celery salt

Wash celery hearts (usually sold in cellophane packages); trim off ragged leaves. Tie a string around the top of each heart. Cook hearts in boiling, salted water for 15 to 20 minutes, or until tender. Drain; remove strings. Arrange cooked celery on a hot serving platter.

While celery is cooking, prepare sauce by rubbing a bowl generously with garlic, leaving pieces of about 1 clove garlic in the bowl. Pour in catsup, salad oil, and vinegar. Season with celery salt, and mix well. Spoon sauce over each celery heart before serving. Makes 18 servings.

DEEP-DISH FRESH APPLE PIE

     6 medium-sized apples
     1 cup raisins
     ⅔ cup sliced almonds
     1 cup sugar
     ½ cup orange juice
        Juice and grated peel of 1 lemon
     1 teaspoon cinnamon
     ¼ teaspoon salt
        Pastry for 2-crust 9-inch pie

Peel and chop apples; combine with raisins, almonds, sugar, orange juice, lemon juice and peel, cinnamon, and salt. Roll out ⅔ of pastry. Line 6 by 10-inch baking pan. Turn in apple mixture. Roll out remaining pastry to make top crust; place on apple mixture; seal pastry edges; slash top. Bake in hot oven (425°) for 15 minutes. Reduce heat to 350°, and bake for 40 minutes longer. Makes 8 servings.

Traditional Thanksgiving Dinner

MANY PEOPLE staunchly maintain that it isn't Thanksgiving unless a golden brown turkey dominates the festive table. This Thanksgiving dinner menu is traditional, inasmuch as it has the turkey and the cranberry sauce, but it has a few new touches to give it originality ⋘ This is designed to be a five-course meal—appetizers, soup, turkey with accompaniments, salad with cheese, dessert and coffee—and should be served in a leisurely way (especially suited to a big Thanksgiving dinner). A few minutes between courses also makes organization easy ⋘ Toast the bread for the canapés ahead of time, but spread the canapés just before serving. The miniature cream puffs that garnish each serving of soup can be made a day ahead (or make them well in advance and freeze them). Prepare the turkey and stuffing

CAVIAR AND OYSTER CANAPÉS

CONSOMMÉ PROFITEROLLES

ROAST TURKEY, ALMOND STUFFING

PRUNE AND BACON GARNISH

CRANBERRY SAUCE

MASHED POTATOES

GREEN BEANS WITH GREEN ONIONS

CELERY   RADISHES   OLIVES

ROMAINE SALAD WITH ASSORTED CHEESES

ICE CREAM WITH MINCEMEAT SAUCE

MINTS

the night before and chill separately—but do not stuff the turkey until just before roasting. Make the prune and bacon garnish ahead and chill; bake it while the turkey is "resting" out of the oven for 20 to 30 minutes before carving. Slice the cheese just before dinner to let it reach full flavor and room temperature; keep it covered with foil or clear adhesive wrap.

CAVIAR AND OYSTER CANAPÉS

- 10 slices white bread
- 1 jar (3½ oz.) caviar
- 20 smoked oysters
  Lemon juice

Toast bread slices lightly on both sides, and then cut in 1½-inch circles. Spread with caviar and top each circle with a smoked oyster. Sprinkle lightly with lemon juice. Makes 20 appetizers.

CONSOMMÉ PROFITEROLLES

Profiterolles are miniature cream puff shells. You can make them from prepared cream puff mix or your own recipe for cream puffs. Drop ¼ teaspoonfuls of dough on an ungreased cooky sheet. Bake in a hot oven (425°) for about 15 minutes.

Use your favorite canned consommé, but flavor each 10½-ounce can with 1 tablespoon sherry. Serve hot in cups garnished with the profiterolles —3 or 4 on each serving.

ROAST TURKEY, ALMOND STUFFING

Roast turkey as usual with stuffing. Add ¼ cup slivered toasted almonds to each cup of your favorite bread dressing, or use this recipe for a 16-pound turkey:

- 2 cups minced onion
- 1 pound melted butter
- 2 cups thinly sliced celery
- 2 teaspoons salt
- 1 teaspoon each thyme, marjoram, savory, and sage
- 10 cups toasted stale bread crumbs
- 2½ cups slivered toasted almonds

Cook onion in butter until golden. Combine with other ingredients. Squeeze some dressing together tightly in your hand; if it won't stay together when released, add a little hot water. Makes about 16 cups.

PRUNE AND BACON GARNISH

Remove pits from large cooked prunes, and insert a stuffed green olive. Wrap each with half a slice of bacon, and bake in a moderate oven (350°) until the bacon is crisp, about 20 minutes.

GREEN BEANS WITH GREEN ONIONS

Cook green beans as usual, planning on 3 pounds fresh beans for 8 servings. For each pound, add ¼ cup chopped green onions that have been sautéed in 1 tablespoon butter.

ICE CREAM WITH MINCEMEAT SAUCE

Top each serving of vanilla ice cream with a dollop of hot brandied mincemeat. Serve at once. For a more spectacular dessert, heat mincemeat at the table in a chafing dish; light ¼ cup warm brandy (for each pint of mincemeat), and pour into mincemeat. Spoon sauce over the ice cream while it's still burning.

Sit-Down Dinner for Eight

THE DAY BEFORE the party: Section grapefruit and stuff prunes; mix ham loaf; bake and whip sweet potatoes; bake cream puffs and cook pudding for filling (fold the whipped cream into the pudding and fill the cream puffs just before serving time). The rolls may be made ahead on the day of the dinner from refrigerator yeast dough and reheated just before serving. To make clean-cut slices, schedule loaf to come out of the oven 20 minutes before serving time.

GRAPEFRUIT PINWHEELS WITH
CHEESE-STUFFED PRUNES

GLAZED HAM LOAF, HORSERADISH SAUCE

WHIPPED SWEET POTATOES

PEAS AND SAUTÉED MUSHROOMS

CRESCENT ROLLS, ORANGE MARMALADE

BUTTERSCOTCH CREAM PUFFS

GRAPEFRUIT PINWHEELS WITH CHEESE-STUFFED PRUNES

2 small packages (3 oz. each) softened
    cream cheese
3 tablespoons mayonnaise
    Dash of salt
¼ cup finely chopped pecans
16 large pitted, cooked dried prunes
4 large grapefruit
1 bunch endive

Cream together the cheese, mayonnaise, and salt; mix in the chopped nuts. Stuff some of the cheese mixture into each prune. Peel and section grapefruit. For each serving arrange 6 or 7 fresh grapefruit sections in the shape of a pinwheel on a bed of endive on salad plates. Center 2 stuffed prunes in each pinwheel. Makes 8 servings.

GLAZED HAM LOAF WITH HORSERADISH SAUCE

2 pounds uncooked smoked ham, ground
1½ pounds fresh pork, ground
1 cup cracker crumbs
2 eggs
1 cup hot milk
1 cup spiced peach syrup

Mix together thoroughly the ground meats, cracker crumbs, and eggs. Add hot milk and mix again. Shape into a loaf and place in a 9-inch-square pan. Pour over as much peach syrup as will soak into the loaf. Bake in a moderate oven (350°) for 45 minutes, basting several times with the remaining spiced syrup. Accompany with horseradish sauce. Makes 8 generous servings.

Horseradish sauce:

½ cup whipping cream
1 tablespoon prepared horseradish
1 teaspoon sugar
½ teaspoon lemon juice

Whip cream until stiff, and fold in horseradish, sugar, and lemon juice. Spoon into a sauce bowl. Chill for several hours. Makes about 1 cup.

WHIPPED SWEET POTATOES

Cook about 4 pounds sweet potatoes in boiling water until tender; peel and mash. Beat, gradually adding enough milk or cream to make soft and fluffy. Beat in 4 tablespoons butter. Season to taste with salt and ground nutmeg. Makes 8 servings.

PEAS AND SAUTÉED MUSHROOMS

3 packages (10 oz. each) frozen peas or
    6 pounds fresh peas, shelled
    Boiling salted water
½ pound fresh mushrooms, sliced
4 tablespoons (¼ cup) butter
    Salt to taste

Cook peas in boiling salted water just until tender. Sauté mushrooms in butter. Drain peas, toss with mushrooms, season with salt. Makes 8 servings.

BUTTERSCOTCH CREAM PUFFS

8 medium-sized cream puffs (use a package
    mix or your own favorite recipe)
1 package butterscotch pudding
2 cups milk
1 cup (½ pint) whipping cream

Bake cream puffs and cool. Cook butterscotch pudding with milk as directed; let cool. Just before serving, or as early as 2 hours in advance, whip cream and fold into pudding. Just before serving, slit cream puffs; spoon in filling. Makes 8 servings.

Two-Bird Thanksgiving Dinner

MIXED GREENS WITH ORANGE AND AVOCADO

ROAST TURKEY

CHESTNUT AND OYSTER STUFFING

GIBLET GRAVY

ROAST GOOSE

APPLE AND PRUNE STUFFING

BRUSSELS SPROUTS, ONION BUTTER

BAKED SWEET POTATOES

JELLIED CRANBERRY MOLD

BUTTERED DINNER ROLLS

 TOMATO PRESERVES

CELERY HEARTS   OLIVES   PICKLES

PRESERVED KUMQUATS

SPICED CRABAPPLES

RUM MINCE PIE   PUMPKIN CREAM PIE

THE FAMILY CIRCLE traditionally widens on Thanksgiving to take in relatives, and often friends; and nowadays many people invite exchange students and others from foreign lands to share in this authentically American celebration. With such a large group to serve, thoughtful planning, advance preparation, and careful stage managing are of major importance. ⤳ This is a two-bird menu, featuring an 8-pound roast goose and a turkey weighing about 10 pounds. Both are traditional entrées for this occasion. Guests can take their preference, and father and grandfather each can carve a bird. Let the guests enjoy their first-course salad while they watch the carving ⤳ Unless your dining table is unusually large, you will probably need to improvise so that your guests can be seated comfortably. The large table shown here, which seats up to 14, is simply a 4 by 8-foot panel of fir plywood (½, ⅝, or ¾ inch thick) set on sawhorses. It could be set up in a living room, quite appropriate for the occasion and preferable to crowding guests into a dining alcove or modest-sized dining room. The carving table at the rear lets both father and grandfather carve at the same time; then it can be moved away.

A handsome striped percale, king-sized bed sheet serves as a tablecloth for the large table, and a twin-bed sheet covers the carving table. (Or you could stitch and hem yardage.) The centerpiece is an idea frequently used in Europe. Flags of the nations represented around the table are on display. These are inexpensive paper flags sold in stationery stores. If you can't find them, let the children make flags with water colors or pastel crayons, using the encyclopedia as a reference.

Start your dinner preparations the day before. Wash the salad greens and prepare the salad dressing. Make the jellied cranberry mold and chill it in the refrigerator overnight. Make both stuffings and refrigerate; *do not* stuff the birds until time to roast. Prepare the onion butter in advance, and reheat it just before serving on sprouts. Make both pies the day before; store the pumpkin cream pie in the refrigerator and serve it chilled; leave the rum mince pie at room temperature and warm it slightly in the oven before serving.

Truss and roast the turkey in your usual way; directions follow for roasting the goose. You can combine the giblets from both birds; cook and add to all or part of the gravy (perhaps you'll want to offer two bowls of gravy, one with and one without giblets).

MIXED GREENS WITH ORANGE AND AVOCADO

- ¼ cup vinegar
- 2 teaspoons grated orange peel
- ½ cup orange juice
- Juice of 1 large lemon
- ¼ cup sugar
- ½ teaspoon each dry mustard and salt
- 1 cup salad oil
- 3 large oranges
- 2 large avocados
- 2 medium-sized sweet onions
- 2 heads romaine
- 1 head leaf lettuce
- 1 head iceberg lettuce

In a quart jar, combine vinegar, orange peel, orange juice, lemon juice, sugar, mustard, salt, and salad oil. Cover, shake well, and refrigerate. Shake again before using.

Cut all rind off oranges, slice fruit; cut each slice in 2 or 3 pieces. Peel and cut the avocados into large cubes. Peel onions and slice very thinly; divide into rings. Combine oranges, avocados, and onions; over them pour some of the dressing, cover; refrigerate for several hours.

Just before serving, tear the crisp greens into a large salad bowl. Add oranges, avocados, onions, and dressing. Mix gently. Makes 12 servings.

To carve goose, cut off tips and first joints of wings, cut through skin on back to expose hip joints. Insert knife tip to loosen joints, then free meat from bone above joints.

Stuffings for the turkey and the goose start with the same basic mixture. You divide this and add ingredients to make two distinctly different stuffings. You can make both the day before and refrigerate; *do not* stuff birds until time to roast.

You can use dried chestnuts (available in Italian or Chinese markets) for the Chestnut and Oyster Stuffing. They're already shelled and skinned, but it is sometimes necessary to pick out some of the skin that is lurking in the interstices after they are cooked. Soak chestnuts overnight in warm water. To cook, cover them with water, bring to a boil, and cook until tender, about 1 hour.

Basic Mixture:

2½ quarts bread cubes, lightly toasted
1 large onion, finely chopped
3 cups finely chopped celery

Apple and Prune Stuffing for Goose:

3 apples, peeled and chopped
   (about 2 cups)
1½ cups soft dried prunes, cut in pieces
1 teaspoon salt
¼ cup lemon juice
2 tablespoons melted butter or margarine

Chestnut and Oyster Stuffing for Turkey:

2 cups cooked dried chestnuts,
   coarsely chopped
8 to 10 medium-sized oysters, each cut
   in several pieces
1 shredded wheat biscuit, crushed
1½ teaspoons Worcestershire
1 small clove garlic, mashed
1 teaspoon salt
½ teaspoon poultry seasoning
¼ teaspoon each thyme, rosemary,
   and marjoram
⅛ teaspoon pepper
½ cup (¼ pound) butter, melted

Combine the bread cubes with onion and celery. Divide mixture in half.

To the first half, add apples, prunes, and salt; mix lemon juice with the melted butter and pour over; toss to blend.

To the second bowl of basic stuffing mixture, add the chestnuts, oysters, shredded wheat, and remaining seasonings. Over this pour melted butter; mix well.

Stuffing is enough for a 10 to 14-pound turkey and an 8 to 10-pound goose.

ROAST GOOSE

Rinse goose with cold water; remove any large layers of fat from the body cavity. Wipe the bird dry. Sprinkle inside with salt and pepper. Stuff the wishbone cavity with Apple and Prune Stuffing; bring neck skin over back and fasten with a skewer. Turn bird over and fill the body cavity with stuffing. Insert skewers or toothpicks across

Steadying wing with fingers or fork, cut off remaining wing section by forcing knife tip at 45° angle into breast to joint; sever joint, turning knife while pulling wing.

With fork firmly anchored in thigh, cut between leg and body while pressing leg down to cutting board—this should break loose the hip joint. Cut on through to free the leg.

Remove side of breast by inserting knife between the meat and the keel bone. Cut to breastbone; follow along wishbone to wing joint. Cut meat free from bone, lifting with fork.

the opening, and lace shut with cord. Loop cord around ends of drumsticks and draw them slightly in toward the body. Place breast-side-down on a rack in an uncovered pan. Roast in a moderately slow oven (325°); it is not necessary to baste. Spoon or siphon off the fat as it accumulates in the pan during roasting. When it is about two-thirds done, as figured against the following time-table, turn the bird breast up and finish roasting.

Plan to have the goose finish cooking about ½ hour before dinner is scheduled. The drumstick meat should feel soft when the bird is done.

Weight in Pounds

(ready-to-cook)	Time in Hours
4 to 6	2¾ to 3
6 to 8	3 to 3½
8 to 10	3½ to 3¾
10 to 12	3¾ to 4¼
12 to 14	4¼ to 4¾

The anatomy of a goose differs markedly from that of a turkey in one particular: the hip joints are located almost at the backbone. Finding and cutting these two joints is the one tricky part of carving. Loosen these joints in the kitchen, with the bird resting breast side down; cut meat free from bone above joints. Then arrange the goose, still intact, breast up on the carving board. (If necessary, place bread slices under the goose to steady it.) At the table, proceed with the carving. Cut off wing sections and legs. Remove each side of breast in one whole piece: Insert knife between meat and keel bone, cut to breastbone, follow along wishbone to wing joint Cut meat free, lifting with fork. Cut breast meat into serving-size pieces.

BRUSSELS SPROUTS, ONION BUTTER

> 2 medium-sized onions, sliced
> 6 tablespoons butter or margarine
> 4 packages (10 oz. each) Brussels sprouts
>   or 3 to 4 pounds fresh sprouts
> 1 cup chicken stock (canned or made from
>   dehydrated base)
>   Salt and pepper to taste

Sauté the onion in butter very slowly until soft and golden brown. Cook the sprouts in chicken stock in a large kettle, steaming them just until tender. Drain; toss with onion butter; season with salt and pepper. Makes 12 servings.

BAKED SWEET POTATOES

Plan on 1 sweet potato for each serving. Scrub and dry each; rub with a little salad oil or butter. Bake in a moderate oven (350°) for 45 to 50 minutes or until tender. To serve, cut a 1½-inch cross in top of each. Holding potato with clean towel, press from bottom until interior partially bursts through top; break up lightly with fork. Top with butter, salt, and paprika.

JELLIED CRANBERRY MOLD

> 2 pounds fresh cranberries
> 2 cups boiling water
> 4 cups sugar
>   Apple slices and walnut halves for garnish

Pick over the berries; wash and drain. Turn into a large kettle, add water, and cook until the skins burst (about 10 minutes). Force berries and juice through a coarse strainer. Add sugar and cook until the sugar is completely dissolved (about 5 minutes). Pour into two 1-quart molds. Chill overnight. Unmold; garnish with unpeeled apple slices (dipped in lemon juice) and walnut halves. Makes 2 quarts.

RUM MINCE PIE

For best flavor, serve this rum mince pie while it's warm. The addition of mangoes (or peaches) mellows the rich sweet flavors of mincemeat.

> 1 jar (1 lb. 14 oz.) ready-to-use mincemeat
> 1½ cups sliced canned mangoes or peaches
>   Pastry for a double-crust 9-inch pie
> 3 tablespoons rum (optional)

Mix the mincemeat and mangoes together; spoon into a pastry-lined 9-inch pie pan, smoothing to the edge. Top with spoke-type pastry top or a lattice top. Bake in a hot oven (400°) for about 30 minutes or until crust is browned. After removing from the oven, spoon rum through openings in the top. Makes 6 to 8 servings.

PUMPKIN CREAM PIE

Ice cream is the secret ingredient in this quick pumpkin pie. Make it the day before, if you wish, and add the garnish of orange wedges and whipped cream shortly before serving.

    1 can (1 lb.) pumpkin
    ½ cup sugar
    ½ teaspoon each salt, cinnamon, nutmeg,
         cloves, and ground ginger
    1 envelope (1 tablespoon) unflavored
         gelatin
    ¼ cup orange juice
    1 pint vanilla ice cream
        Baked 9-inch pie shell
        Sweetened whipped cream
        Mandarin orange wedges, drained
           thoroughly

In a saucepan, combine pumpkin and a mixture of the sugar, salt, cinnamon, nutmeg, cloves, and ginger; heat through. When hot, stir in the gelatin dissolved in the orange juice; remove from heat and cool to room temperature. Meanwhile, spoon ice cream into bowl so it will soften slightly. Beat the softened ice cream with electric mixer until smooth, add cooled pumpkin mixture, and beat until completely blended. Turn into baked pie shell and refrigerate for at least 2 hours. Garnish with whipped cream and the mandarin orange wedges. Makes 6 to 8 servings.

Mandarin orange wedges and fluted whipped cream garnish this pumpkin pie. Store it in refrigerator; serve chilled.

Mince pie takes on a new appearance when you add sliced canned mangoes or peaches and fancy top pastry.

Picnic Dinner Party

WHY NOT have your next dinner party in a shaded glen—a picnic buffet served out-of-doors and away from home? Here's a picnic menu for six, designed especially for adult tastes. For all of its dining room manners, you'll find that the dishes are as easy to prepare, transport, and serve as the more traditional picnic foods ❧ To eliminate the usual picnic chore of building a fire, borrow a convenience from the buffet table: canned alcohol fuel. If you have a chafing dish, by all means take it along—its elegance is quite in keeping with the menu—and let it triple as carrying container, heating implement, and serving dish for the entrée. Otherwise, you can duplicate the function of the chafing dish by assembling an uncomplicated cooker like the one shown in the photograph—a light metal stand (this one is a holder for a

OPEN-FACE SHRIMP SANDWICHES

FRESH MUSHROOM CREAM SOUP

PILOT CRACKERS

 BUTTER-FRIZZLED CORNED BEEF ROLLS

MARINATED BABY BEETS AND ONIONS

SPINACH GREENS SALAD WITH PINE NUT DRESSING

BREAD STICKS

MUSCAT GRAPES

DRY MONTEREY JACK   GRUYÈRE

casserole) with ignited alcohol fuel placed beneath. Most of these dishes can be prepared a day ahead—soup, corned beef rolls, beets and onions (which are better if they stand overnight), and salad dressing. Just before you depart, make the sandwiches and coffee, and reheat the soup. In each of the recipes, there is a suggestion for carrying the food to the picnic.

OPEN-FACE SHRIMP SANDWICHES

Cut sliced, firm-textured white or whole wheat bread into crust-free rounds, strips, or squares; or use thinly sliced buffet rye bread. Butter bread lightly; if you wish, spread also with mayonnaise, mustard, or commercial sour cream. On each slice, neatly arrange small whole cooked shrimp (fresh, frozen, or canned) or cooked prawns, split in half lengthwise. Garnish with minced parsley, dill weed, or paprika. Place sandwiches in a single layer on a tray and cover. Carry to picnic in ice chest. Allow 2 or 3 sandwiches for each serving.

FRESH MUSHROOM CREAM SOUP

1 pound fresh mushrooms, chopped
½ cup (¼ pound) butter or margarine
¼ cup flour
1 cup light cream
2 cups milk
Salt to taste

Simmer mushrooms in ¼ cup of the butter for 10 minutes; whirl smooth in a blender (or rub through a wire strainer). Melt the remaining ¼ cup butter, and blend with flour and cream; cook, stirring until thickened. Add mushrooms and juices, milk, and salt to taste. Heat to simmering; pour into vacuum bottle. Serve in cups. Makes 6 servings.

BUTTER-FRIZZLED CORNED BEEF ROLLS

1½ pounds freshly cooked (not canned)
    corned beef
12 to 16 white or black figs
    (peeled, if needed)
    Lemon juice
½ cup (¼ pound) butter or margarine
1½ tablespoons each brown sugar and
    dry mustard

Cut corned beef in ⅛-inch-thick slices that are as large in diameter as possible. (Or purchase corned beef at a delicatessen.) Cut figs in halves and dip in lemon juice. Roll each slice of corned beef around a piece of fruit and secure meat with a toothpick.

Melt butter in a wide (about 14 inches), shallow pan. Blend in brown sugar and mustard. Remove from heat. Coat each meat roll in butter and arrange one layer deep in pan; place any extras in another pan, to be heated for second servings. Cover and chill. Carry to picnic in ice chest. At picnic, heat over direct flame until butter bubbles and rolls are heated; turn only once as rolls are rather fragile. To hasten heating, place 2 or 3 cans of canned alcohol fuel beneath pan and ignite. Makes 6 servings.

MARINATED BABY BEETS AND ONIONS

2 cans (1 lb. each) small whole beets
2 medium-sized mild salad onions,
    thinly sliced
½ cup red wine vinegar
1 teaspoon dill weed
1 to 2 tablespoons sugar
½ teaspoon salt
¼ teaspoon pepper

Drain beets, reserving 1 cup of the liquid. In a deep bowl, combine beets and reserved liquid with onions, vinegar, dill weed, sugar, salt, and pepper. Let chill several hours (overnight is best). Carry beets and onions to picnic in a tightly covered container in ice chest. Makes 6 servings.

SPINACH GREENS SALAD WITH PINE NUT DRESSING

½ cup chopped pine nuts
¼ cup salad or olive oil
3 tablespoons tarragon vinegar
¼ teaspoon grated lemon peel
½ teaspoon salt
    Dash nutmeg
1½ quarts crisp, fresh spinach

Combine pine nuts, salad oil, vinegar, lemon peel, salt, and nutmeg. Carry to picnic in a small jar. Carry spinach to picnic in plastic bag in ice chest. Just before serving, break spinach into bite-size pieces and toss with dressing. Makes 6 servings.

Polynesian Buffet

THE COLOR and informality of this buffet are well suited to a poolside setting. The foods are adaptations of both Tahitian and Hawaiian dishes ⋘ This is a buffet meal that is easy on the hostess. The Masked Fish Polynesian and the Raw Fish Tahitian Style are made in the morning, then chilled in the refrigerator. You may assemble the Tahitian Spinach and Hawaiian Chicken in Papaya ahead of time and finish cooking them while the party is in progress ⋘ It's logical that Polynesians seldom use a formal floral centerpiece. Their food is ablaze with color, and everything goes on the table at once. If you do want a centerpiece, fruit makes a handsome one and stands up well even though you may keep it on the table outside for several hours. You might tuck several blossoms into the arrangement at the last minute.

HAWAIIAN CHICKEN IN PAPAYA

POISSON CRU (RAW FISH TAHITIAN STYLE)

FAFA (TAHITIAN SPINACH)

MASKED FISH POLYNESIAN

ICE CREAM BALLS IN COCONUT

HAWAIIAN CHICKEN IN PAPAYA

Papaya serves as both a baking and serving container. You fill the fruit with chicken, peas, and a mushroom sauce. The papaya holds in the mingled flavors as the mixture steams.

> 4 *large chicken breasts*
> 8 *small chicken thighs*
> 4 *tablespoons (¼ cup) butter or margarine*
> 8 *large papayas*
> 2 *tablespoons flour*
> 1 *can (4 oz.) button mushrooms*
>   *Water (approximately ⅔ cup)*
> 1 *can (6 oz.) brown mushroom sauce*
>   *Salt and pepper*
> ½ *package (10 oz.) frozen peas, thawed*

Cut chicken breasts in half so they will fit inside the papayas. Fry chicken in butter slowly until golden brown and barely tender. While chicken is cooking, cut a cap from each papaya. Scoop out the seeds. Remove chicken from pan. Pour off all but 2 tablespoons of the drippings; blend in the flour. Drain liquid from mushrooms, and add to it enough water to make 1 cup; pour into pan, and stirring, cook until sauce is smooth and thickened. Stir in mushrooms and mushroom sauce. Taste, and add salt and pepper if desired.

Now, fill each papaya with 1 or 2 pieces of chicken, 3 or 4 tablespoons of mushroom sauce, and a tablespoon of peas; replace the caps. Place papayas in a shallow baking pan; pour in ½ inch of water. Bake in a moderate oven (350°) for 1½ hours, or until papaya is tender. Makes 8 servings.

POISSON CRU

This colorful fish dish, a relish that tastes much like *lomi* salmon, is cooked by lime juice rather than heat.

> 2 *pounds boned and skinned halibut*
> 1 *tablespoon salt*
> ⅔ *cup lime juice*
> 4 *green onions and tops, chopped*
> ½ *green pepper, seeded and chopped*
> 1 *large tomato, peeled and chopped*
> 2 *tablespoons chopped parsley*
> ¾ *cup coconut milk (see recipe for Fafa,*
>   *below) or French dressing*
> 1 *hard-cooked egg*

Cut fish into bite-size pieces; mix lightly with salt and lime juice, then chill in refrigerator for at least 3 hours. Drain well; add the chopped onions and tops, green pepper, tomato, and parsley; mix well. Pour over coconut milk or French dressing, and chill for 1 hour. Slice the hard-cooked egg and arrange over fish before serving. Makes 8 servings.

Serve papayas with caps on so filling stays hot. Ti leaves line serving plate, add to party's "Island" atmosphere.

To prepare papaya for chicken filling, cut cap about 2½ by 4½ inches from each papaya. Remove seeds.

Slide browned chicken into papaya gently so fruit does not split. Spoon peas, sauce over and around chicken.

FAFA

In this dish, spinach is substituted for the tiny young taro leaves generally used by Polynesian cooks. The spinach is seasoned with onion and enriched with bacon and coconut milk. Salt pork or ham can be used in place of bacon if you wish.

    3 bunches spinach
    ¼ cup lime juice
    6 slices bacon, cut in small pieces
    1 medium-sized onion, chopped
    1 cup coconut milk

Wash, trim, and chop spinach; place in a covered saucepan, and using the water that clings to the leaves, steam for 5 minutes; drain thoroughly, then turn into a 2½-quart casserole. Sprinkle over the lime juice. Cook bacon until half done; add the chopped onion and continue to sauté until onion is wilted; pour bacon, onion, and drippings over spinach. Pour over coconut milk. (Use frozen coconut milk, or make coconut milk as follows: Pour 2 cups boiling water or scalded milk over 4 cups finely grated fresh coconut; let stand for 20 minutes. Strain through a double thickness of cheesecloth. Squeeze tightly to remove all liquid. Makes 2 cups.) Cover and bake in a moderate oven (350°) for 45 minutes. Before serving, mix bacon through the spinach with a fork. If desired, pour over a little more coconut milk. Makes 8 servings.

MASKED FISH POLYNESIAN

For the place of honor on the buffet table, this Masked Fish Polynesian is a good choice. The pickled beet and green pepper cutouts, which decorate the fish, and the garnishes are good munching foods, too.

    1 whole white fish, approximately 5 to 7
         pounds (corbina, ling cod)
       Salt to taste
    ½ cup water
    2 envelopes (2 tablespoons) unflavored
         gelatin
    ½ cup cold water
    2 cups mayonnaise

Garnishes:

    Thinly sliced pickled beets, cut into ovals
         and half circles
    Green pepper wedges and rings
    Radish roses
    Cooked prawns
    Water cress

Remove the tail from the fish and cut off the head, leaving the collar intact. Sprinkle inside of fish with salt. Place on a sheet of heavy aluminum foil, cup the edges, then pour in the ½ cup water. Wrap foil over fish; fold and crimp edges together. Place on a shallow pan and bake in a moderate oven (350°) for 30 minutes, or until fish flakes with a fork. While still warm, fold back foil and pull off skin. Chill fish in refrigerator. When very cold, carefully transfer to a large serving platter or chop plate.

Soften gelatin in cold water; melt over hot water, then stir into mayonnaise. Chill until syrupy; quickly spread all but ¼ cup of sauce over cold fish; chill.

If the remaining masking sauce has set, reheat it over hot water to soften, then chill again until syrupy. Now decorate the fish with beet ovals and green pepper wedges, dipping the backs of the "cutouts" into the syrupy mixture before placing them on the fish. Arrange beet half circles in a fan for the fish's tail. Place green pepper rings at the head. Garnish with radish roses, prawns, and water cress. Serve well chilled.

ICE CREAM BALLS IN COCONUT

Roll balls of vanilla or coconut ice cream in freshly grated coconut early in the day. Keep them in the freezer until serving time.

A Simple Dinner for Guests

THIS DINNER is a treat for guests, but it's easy on the hostess. It features anchovy turnovers, veal scaloppine, broccoli, rice, and pears with Zabaglione Cut the fresh vegetable sticks ahead of time and keep them crisp in ice water. Make the turnovers in advance and chill them until you are ready to bake them just before serving time. Cook the veal scaloppine and vegetables while the rice bakes.

ANCHOVY TURNOVERS

FRESH VEGETABLE STICKS

VEAL SCALOPPINE

BROCCOLI OR ZUCCHINI

TWO-TONE RICE

PEARS WITH ZABAGLIONE

ANCHOVY TURNOVERS

- 1 cup flour
- 1 small package (3 oz.) cream cheese
- ½ cup (¼ pound) butter or margarine
- 1 tube anchovy paste

Sift flour, measure, and sift again into a mixing bowl. Cut in cream cheese and butter. Roll into a ball, and chill for about 2 hours. Roll out dough ⅛ inch thick and cut into 2-inch rounds. Put about ¼ teaspoon anchovy paste in the center of each round. Moisten edges and press together, turnover fashion. Prick tops. Place on a baking sheet and chill until serving time. Then bake in a moderately hot oven (375°) for 10 minutes. Serve at once. Makes about 5½ dozen.

VEAL SCALOPPINE

- 2 to 2½ pounds veal cutlets, sliced thin
- 2 tablespoons flour
  Salt and pepper
- 3 tablespoons each olive oil and butter
- 1 lemon, very thinly sliced
  Juice of 1 lemon
  Few drops garlic juice (use a press)
- 2 tablespoons minced parsley
- ¼ cup water
  Salt to taste

Pound veal cutlets slightly, and dust with flour and salt and pepper to taste. Cook them quickly on both sides in olive oil and butter. When brown on both sides, remove to a platter and keep warm.

In the pan, brown lemon slices and arrange on meat. Add lemon juice to pan along with garlic juice, parsley, and water. Bring to a boil, stirring the crusty bits from the pan. Add salt if necessary. Pour over the meat. Makes 6 servings.

TWO-TONE RICE

- ¾ cup each well-washed wild rice and uncooked white rice
- 3 cups consommé
- 2 tablespoons each soy and minced onion

Cook wild rice in 1½ cups of the consommé for 10 minutes. Meanwhile, place white rice in a 1-quart baking dish in a slow oven (300°) to toast until golden brown. Stir in the remaining 1½ cups consommé, soy, minced onion, and partially cooked wild rice. Bake in a moderate oven (350°) for 30 minutes. Makes 6 servings.

PEARS WITH ZABAGLIONE

- 6 ripe fresh pears
- 2 cups sugar
- 1 cup water
- 1 teaspoon vanilla

Zabaglione:

- 4 egg yolks
- 3 tablespoons sugar
- 4 tablespoons Marsala or sherry

Peel pears, cut in half, and core. Cook a syrup with sugar, water, and vanilla. Poach pears in it for 5 minutes. Chill in syrup; drain. (Save syrup for another use.) For the sauce, put egg yolks in the top of a double boiler and beat until light. Beat in sugar. Heat Marsala and beat in gradually, then place mixture over hot water and cook until thick, beating constantly. Do not overcook or it will curdle. Chill sauce and spoon over pears, or serve it warm. Sprinkle with toasted slivered almonds, if desired. Makes 6 servings.

Fillet of Sole Dinner

PLAN TO DO MOST of the preparation just before serving this dinner, but cook and chill the beans for the salad ahead of time.

AVOCADO WITH PROSCIUTTO

FILLET OF SOLE WITH CLAMS

RISI PISI   WHOLE WHEAT ROLLS

ITALIAN GREEN BEAN SALAD

CHOCOLATE SOUFFLÉ

AVOCADO WITH PROSCIUTTO

You can serve this as an appetizer, along with a beverage, or as a first course. If it is served as an appetizer, cut the ripe peeled avocado in cubes (about ¾ inch) and wrap in very thinly sliced pieces of prosciutto (Italian ham). Fasten together with toothpicks. If served as a first course, alternate slices of prosciutto and avocado on individual plates, overlapping them.

FILLET OF SOLE WITH CLAMS

　　2 cups each water and dry white table wine
　　¼ teaspoon thyme
　　1 small whole onion, peeled
　　1 small carrot, sliced
　　½ bay leaf
　　1 sprig parsley
　　6 small fillets of sole
　　2 cans (7 oz. each) minced clams
　　3 tablespoons each butter and flour
　　½ cup heavy cream
　　6 whole fresh mushrooms
　　　 Butter

Make a court bouillon by simmering together for 10 minutes the water, wine, thyme, onion, carrot, bay leaf, and parsley; strain. Poach sole fillets in the court bouillon for about 4 minutes, or until they lose their translucent look. Remove to a well-buttered, shallow baking dish. Drain the liquid from clams, and add the liquid to the court bouillon; boil until it is reduced to 1½ cups.

In a saucepan, melt butter, stir in flour, add the reduced stock and cream, and cook until thick and smooth. Add clams, correct seasoning, and pour over the fillets. Garnish each fillet with a butter-broiled mushroom; place under broiler to brown for a minute before serving. Makes 6 servings.

RISI PISI

Combine 3 cups hot cooked fresh peas, 3 cups hot boiled rice, 3 tablespoons melted butter, and 2 tablespoons minced parsley. Makes 6 servings.

ITALIAN GREEN BEAN SALAD

Cook 2 packages (10 oz. each) frozen Italian green beans according to directions. Drain and chill. At serving time, arrange individual servings on lettuce-lined salad plates. Garnish with pimiento strips. Serve with dressing made of 1 part wine vinegar, 3 or 4 parts olive oil, and salt and pepper to taste. Makes 6 servings.

CHOCOLATE SOUFFLÉ

　　2½ ounces unsweetened chocolate
　　½ cup sugar
　　5 tablespoons hot water
　　5 tablespoons butter
　　3 tablespoons flour
　　1 cup milk
　　½ teaspoon salt
　　4 egg yolks
　　5 egg whites
　　1 teaspoon vanilla

Melt the chocolate over hot water. Add ¼ cup of the sugar and the hot water, and stir until smooth. In a saucepan, melt butter. Stir in flour to make a smooth paste; gradually add milk, and bring slowly to a boil. Add chocolate mixture and salt. Cool slightly, then combine with the very well-beaten egg yolks. Cool to lukewarm.

Beat egg whites until almost stiff; add remaining sugar gradually, beating until glossy. Add the vanilla. Combine one-third of the whites very thoroughly with the chocolate mixture, then carefully fold in remaining whites. Pour into a buttered 2-quart soufflé dish and bake in a moderately hot oven (375°) for 25 minutes. (This will give you a soufflé with a nice crusty bottom and sides, and a creamy interior. If you prefer a firmer soufflé, bake at 325° for about 40 minutes.) Makes 6 servings.

A Mexican Menu for Christmas Eve

Our Mexican Neighbors have developed to a fine art the gay celebration of religious holidays. They don't have the tree or the Santa Claus that we inherited from Germanic ancestors, but we see eye to eye on Christmas feasting. This Christmas Eve menu features *Mole de Guajolote* (turkey in a spicy chocolate sauce), one of the most festive of Mexican dishes Decorate your table with souvenirs that you or friends or relatives have brought back from Mexico. Play records of Mexican music, or round up your own *mariachis* to sing and play.

GUACAMOLE WITH POMEGRANATE SEEDS

TOSTADAS (TOASTED TORTILLA WEDGES)

MOLE DE GUAJOLOTE   SOPAIPILLAS

RICE   GREEN SALAD

BAKED PINEAPPLE, NATILLAS

GUACAMOLE WITH POMEGRANATE SEEDS

> 3 large ripe avocados
> 1 clove garlic, pressed
> 1 can (4 oz.) peeled green chilies, chopped
>   (optional)
> 1 teaspoon salt
>   Additional salt, cayenne, and
>   lemon juice to taste
>   Pomegranate seeds

Mash avocados with a fork until smooth, but with definite chunks showing. Add pressed garlic, chilies, if desired, and the 1 teaspoon salt. Add additional salt, cayenne, and lemon juice to taste. Sprinkle top with pomegranate seeds. Serves 8 to 12.

TOSTADAS

A tostada is any toasted tortilla, garnished or not. In this case they are corn tortillas, each cut in six pie-shaped wedges and cooked in deep fat (370°) until crisp and brown. Make as many as you like. Drain on paper toweling.

MOLE DE GUAJOLOTE

This is a classic Mexican dish supposedly created by the nuns of Puebla in preparation for the visit of a church dignitary. They put practically everything in the kitchen into their creation, and it has been a national feast dish ever since. This is a simplified version using chili powder instead of many varieties of chili peppers.

> 12-pound turkey, disjointed, or 4 pounds
>   turkey breasts and 3 pounds turkey
>   thighs
> ½ cup flour
> 1 teaspoon salt
> ½ cup rendered turkey fat or shortening
>   Water
> 2 teaspoons salt

Mole Sauce:

> 2 large or 3 medium onions, chopped
> 1 large or 2 medium cloves garlic, chopped
> ½ cup seedless raisins
> 2 squares (2 oz.) unsweetened chocolate,
>   cut in small pieces
> ¼ teaspoon each ground anise seed, coriander
>   seed, cumin seed, and cloves
> ½ cup peanut butter
> 1 can (8 oz.) tomato sauce
>   About ¾ cup chili powder
> 2 toasted bread slices
> 3 or 4 dry tortillas, toasted
> 2 tablespoons sesame seed, toasted
> 6 cups turkey broth
> 1 tablespoon sugar

Rub turkey with flour which has been seasoned with the 1 teaspoon salt. Brown in turkey fat or shortening (the Mexicans usually use lard). Put in a large pot, cover with water, add 2 teaspoons salt, and cook until tender. Cool and, for easier buffet serving, remove bones and cut meat in larger serving pieces. Return bones to stock, adding neck, gizzard, wing tips, and other portions not used. Simmer to make a strong turkey broth.

To make sauce: Add onions to pan in which you browned the turkey, and cook until lightly browned, adding more shortening if necessary. Add garlic, raisins, chocolate, and the seeds and cloves (if you can't get the seeds in ground form, pound whole ones in a mortar until powdered). Add peanut butter, tomato sauce, and chili powder. Break bread and tortillas into pieces, add with sesame seeds to the onion mixture, and whirl all in a blender until smooth, using 2 cups of turkey broth for the necessary liquid. (If you don't have a blender, grind the raisins, chocolate, bread, and tortillas; mix with the other ingredients; and force through a sieve or food mill.) Add another 4 cups turkey broth and the sugar. Strain and add more salt or chili powder to taste.

Add turkey meat to the mole sauce, heat on top of the range or in the oven, and serve with rice (3 cups raw rice, cooked, makes 12 servings.) Makes 10 to 12 servings.

4 cups flour
1¼ teaspoons salt
3 teaspoons baking powder
3 tablespoons sugar
2 tablespoons shortening
Milk (about 1¼ cups)

Sift flour, measure, and mix with other dry ingredients, rub in shortening with finger tips, and add milk to make a soft dough just firm enough to roll. Allow dough to stand for 30 to 60 minutes, then on lightly floured board roll ¼ inch thick and cut in diamond-shaped pieces. Fry in deep fat at 390° to 400°. Turn at once so they will puff evenly, then turn back to brown both sides. Drain on paper toweling. Serve with butter, as a bread equivalent. Makes 4 dozen or more.

(To make sopaipillas for a dessert, increase sugar to ⅓ cup, add 4 beaten eggs and decrease amount of milk accordingly. Serve with powdered sugar or honey, or an anise-flavored syrup.)

1 large or 2 medium-sized fresh ripe
    pineapples
¼ cup sugar (approximately)
2 or 3 tablespoons rum or 1 teaspoon
    rum flavoring
4 tablespoons (¼ cup) butter

Lay pineapple on its side and take off a thick slice that does not include the green top. Carefully scoop out the insides and cut into bite-size pieces. (Or if you prefer, stand the pineapple up and cut off its top to remove the insides.) Sweeten to taste with about ¼ cup sugar. Flavor with rum or rum flavoring. Put pineapple pieces back into pineapple "shell." Dot the top with butter, cover with foil (including the green leaves), and bake in a moderate oven (350°) for 20 minutes. Replace the top and bring it to the table on a plate to serve warm, topped with *Natillas*, a cold sauce.

Natillas:

1 pint light cream
¼ teaspoon salt
¼ cup sugar
1 egg
2 egg yolks
1 teaspoon each cornstarch and vanilla

Scald cream. Add salt, sugar beaten with the 1 egg, 2 egg yolks, cornstarch, and vanilla. Cook over hot water, stirring constantly, until smooth and slightly thickened. Chill. Serve on top of the pineapple.

Baked pineapple for dessert is served dramatically from plumed pineapple shell. Chilled sauce is spooned over the warm pineapple slices.

An Autumn Dinner

TURKEY DIABLO with broiled pineapple turns cold turkey slices into a crusty hot dish that's company fare. Use canned abalone for the abalone cocktail. The crisp cauliflower slaw is a good accompaniment to the turkey and pineapple. Round out the menu with buffet-sized French bread and French-fried potatoes—or serve canned shoestring potatoes. A simple dessert of fruit, cheese, and salted nuts tops off the meal ✺ The sauce for the turkey can be made ahead of time; reheat it while the turkey slices and pineapple broil. Combine the cocktail ingredients an hour before serving and chill. Make the French-fried potatoes ahead, wrap them in foil, and reheat in a moderate oven (350°) for 15 minutes; open foil to re-crisp

ABALONE COCKTAIL

TURKEY DIABLO WITH BROILED PINEAPPLE

FRENCH-FRIED POTATOES

CAULIFLOWER SLAW

FRUITS, ALMONDS, AND CHEESE

during the last 5 minutes. (Or use frozen French-fried potatoes and prepare them according to package directions.) Prepare the slaw ingredients ahead and combine them at serving time. Set the cheese out far enough ahead so that it will be at room temperature by serving time.

ABALONE COCKTAIL

1 can (about 15 oz.) abalone
1 cup finely minced celery
¼ cup minced sweet red onion
2 tablespoons each lemon juice, soy, and
      peanut or sesame seed oil
   Salt to taste
   Dash cayenne

Drain and dice abalone, and mix with other ingredients. Serve in cocktail glasses or on lettuce. Makes 6 servings.

TURKEY DIABLO

6 thick slices cold, cooked turkey breast
½ cup salad oil
1 teaspoon dry mustard
   Freshly ground black pepper
   Fine cracker crumbs or dry bread crumbs
   Pineapple slices
   Salad oil
1 can (10½ oz.) bouillon
½ cup tarragon vinegar
1 tablespoon prepared mustard
2 tablespoons butter

Dip turkey slices in a mixture of the ½ cup salad oil, dry mustard, and a few grindings of black pepper. Roll in fine cracker or dry bread crumbs and broil until brown on both sides. At the same time, broil pineapple slices in salad oil, and have them ready to serve on the side. Serve the turkey with a sauce made this way: Cook bouillon quickly until reduced to ½ cup. Also cook vinegar until reduced one-half. Combine the two, and add the prepared mustard and butter. Serve as soon as the butter is melted. Makes 6 servings.

CAULIFLOWER SLAW

1 large head cauliflower
¼ cup minced green onion
½ cup minced celery leaves
1 cup (½ pint) commercial sour cream
½ cup French dressing
2 teaspoons caraway seeds
   Salt to taste

Slice raw cauliflower thinly, and combine with other ingredients. Makes 6 servings.

Elegant Roast Chicken Dinner

SERVE THIS as a four-course meal—the appetizer in the living room before dinner, the chilled crab cocktail as a second course served at the table, then the chicken with the vegetables, and lastly, dessert and coffee.

ARTICHOKE APPETIZER

FRESH CRAB AND AVOCADO COCKTAIL

ROAST CHICKEN, PECAN STUFFING

ASPARAGUS   GINGERED CARROTS

BROWNED NEW POTATOES

STRAWBERRY RING SHORTCAKE

ARTICHOKE APPETIZER

Wreath a plate with several layers of cooked artichoke leaves (from about 4 medium-sized artichokes), tips pointing out. In the center, put a bowlful of the following dunking sauce:

- 2 *small packages (3 oz. each) softened cream cheese*
- *Few drops garlic juice (use a press with a fresh clove garlic)*
- ¼ *cup commercial sour cream*
- 2 *teaspoons wine vinegar*
- ¼ *cup minced ripe olives*
- *Salt to taste*

Combine sauce ingredients. Mix well, adding a few drops cream if necessary to make sauce the proper consistency for dunking. Makes about 1 cup sauce, enough for appetizers for 6.

CRAB AND AVOCADO COCKTAIL

- 2 *large ripe avocados*
- ½ *pound flaked crab meat*
- ½ *cup mayonnaise*
- 2 *teaspoons lemon juice*
- 1 *tablespoon light cream*
- *Additional mayonnaise*
- 6 *crab legs*

Dice avocados. Mix crab meat with the ½ cup mayonnaise, lemon juice, and cream. Mix lightly with diced avocado, and put in cocktail glasses. Top each serving with mayonnaise and a crab leg. Makes 6 servings.

ROAST CHICKEN, PECAN STUFFING

Select a large (5-pound) roasting chicken. Stuff and truss, cover with cheesecloth dipped in melted butter, and bake, breast side up, in open roasting pan in a hot oven (400°) for 3 hours, or until drumstick moves easily.

Stuffing:

- ½ *cup minced onion*
- 1 *cup (½ pound) butter or margarine*
- 4 *cups dry bread crumbs*
- 1 *cup chopped pecans*
- *Salt to taste*
- *Light cream or dry white table wine*

Cook onion in butter until wilted. Add it and all the butter to bread crumbs and pecans; toss to mix. Season to taste with salt, and add just enough cream or wine to hold stuffing together. Makes 6 servings.

ASPARAGUS

Cook 3 pounds fresh asparagus, covered, in boiling salted water until tender, 10 to 20 minutes. Drain; season with butter, salt, and pepper. Makes 6 servings.

GINGERED CARROTS

- 2 *pounds baby carrots, peeled*
- 4 *tablespoons (¼ cup) butter*
- 1 *tablespoon minced candied ginger or grated green (fresh) ginger*

Cook carrots until tender; drain. Put carrots in heavy pan with butter and ginger, and cook until lightly browned. Makes 6 servings.

NEW POTATOES

Cook 3 pounds potatoes in their skins; roll in melted butter, then in minced watercress. Makes 6 servings.

STRAWBERRY RING SHORTCAKE

Bake sweetened, enriched biscuit dough (2 cups mix) in 9-inch ring mold. Turn out on plate, fill center, and surround the ring with 1 quart fresh berries, sliced and lightly sugared. Make sauce by combining 2 cups commercial sour cream, ½ cup honey, and, if you wish, ¼ teaspoon finely crushed or ground cardamom seed. Makes 6 to 8 servings.

Sukiyaki Supper

JAPANESE COOKING has developed many traditions through some 2,500 years. The method of cooking is simple. Food is cut in uniform bite-size pieces. Though vegetables are always cooked, they keep their natural colors and slight crispness because of their short cooking period. Perhaps most important is arrangement, for Japanese food appeals to the eye as well as the palate ❧ This menu for a sukiyaki supper lends itself nicely to informal entertaining in the Japanese fashion. You might even let your guests have the fun of helping with the preparation of the food ❧ It's easy to turn your home into a Japanese tea house. Cover the floor with matting, serve the food from a low coffee table. If Japanese dishes are not available, you can use small individual bowls and plates. Chopsticks are in order, too.

GOMA ZU

SUKIYAKI   EGG

RICE

LIMA BEAN KINTON

GREEN TEA

Sliced cucumber, abalone, and celery marinate in a sweet and sour sauce for a crisp pickled salad. Serve chilled on small individual porcelain or pottery dishes.

> 1 tablespoon sesame seeds
> 1 tablespoon sugar
> ¼ teaspoon each salt and monosodium glutamate
> 1 teaspoon cornstarch
> 2 tablespoons fish stock or water
> ½ cup vinegar
> 2 small cucumbers
> ½ can (1 lb. size) abalone
> 1 large stalk celery

Toast sesame seeds in a moderate oven (350°) for 5 minutes. Make a paste of the sugar, salt, monosodium glutamate, constarch, and fish stock or water, and pour into vinegar. Stirring constantly, simmer until liquid is thick, about 5 minutes. Add sesame seeds. Cool. Strain liquid through a double thickness of cheesecloth. Peel cucumbers, cut in thin crosswise slices, and sprinkle with salt. Cut abalone in very thin strips 2 inches long and ½ inch broad. Chop the celery fine. Combine cucumbers, abalone, and celery with vinegar mixture. Chill. Makes 4 servings.

Cook this mixture of meat and vegetables at the table in a chafing dish or on a small burner.

> 1½ pounds fillet of beef, cut in very thin strips across the grain
> 1 can (12 oz.) cooked long rice
> 1 can (8 oz.) bamboo shoots, cut in thin slices
> 2 medium-sized onions, cut in eighths and then thinly sliced
> 1 can (4 oz.) mushrooms
> 2 green onion tops, cut in 1-inch-long pieces
> 1 fresh soybean cake (3 inches square), cut in ½-inch cubes (optional)
> 3 small pieces beef suet
> ½ cup sugar
> ½ cup sherry
> 1 cup soy
> 1 teaspoon monosodium glutamate

Arrange beef, rice, bamboo shoots, onions, mushrooms, onion tops, and soy bean cake attractively on a large platter, keeping each item separate. In the container to be used for cooking, heat suet and sauté meat until golden brown. Stir in rice, bamboo shoots, onions, and mushrooms. Cook for 10 minutes. Then add sugar, sherry, soy, and monosodium glutamate, and mix well. Add green onion tops and soybean cake, if desired, just before serving. Since sukiyaki should be served hot, begin cooking second portion after serving first. Makes 4 servings.

EGG

Serve one raw egg in each small individual bowl. Let each guest beat egg slightly with chopsticks. Dip each biteful of hot sukiyaki into egg.

RICE

Cook 1½ cups white rice. Serve in a large bowl, letting each guest dip rice into individual dishes.

LIMA BEAN KINTON

Orange slices offset the sweetness of this lima bean confection which is served with green tea.

> 1 *can (1 lb.) lima beans and liquid*
> ¼ *teaspoon salt*
> ½ *cup sugar*
>   *Green food coloring*
> 12 *sections mandarin oranges*

Peel skins from lima beans and mash beans. Place bean pulp and liquid, salt, and sugar in a small saucepan. Stirring occasionally, cook slowly until mixture forms a ball, about 20 minutes. Cool. Force mixture through a fine sieve or food mill. Mix in enough coloring to make a bright green. Roll mixture into 12 small balls. Cut a lengthwise slit halfway into the middle of each ball. Tuck one orange section in each, pressing sides together to hold orange in place.

Easter Dinner

THIS DINNER, designed for family and guests, could be served at noon or at night. You can make the bombe dessert a day ahead and cook the yams for the soufflé, if you wish. The rest of the menu won't require much attention on Easter Day 🌷 Time the baking of the ham so it can come out of the oven about 15 minutes before carving so slicing will be easy. Make the appetizer spread a few hours ahead and chill; spread crackers just before serving, or let guests spread their own appetizers 🌷 You can cook the celery and make the cream sauce separately ahead of time, then reheat the cream sauce and add the celery just before serving. Cook the asparagus and bake the yam soufflé just before serving.

CRAB AND WATER CHESTNUT APPETIZER

BAKED HAM   CELERY AMANDINE

YAM SOUFFLÉ

ASPARAGUS

EASTER BOMBE

> 1 pound (2 cups) fresh, frozen, or canned
> crab meat
> ½ cup minced water chestnuts
> 2 tablespoons soy
> ½ cup mayonnaise
> 2 tablespoons minced green onions
> About 36 crisp crackers

Chop crab meat and combine with water chestnuts, soy sauce, mayonnaise, and green onions. Serve with crisp crackers and a beverage.

BAKED HAM

Choose whichever type of ham you prefer from the many available—ready-cooked, tenderized, old-fashioned, Virginia, canned—and cook it according to directions. After the ham is cooked, remove skin if necessary. Mix 2 egg yolks with 1 cup strained apricot jam, and spread over the entire surface, then dust with ½ cup ground pecans (or fine cracker crumbs) and return to a moderately hot oven (375°) to brown for about 25 minutes. Stud the ham with halves of candied cherries and chunks or slices of well-drained and dried pineapple. These decorations can be fastened on with colored toothpicks. You might surround the meat on the platter with lacy celery leaves or parsley.

CELERY AMANDINE

> 4 cups matchlike pieces cut from
> tender celery
> Boiling salted water
> 2 cups cream sauce
> ¼ to ½ cup slivered almonds
> Salt and pepper to taste

Cook celery in salted water until tender-crisp, about 2 minutes. Drain and mix with cream sauce and slivered almonds. Season to taste with salt and pepper, and reheat before serving. Makes 8 servings.

YAM SOUFFLÉ

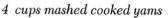
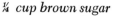

> 4 cups mashed cooked yams
> ¼ cup brown sugar
> 1 teaspoon salt
> 1 tablespoon grated orange peel
> 2 cups milk
> 6 eggs, separated

Put yams, sugar, salt, orange peel, milk, and well-beaten egg yolks in a pan and cook, stirring, until thickened. Add more salt if needed, and allow to cool for about 15 minutes or so. Beat egg whites until stiff but not dry; thoroughly fold half of the whites into yam mixture; then fold remainder in casually. Pour into a buttered 3-quart soufflé dish and bake in a moderate oven (350°) for 55 minutes. Makes 8 servings.

ASPARAGUS

If you have this early spring vegetable, try serving it as a separate course, cooked tender-crisp (never limp!), and served simply with melted butter. (You will need about 4 pounds asparagus for 8 servings.) If fresh asparagus is not available, have a salad of the frozen or canned variety.

EASTER BOMBE

This bombe should look like a huge Easter egg, so an oval mold is best.

If you use homemade ice cream or a high quality commercial ice cream, 2 quarts will fill a 2-quart mold. However, some commercial ice creams are whipped so that they contain a large quantity of air. These lose volume when pressed into the molds, so you will need more than 2 quarts of ice cream.

Before filling the mold, chill it thoroughly in the freezer or in a pan filled with cracked ice. Have the ice cream soft enough so that it can be spread easily.

Fill the mold with vanilla ice cream to which you have added mixed candied fruits soaked in kirsch or any fruit juice of your choice. (For each quart of ice cream, use ½ cup fruit and 2 tablespoons kirsch or juice.)

Smooth top of ice cream with spatula; then cover it with a sheet of waxed paper or aluminum foil. Put on cover and press down firmly; or use heavy foil, pressed down around sides. Freeze 5 to 6 hours, or longer if desired.

Unmold bombe as you would a gelatin mold. Uncover, dip bottom of mold quickly in hot water, and turn out on a well-chilled plate. Cover completely with vanilla-flavored whipped cream, smoothed carefully so the bombe looks like half an egg. Return to the freezer to set; then, using a pastry bag, decorate like an Easter egg with whipped cream tinted with vegetable colors. Once more freeze long enough to set (overnight, if you wish), and serve the "egg" surrounded by fresh spring flowers.

A Guest Dinner

Low in Calories

THE CONSIDERATE HOSTESS faces up to a new problem these days: How to plan the dinner menu that pleases guests who are counting calories yet satisfies those who are not. This dinner is designed for just this double purpose. Sherried scallops with almonds certainly doesn't have the sound or flavor of a typical diet dish, and it appears even less so when prepared at the table in a chafing dish or an electric frying pan ❧ Start the delicate scallop entrée at the table as soon as you serve the soup. Radishes rather than crackers are for those who are counting calories, but even including a few grapes and one thin cooky with the golden fruit soufflé, the meal is well within 600 calories. You might include hot buttered bread for guests who are less diet-conscious.

CLEAR SOUP WITH CHIVES

RADISHES   CRISP CRACKERS

SHERRIED SCALLOPS WITH ALMONDS

LEMON BROCCOLI   FRESH TOMATO RISSOTO

MANDARIN SOUFFLÉ

GRAPE CLUSTERS   THIN COOKIES

CLEAR SOUP WITH CHIVES

Serve hot cups of well-seasoned, fresh (fat-free) or canned beef broth with finely snipped chives sprinkled over each serving. Accompany with radishes, crisped in ice water, or crackers.

SHERRIED SCALLOPS WITH ALMONDS

   3 tablespoons sliced, unblanched almonds
   1½ teaspoons butter or margarine
   2 tablespoons chicken broth (fresh, canned, or made with stock concentrate)
   ¼ teaspoon salt
   1½ pounds scallops, cut in halves or quarters
   2 tablespoons sherry

In a chafing dish over full flame (or electric frying pan set at about 325°) lightly brown almonds in butter; set almonds aside. Add chicken broth and salt to pan; bring to a boil. Add scallops; cover and simmer about 8 minutes or until scallops lose transparency, stirring occasionally. Return almonds to pan along with sherry, and simmer for 2 minutes more. Makes 4 servings.

LEMON BROCCOLI

Allow ⅓ pound broccoli spears for each serving. Add several thin strips of pared fresh lemon peel to cooking water and cook until broccoli is just done. Garnish with julienne strips of lemon peel. Non-weight watchers can dot their servings with butter, but the additional richness really is extraneous here.

FRESH TOMATO RISSOTO

   2 small tomatoes, peeled and diced
   ¾ cup long grain rice
   2 green onions including tops, thinly sliced
   ½ teaspoon each sweet basil and salt
   1¾ cups chicken broth (freshly made, canned, or made from stock concentrate)

Combine tomatoes in a casserole (1 or 1½-quart) with rice, green onions, sweet basil, and salt. Heat chicken broth to boiling and pour over rice. Cover and bake in a moderately hot oven (375°) for about 35 minutes or until rice is cooked; stir occasionally. Makes 4 or 5 servings.

MANDARIN SOUFFLÉ

   1 envelope (1 tablespoon) unflavored gelatin
   1 cup freshly squeezed orange juice
   1 cup fresh orange sections or drained, canned mandarin orange sections
   ½ teaspoon grated orange peel
     Dash salt
   3 egg whites
   ¼ cup sugar
     Additional orange sections for garnish (or a few chocolate curls peeled from a chocolate bar with a vegetable peeler)

Soften unflavored gelatin in orange juice, and dissolve over hot water. Add orange sections, orange peel, and salt. Whip egg whites until stiff, and beat in sugar, 1 tablespoon at a time, until whites hold soft peaks. Fold in gelatin mixture. Spoon into stemmed glass serving dishes. Chill until set. Garnish with additional orange sections or chocolate curls. Makes 4 or 5 servings.

A Dinner for December

THIS PARTY MENU is filled with shortcuts. The bisque starts with canned soup. You buy the turkey already boned and rolled. The salad is made ahead and chilled. The rolls are refrigerator rolls or the ready-to-bake kind. Sherbet from the freezer is served with confetti sauce, which may be made as much as a day ahead. Prepare the mushroom casserole before the guests arrive, but bake it along with the rolls just before serving.

SPLIT PEA BISQUE   RADISHES

ROAST TURKEY ROLL

SCALLOPED MUSHROOMS

GREEN BEAN SALAD

HOT BUTTERFLAKE ROLLS

LIME SHERBET, CONFETTI SAUCE

SPLIT PEA BISQUE

Blend 3 cans (10½ oz. each) condensed split pea soup with equal measure light cream or milk. Heat to simmering, season with ¾ teaspoon crushed anise seed or ¾ teaspoon dried tarragon. Serve in cups. Makes 12 servings.

ROLLED TURKEY ROAST

Select a 5-pound frozen boned and rolled turkey roast (3 lbs. to 10 lbs.—hen rolls are 3 to 6 lbs.; tom rolls are 7 to 10 lbs.). Place frozen, on a rack in a roasting pan. In a very hot oven (450°) roast hen roll for 30 minutes or tom roll for 45 minutes. Reduce oven temperature to moderate (350°) and roast until thawed enough to insert a meat thermometer in thickest portion; continue roasting until turkey reaches 170° to 175° (about 35 minutes per pound). Let stand 10 to 15 minutes. Slice thinly on a diagonal. Makes 12 servings.

SCALLOPED MUSHROOMS

3 pounds chopped fresh mushrooms
½ cup (¼ pound) butter or margarine
1 cup heavy cream
1 teaspoon salt
½ teaspoon pepper
⅛ teaspoon cayenne
Shredded processed Gruyere or medium soft Monterey jack cheese (about 3 cups)
Whole mushroom caps, canned or cooked in butter (optional)

In a large frying pan, sauté mushrooms over medium heat in butter for about 5 minutes. Add cream, and continue to cook until liquid is almost all gone, stirring when needed. Season with salt, pepper, and cayenne. Spoon mixture into 12 greased scallop shells, individual casseroles, or a shallow casserole (about 2-quart size). Cover generously with shredded cheese. Bake in a hot oven (400°) until cheese is melted and lightly browned —about 10 minutes. If you wish, garnish with whole mushroom caps. Makes 12 servings.

GREEN BEAN SALAD

Cook 6 packages (9 oz. each) frozen cut green beans as directed; cool. Make dressing by combining ¾ cup salad oil with ¾ cup wine vinegar; stir in 1½ teaspoons salt, ¾ teaspoon each garlic salt and pepper, and ¼ cup finely sliced canned pimiento. Shortly before serving, spoon cooled beans into a lettuce-lined bowl, pour dressing over top; chill until served. Makes 12 to 15 servings.

LIME SHERBET WITH CONFETTI SAUCE

1 can (9 oz.) crushed pineapple with syrup
½ cup light corn syrup
1 tablespoon lemon juice
¼ teaspoon almond extract
¼ teaspoon salt
⅓ cup halved or quartered candied cherries
¼ cup sliced or diced candied citron
1 tablespoon rum (or rum flavoring to taste)
2 to 3 tablespoons chopped Brazil nuts or pecans (optional)
1½ quarts lime sherbet

Combine all the ingredients except sherbet, stirring to blend them. Cover and chill for several hours to mellow the flavors. Serve sauce spooned over lime sherbet. Makes 12 servings.

CLAMS (OR OYSTERS) CASINO

MINIATURE BROWN BREAD AND BUTTER SANDWICHES

RIB ROAST OF BEEF   HORSERADISH SAUCE

HERBED YORKSHIRE PUDDING

SPINACH WITH MUSHROOMS

ROMAINE SALAD

CAMEMBERT CHEESE   TOASTED CRACKERS

STEAMED FRUIT PUDDING   HARD SAUCE

A Christmas Dinner

Featuring

Roast Beef

ROAST BEEF DINNER is a Christmas tradition for many people. In this menu it follows a first course of Clams Casino—or Oysters Casino, if you prefer. You can make the Yorkshire pudding and cook the spinach after the beef comes out of the oven—let the roast "rest," covered, to develop juices. Serve the salad as a separate course, accompanied by Camembert cheese and toasted crackers. Make the dressing ahead, but tear the crisp greens and toss the salad just before serving. Flaming plum pudding tops off the meal.

CLAMS OR OYSTERS CASINO

Allow 6 clams or oysters in the shell for each serving. Have a pie pan or ovenproof plate for each serving, and half fill it with ice cream salt (or crumbled aluminum foil). Heat the pie pan of salt in a 400° oven for 15 minutes. Open clams or oysters (or have it done at the market) and discard top shells. Leave meat and juices in bottom shells, and arrange them on salt or foil so they are level.

Sprinkle each mollusk with salt and with a mixture (about 1 teaspoon) of chopped green and red pepper. (Use canned pimiento if you can't find red pepper.) Top each with a fourth of a thin slice of bacon, and put the pans in the hot oven (400°) until the bacon is crisp. Do not overcook. Serve in the dishes in which they were cooked, with a wedge of lemon and brown-bread-and-butter sandwiches.

RIB ROAST OF BEEF

Select a large, well-aged roast, preferably 5 or 6 ribs, allowing 1 pound for each person. Have chine cut, and ribs cut short. Sprinkle with salt and place, fat side up, in an open roaster. Start in a very hot oven (450°) long enough to brown; this will take about 20 minutes. Reduce heat to moderately low (325°), and cook until the meat thermometer reaches 120° for very rare, 140° for medium rare (about 18 minutes per pound), 150° for well done. (The temperature rises slightly after the meat is taken from the oven.) Remove and cover to keep warm and develop juice while the Yorkshire pudding is being made. Serve the roast on a large platter.

HORSERADISH SAUCE

  ¼ cup drained prepared horseradish
  ½ teaspoon salt
  1 cup (½ pint) commercial sour cream

Combine horseradish, salt, and sour cream. Serve in a small bowl. Makes enough for 6 servings.

HERBED YORKSHIRE PUDDING

  Beef drippings
  3 eggs
  1¼ cups milk
  1 cup flour
  1 teaspoon salt
  1 tablespoon minced parsley
  ¼ teaspoon each rosemary and thyme

Set the oven at hot (450°). Pour 1½ tablespoons of hot drippings from beef into each individual glass baking dish or each section of muffin or popover pans. Beat eggs until fluffy. Sift flour, measure, and add with other ingredients to the eggs. Mix just enough to make smooth. Pour into the dishes and bake for 15 minutes. Reduce heat to moderate (350°) and bake another 10 to 15 minutes, or until puffy and brown. Serve at once to 6 to 8 persons.

SPINACH WITH MUSHROOMS

  ½ pound mushrooms, sliced
  4 tablespoons butter
  1 clove garlic, crushed
  3 tablespoons flour
  1 cup light cream
  2 pounds washed spinach
  Salt and pepper
  Pimiento

Sauté mushrooms in 2 tablespoons of the butter for 5 minutes. Reserve. Make a sauce by cooking crushed garlic in the remaining 2 tablespoons butter until soft; mash garlic smooth, stir in flour, and cook for 2 minutes. Add cream and cook until thickened.

Cook spinach (in water that clings to leaves after washing) until wilted but still bright green. Drain and chop very fine. Combine with mushrooms and cream sauce. Season to taste with salt and pepper, put in a serving dish, and decorate with stars cut from pimiento. Makes 6 servings.

ROMAINE SALAD

    1 large head romaine
    ½ cup each olive oil and bland salad oil
    ¼ cup red wine vinegar
    1½ teaspoons salt
        Freshly ground black pepper
    ¼ cup each minced parsley and chives
    1 teaspoon tarragon

Dress crisp leaves of romaine with French dressing made by combining the remaining ingredients. Makes 6 servings.

STEAMED FRUIT PUDDING

    ⅓ cup butter
    ¾ cup brown sugar (firmly packed)
    1 egg, beaten
    2 tablespoons wine
    ½ cup each currants, chopped raisins, and
        chopped dates
    ⅓ cup each chopped candied pineapple,
        candied cherries, pecans, and citron
    1 cup sifted flour
    ½ teaspoon soda
    ¼ teaspoon each salt and cinnamon
    ⅛ teaspoon each ground allspice, ginger,
        and nutmeg
        Sugar

Cream butter, brown sugar, and egg. Add wine, currants, raisins, dates, candied pineapple, candied cherries, pecans, and citron. Sift into fruit mixture the flour, soda, salt, cinnamon, allspice, ginger, and nutmeg. Stir thoroughly.

Grease molds well; sprinkle with sugar. Fill ⅔ full; cover tightly. Steam 4 hours for 1-quart mold, 1 hour 45 minutes for individual molds. Cool; unmold. Makes one 1-quart pudding or 6 small ones.

HARD SAUCE

Beat 2 cups sifted powdered sugar into ½ cup (¼ pound) soft butter until mixture is fluffy. Beat in rum or brandy to taste. Pile into serving dish. Makes about 1½ cups sauce.

Indian ❋ Dinner

INDIAN CURRY is a dish that's subject to endless variation. Curry itself is a combination of from 8 to 20 spices ground together to make a powder. This powder is used to flavor a variety of dishes, which can have as their basic ingredient meat, sea food, fowl, or vegetable. The resulting dish can be used as a one-dish family meal, or it can be part of a party meal ᕕᕗ In India, this would be a party meal, because it includes not only meat but also rice and bread. It would be served in brass or copper containers arranged in a semicircle on a large, flat plate about the size of a chop plate ᕕᕗ Guests at such a dinner would sit on the floor on long straw

PULAO (FRIED RICE WITH PEAS)

MURGAI CURRY (CHICKEN CURRY)

SABZI (VEGETABLE CURRY)

DAL (SPLIT PEA SOUP)   TOMATO CHUTNEY

RAITA (YOGURT DIP)   PURI (FRIED BREAD)

KHEER (CARROT PUDDING)

mats or rugs. The dishes would be placed on the matting or on tables about equal to the height of our coffee tables. The food would be eaten with the fingers—picked up by the tips of the first two fingers and the thumb of one hand. Fried bread would be used as a "pusher."

PULAO

Peas and rice are mixed, along with some well-chosen spices, in this dish that the Indians call *Pulao*. You can cook Pulao ahead of time and re-heat it over hot water.

1 large onion, sliced
1 cup shortening, butter, or margarine
1 pound white rice
4 cups water
1 tablespoon salt
1 teaspoon curry powder
½ teaspoon ground cumin
⅛ teaspoon each cayenne, ginger, black pepper, and turmeric
1 package (10 oz.) frozen peas, thawed
½ cup (¼ pound) butter or margarine

In a heavy saucepan, sauté onion in shortening until clear. Add rice and sauté until rice turns white, about 5 minutes. Pour in water. Add salt, curry powder, cumin, cayenne, ginger, pepper, and turmeric. Stir to mix seasonings. Cover tightly and simmer slowly, without stirring, for 25 minutes. Remove cover and place peas and butter on top. Cover and cook slowly for 5 minutes longer, or until peas are tender. Just before serving, turn under once to mix in the peas and melted butter. Makes 8 servings.

To shape rice, spoon into shallow bowl about 4 inches in diameter. Pack rice down slightly, then invert on plates.

MURGAI CURRY

2 broiler-fryers (approximately 2½ pounds each)
1 teaspoon salt
¼ teaspoon turmeric
1 cup shortening or salad oil
2 large onions, sliced and separated into rings
10 whole cloves
1 bay leaf, crumbled
2 medium-sized potatoes, peeled and cut into 1-inch cubes
2 large carrots, sliced

Cut chicken into pieces and rub with salt and turmeric. Heat shortening in a large, heavy kettle, and sauté onions, cloves, and bay leaf until onion is clear. Add the chicken and cook, turning constantly, until skin becomes golden. Stir in the potatoes and carrots. Cover and cook over low heat while you fry the seasoning spices.

Seasoning ingredients:

1 tablespoon shortening
2 teaspoons curry powder
½ teaspoon chili powder
¼ teaspoon cinnamon
⅛ teaspoon ginger
Dash ground cardamom
2 cups water
½ teaspoon turmeric
2 teaspoons salt
2 medium-sized tomatoes, chopped

In a separate pan, melt the shortening and stir in the curry powder, chili powder, cinnamon, ginger, and cardamom. Cook until spice mixture turns a deep brown color, about 5 minutes. Spoon over the chicken. Pour the water into the spice pan and

The curry powder blends used in these Indian dishes include a wide assortment of spices.

add the turmeric and salt, stirring until dissolved. Pour over the chicken. Stir in the chopped tomatoes.

Cover and simmer for 20 minutes, or until diced potatoes and carrots are barely tender. Remove cover and continue to simmer until liquid evaporates and sauce is thickened, about 10 minutes longer. Makes 8 servings.

SABZI

This curry-flavored combination of vegetables which the Indians call *Sabzi*, is typical of northwestern India. In other regions you will find different combinations: tomato, peas, and squash; or eggplant, peas, and spinach; or potato, cabbage, and peas.

> 1 medium-sized onion, coarsely chopped
> 2 tablespoons salad oil
> 2 potatoes, cut in large cubes
> 1 cauliflower, separated into flowerets
> 2 carrots, diced
> 1 medium-sized eggplant, cut in large pieces
> 2 tomatoes, cut in wedges
> 1 tablespoon salt
> ½ teaspoon pepper
> ¼ teaspoon each powdered ginger and cumin
> ⅛ teaspoon cayenne
> 1 teaspoon curry powder
> 2 bay leaves, crumbled
> 1½ cups water

In a heavy saucepan, sauté the onion in salad oil until clear. Add the potatoes, cauliflowerets, carrots, eggplant, and tomatoes. Season with salt, pepper, ginger, cumin, cayenne, curry powder,

Chicken for the Murgai Curry is turned or stirred constantly while browning.

and bay leaves. Pour in water. Cover and simmer for 25 minutes, or until the vegetables are tender; drain thoroughly. Makes 8 servings.

Sabzi has interesting form when cooked because the six kinds of vegetables are cut into various shapes.

DAL

Unlike our soups, the Indian's *Dal* (a stiff, smooth split pea porridge) is more often used as a dip for bread. Cinnamon and cumin make it slightly sweet. If made in advance, reheat over a pan of hot water.

> 1 cup yellow split peas
> 5 cups water
> 6 tablespoons butter or margarine
> ½ teaspoon cumin seed
> ⅛ teaspoon each dry mustard, chili powder, and ground cinnamon
> ½ bay leaf, crumbled
> 3 tablespoons water
> 1 teaspoon salt

In a heavy saucepan, bring peas and 4 cups of the water to a boil; simmer uncovered for 30 minutes, or until almost all the water is absorbed. Pour in the remaining 1 cup of water and simmer for 20 minutes longer, or until the peas are cooked and the soup is thick.

Melt butter in a separate pan, and add the cumin seed, mustard, chili powder, cinnamon, and bay leaf. Cook on medium heat, letting butter bubble, until the cumin seeds start jumping, about 5 minutes. (Butter turns slightly brown.) Pour butter mixture into the cooked peas; rinse out the pan with the 3 tablespoons water and add to peas. Add salt. Stir soup thoroughly and keep warm for 20 minutes to let flavors blend. Makes 8 servings.

TOMATO CHUTNEY

Most cooks embellish their curry dinners with a variety of condiments: chutney, pickled vegetables, tiny pieces of crisp bacon, chopped almonds and peanuts, toasted coconut, and chopped hard-cooked egg. At a genuine Indian dinner, you will usually find only one or two—usually chutney, pickled vegetables, or Bombay duck (a salted, dried fish obtainable in some delicatessens). The classic condiment is chutney. It is made from mango, dried plum, green papaya, or tomato. This tomato chutney is from Bengal. It is sweeter and milder than most. If made ahead of time and refrigerated, allow it to warm up to room temperature before serving.

> 1 tablespoon shortening or salad oil
> 1 whole dried red chili pepper
> ½ teaspoon cumin seed
> ¼ teaspoon each nutmeg and mustard seed
> 4 medium-sized tomatoes, peeled and sliced ⅛ inch thick
> ½ lemon
> ⅓ cup raisins (1½ oz. package)
> ½ cup sugar

Melt shortening in a saucepan and add the cumin seed, crumbled chili pepper, nutmeg, and mustard seed. When seeds start to jump, add the tomatoes. Quarter lemon half and place on top. Simmer, stirring frequently, for 15 minutes. Stir in the raisins and sugar. Simmer, stirring frequently, until thickened—about 30 minutes longer. Chill. If desired, pack in sterilized jars and seal. Makes 2 half-pints.

Tomato chutney may be made ahead of time, refrigerated, then warmed to room temperature before serving.

RAITA

After the chutney and the curries, you'll welcome the mouth-cooling sauce the Indians call *Raita*. It can be eaten alone or mixed with any of the other dishes. Toasted cumin seeds give it a warm aroma, offsetting the sour tang of yogurt. (This, too, can be made ahead of time and refrigerated.)

> 1 large cucumber, peeled and finely grated
> 3 cups (1½ pints) yogurt
> ½ medium-sized onion, coarsely chopped
> 1 teaspoon salt
> 1 teaspoon cumin seed

Grate cucumber into yogurt; add onion and salt. Place cumin seeds in a dry, heavy saucepan and heat until seeds start jumping (they will be toasted). Crush seeds with a mortar and pestle to a fine powder. Just before serving yogurt, stir in the toasted cumin. Makes 8 servings.

To make yogurt dip, grate peeled cucumber directly into cold yogurt. Mix in onion, salt, and crushed cumin seed.

PURI

This tender bread comes out of the deep fat all puffed up like a popover. It collapses when it cools, its flaky surface looking rather blistered.

> 4 cups white flour (unsifted)
> 1 teaspoon each salt, baking powder, and sugar
> 3 tablespoons shortening
> 1½ cups water (approximately)
> Shortening or oil for frying

Mix flour, salt, baking powder, and sugar in a large shallow bowl. Add shortening and mix in with your fingers until mixture is crumbly. Gradually pour in half of the water, and knead to make a soft dough. Continue kneading for about 10 minutes. Gradually add the remaining water as needed, and continue kneading for about 10 minutes. (Dough should be firm, like a stiff yeast dough.)

Make a slight depression in the top of the dough and spoon in 1 tablespoon water. Cover with a dampened cloth. Let rest for 30 minutes. Pinch off small balls, about the size of a large walnut. Roll out on a lightly floured board into 5-inch rounds, about 1/16 to 1/32 inch thick.

One at a time drop rounds of dough into hot fat 1 inch deep. (Lightly tap the top of each one as soon as you drop it in the fat.) When dough puffs up and is golden brown underneath, turn over and brown other side. Serve hot. Makes 24 large pieces of fried bread.

Dough for Puri should be kneaded for at least 20 minutes to insure fried bread that is tender with flaky layers.

Roll out dough as thin as possible. The thinner the dough, the more it will expand, puff up when dropped in fat.

KHEER

You need something refreshing after so much rich food—and often a fruit platter of papayas, fresh pineapple, bananas, and dates will provide the answer. If you want something a little more typically Indian, however, try this dish. When lemon or lime juice is squeezed on top of it, it tastes much as if it contained papaya. It can be made the day before and then refrigerated.

¼ cup shelled almonds, blanched
4 large carrots, peeled and finely grated
¼ cup (4 tablespoons) sugar
3 cups milk
½ teaspoon vanilla
2 tablespoons whipping cream
1 lemon or lime, sliced (optional)

Coarsely chop half of the almond meats and mix with the grated carrots, sugar, and milk. Cook in a heavy, covered saucepan over very low heat for 2 hours, or until carrots absorb all the milk; stir occasionally. Cool. Stir in vanilla and whipping cream. Finely chop the remaining nut meats and sprinkle over the top. If you wish, squeeze lemon or lime juice over the servings. Makes 8 servings.

Fry rounds in very hot salad oil or shortening. Bread browns quickly; total cooking time is 1 minute.

Cracked Crab Party

A PLATTER OF CRACKED FRESH CRAB is a treat for guests, and since a crab supper calls for the simplest of menus, this meal is a treat for the hostess, too The light vegetable soup, steaming hot, is a perfect prelude to the chilled crab. To simplify service, you might pass the cups of soup in the living room. The delicate flavor of cracked fresh crab can best be appreciated "as is," or with just the right sauce or dip to enhance its flavor. This menu offers a choice of one hot sauce and two cold ones. Assorted relishes and crusty hot French bread are the only other accompaniments You can make the eating easier and neater—and more fun—by adding a few refinements to your table. Small, inexpensive baskets, one on each dinner plate, are a great help in keeping the accumulation of shells organized as your supper progresses. When your guests help themselves to crab from the center platter, they

WINTER TOMATO SOUP

CRACKED CRAB PLATTER

HOT DEVILED BUTTER   AVOCADO-CREAM DIP

PIQUANT MAYONNAISE DRESSING

RELISH KEBABS

TOASTED FRENCH BREAD FINGERS

APPLE TARTS WITH HOT LEMON SAUCE

can put it directly into their basket, which also collects the discarded shells. Individual wooden or ceramic salad bowls could be used this same way. Your guests will appreciate finger bowls or hot towels—or both. Have them on the table all through the supper. Use any attractive small bowls; fill them with warm water and float a thin lemon slice on top. Use small guest towels or extra linen napkins wrung out in hot water and folded beside each guest's plate. In addition to your regular table service, provide a pick at each place. Unless you have special crab picks, these can be cocktail picks or even small, sturdy, bamboo skewers.

WINTER TOMATO SOUP

½ cup chopped celery
2 tablespoons butter or fresh bacon
   drippings
1 can (1 lb.) stewed tomatoes
1 can (10½ oz.) consommé or
   chicken broth
½ cup dry white table wine or ½ cup
   additional chicken broth
3 tablespoons chopped green onion
   or 1 tablespoon instant
   minced onion
1 tablespoon lemon juice
1 tablespoon cornstarch, blended with
   ½ cup water
Dash curry powder (to taste)
Cheese croutons (optional)

Sauté the celery in butter or bacon drippings until tender, about 5 minutes. Add all remaining ingredients (except croutons); blend well. Simmer for 15 to 20 minutes, stirring occasionally. Garnish with cheese croutons, if you wish. Makes 6 servings.

CRACKED CRAB PLATTER

If you buy the largest crabs you can find (2½ to 3½ pounds each), you can estimate that a crab will serve two people quite generously. If the crabs you buy are small, better allow one crab per person. You can have the fresh cooked crabs cleaned and cracked at the market where you buy them, or do this yourself. Either way, reserve one large, handsome crab whole (or you might take out the body meat, but leave the shell and legs intact) to top off your platter of cracked crab.

Choose a large platter or tray to serve the crab. It is especially attractive arranged on a mound of cracked ice, but be sure the platter is deep enough to collect the water as the ice melts, without overflowing. Divide the crabs into parts: main body sections, large legs, and smaller legs, if used. (You may wish to leave out the small legs and use the meat from these later in a salad or casserole.) Keep the various parts together, alternating them as you arrange the platter. Finally, center the whole crab on top of the mound.

At each place: basket of cracked crab, avocado dip in lettuce cup, French bread, relishes, hot butter served in shell, finger bowl. Huge platter of cracked crab centers party table.

For added embellishment, spear a collection of relishes (lemon wedges, fancy pickles, small tomatoes, and green stuffed olives) on skewers, and stick them into the crab shell at the very top of the pile. You might spear your choice of relishes on a single long skewer to top off the pile of cracked crab. And the platter could be garnished with parsley or crisp romaine leaves.

In addition, you can offer a choice of two or three sauces as dips for bite-size morsels of crab meat. If you have a small chafing dish, bring it to the table for serving Hot Deviled Butter into individual butter cups as needed. The two cold dressings can be served in small lettuce cups or can be spooned directly onto the plates.

HOT DEVILED BUTTER

1 cup (½ pound) butter
2 teaspoons each Worcestershire and prepared mustard
2 tablespoons chili sauce
2 to 3 drops Tabasco
4 teaspoons lemon or lime juice
2 to 3 teaspoons finely chopped parsley

Melt butter. Add Worcestershire, mustard, chili sauce, Tabasco, lemon or lime juice, and parsley. Heat until bubbly. Makes about 1¼ cups.

AVOCADO-CREAM DIP

2 medium-sized avocados
½ cup commercial sour cream
2 tablespoons each lime or lemon juice, light cream or white table wine, and chopped green onion
1 teaspoon seasoned salt
⅛ teaspoon garlic powder
1 chopped green chili pepper (optional)
1 medium-sized tomato, peeled and chopped

Peel and remove pits from avocados. Whirl avocados in blender with sour cream, lime or lemon juice, cream or white table wine, green onion, seasoned salt, garlic powder, and chili pepper. Stir in tomato. Makes 2 cups.

PIQUANT MAYONNAISE DRESSING

¾ cup mayonnaise
1 cup (½ pint) commercial sour cream
2 tablespoons each chili sauce, chopped dill pickle, chopped green pepper or green chili pepper, and chopped green onion
1 tablespoon each chopped pimiento and wine vinegar
¼ cup white table wine or light cream
2 hard-cooked eggs, chopped
Salt to taste

Combine all ingredients. Mix, and chill for several hours before serving. Makes 2 cups.

TOASTED FRENCH BREAD FINGERS

Some connoisseurs like the flavor of garlic-buttered French bread with crab, others prefer the crusty bread simply buttered and toasted. Cut a long loaf in half lengthwise and butter each half generously. (If you flavor the butter with garlic, we suggest you use a fairly light hand.) After lightly toasting the bread halves in your broiler, use scissors to cut each crosswise into fingers. Serve hot.

APPLE TARTS

For the dessert, make tarts, using your favorite recipe for apple pie or crumb-topped apple pie; or you may prefer to buy the tarts at your bakery. Serve with Lemon Sauce. (You might serve dessert with coffee in the living room.)

Lemon Sauce:

⅓ cup sugar
1 tablespoon cornstarch
1 cup boiling water
2 teaspoons grated lemon peel
2 tablespoons each lemon juice and butter

Combine sugar and cornstarch in a saucepan; stir in water and lemon peel. Cook and stir over medium heat until slightly thickened and clear. Remove from heat; stir in lemon juice and butter. Makes about 1 cup, topping for 4 to 6 desserts.

Early Spring Dinner

SCALLOP COCKTAIL

LAMB CHOPS WITH DEVILED HAM

HOMINY SPOON BREAD

ASPARAGUS, SOUR CREAM SAUCE

FRESH STRAWBERRY SHERBET

ALMOND COOKIES

THIS MENU fairly shouts to your guests that it's spring, with almost every item—thick lamb chops, fresh asparagus, early berries—a spring tradition. If you serve this dinner early in the season, it is an exciting introduction to the abundant fresh foods of spring and summer to come 🍃 You can prepare the scallop cocktail ahead except for a last-minute dressing with olive oil. Make the sherbet far enough ahead to allow it to mellow in the freezer for an hour or more. Lamb chops, spoon bread, and asparagus will need attention just before you serve.

SCALLOP COCKTAIL

This is best made with raw scallops. If you prefer a cooked version, poach the cut scallops in 1½ cups dry white table wine for 4 minutes. Drain and proceed as below, but use only 3 tablespoons lemon juice.

1½ pounds scallops
3 tablespoons each minced green onion, parsley, pimiento, and celery
6 tablespoons lemon juice
3 tablespoons olive oil
Salt and pepper to taste

Cut scallops in quarters if large, or leave whole if small. Add green onion, parsley, pimiento, celery, and lemon juice. Mix together and refrigerate overnight. Before serving, add olive oil, salt, and pepper. Serve in cocktail glasses.

LAMB CHOPS AND DEVILED HAM

Have rib lamb chops cut about 1¼ inches thick, and make a slit in the rounded side, cutting to the bone. Spread the inside of this pocket with deviled ham, using about 2 teaspoons for each chop. Broil chops as usual, and top each one with a spoonful of deviled ham and a sprinkling of minced parsley.

HOMINY SPOON BREAD

1 cup hominy grits
3 cups boiling water
1½ teaspoons salt
1 cup milk
½ cup (¼ pound) butter or margarine
4 eggs, slightly beaten
½ cup shredded Cheddar cheese

Cook hominy in the boiling salted water until the grains are tender. Add the milk and cool to lukewarm. Grease a 2-quart casserole thickly with part of the butter. Melt remaining butter and combine with the hominy and the eggs. Pour into the casserole, and bake in a moderate oven (350°) for 35 minutes. Sprinkle the cheese on top, bake for another 10 minutes. Makes 6 to 8 servings.

ASPARAGUS WITH SOUR CREAM SAUCE

Cook asparagus in boiling salted water until tender-crisp, allowing 1 pound for each 2 persons. For the sauce, combine 1½ cups sour cream, 3 slightly beaten eggs, 1½ tablespoons lemon juice, a dash of cayenne, and ¾ teaspoon salt. Cook in the top of a double boiler over hot water until thick, stirring occasionally. Makes enough sauce for 6 to 8 servings of asparagus.

FRESH STRAWBERRY SHERBET

8 cups very ripe strawberries
2 cups sugar
1 cup ice water
2 tablespoons lemon juice

Sprinkle strawberries with sugar and let stand for at least an hour. Mash well; strain through a very fine sieve. Add ice water and lemon juice. Freeze in an old-fashioned crank freezer or an electric freezer. Makes 8 servings.

ALMOND COOKIES

1 cup (½ pound) butter
⅔ cup sugar
¾ teaspoon almond extract
2 eggs
1½ cups flour
¼ teaspoon salt
1 ounce (2 tablespoons) whole blanched almonds

Cream butter; add sugar, almond extract, and eggs. Beat well until light. Sift flour and measure; sift with salt into creamed mixture. Blend well. Drop by half-teaspoonfuls on buttered cooky sheets. Split almonds and top each cooky with a half. Bake in a moderate oven (350°) for 10 minutes, or until nicely browned. Makes about 6½ dozen small cookies.

International Dinner

THIS MENU selects from the cuisines of various nationalities to become a harmonious whole. Prepare the salad early in the day and allow it to marinate. You can also make the pie ahead of time and chill; sprinkle on toffee topping just before serving.

CALIFORNIA CONSOMMÉ

SWEDISH SESAME CRISPS

COQ AU VIN

GOLD AND GREEN SALAD

ENGLISH TOFFEE PIE

CALIFORNIA CONSOMMÉ

Heat 3 cans (10½ oz. each) consommé. Add ¼ cup dry sherry, and garnish each serving with 1 or 2 diced artichoke bottoms. Makes 6 servings.

SWEDISH SESAME CRISPS

Brush wafer-thin pieces of Swedish *flatbröd* with melted butter, sprinkle with sesame seeds, and put under the broiler until brown. This takes a very short time.

COQ AU VIN

    3 to 4-pound chicken, cut in serving size
        pieces
    2 tablespoons flour
    1 small onion, chopped
    3 tablespoons shortening
    3 cups each red table wine and chicken
        stock
      Herb bouquet of bay, parsley, and
        marjoram or thyme
    1 clove garlic, crushed
    18 small onions (about 1 pound), peeled
    ½ pound whole, small mushrooms with
        stems trimmed
    ½ teaspoon salt
      Buttered, toasted French bread slices

Rub chicken with flour. In a heavy kettle, cook chopped onion in shortening; add chicken, and brown well on all sides. Pour in wine and chicken stock; add herb bouquet and garlic (impale garlic on a wooden pick). Add onions, mushrooms, and salt. Cover kettle and simmer for 30 to 45 minutes, or until meat is tender. Remove garlic. Serve garnished with toasted slices of French bread, buttered (or, in the classic manner, with French bread fried in butter). Makes 6 servings.

GOLD AND GREEN SALAD

    1½ pounds carrots, peeled
    1½ cups finely minced parsley
    1 cup salad oil
    6 tablespoons vinegar
      Pinch of thyme
      Freshly ground black pepper
    1½ teaspoons salt
      Lettuce leaves

Slice carrots as thin as possible; this may be done with an ordinary potato peeler, cutting on the diagonal. Cook carrots in boiling water to cover for 2 minutes. Drain carrots and pour over them a mixture of parsley, salad oil, vinegar, thyme, pepper, and salt. Chill at least 2 hours. Serve on leaves of lettuce. Makes 6 servings.

ENGLISH TOFFEE PIE

    4 egg yolks
    ⅓ cup sugar
    ⅛ teaspoon salt
    2 teaspoons unflavored gelatin
    2 tablespoons cold water
    ½ pint (1 cup) whipping cream
    2 tablespoons rum or rum flavoring to taste
    1 baked 9-inch pie shell
    ¼ pound English toffee or Almond Roca

Beat egg yolks until light and thick; add sugar and salt. Soften gelatin in cold water and heat to dissolve over hot water. Mix well with yolks. Whip cream until stiff, combine with egg mixture and rum, and pour into a baked pie shell. Chill. Before serving, chop toffee and sprinkle over top of pie. Makes 6 servings.

Barbecued Pork Dinner

❋ ❋ ❋

THIS IS A DINNER that requires very little attention from the hostess. The pork bastes itself as it turns on the spit. The foil-wrapped corn goes on the grill fifteen minutes before serving. Ingredients for the Summer Waldorf Salad can be combined about an hour ahead and chilled ⤚ Serve the pork on a large platter or wooden plank, and garnish with candied kumquats and fresh water-cress sprigs. It's fun to make the dessert pancakes at the last minute over the charcoal fire or on an electric table griddle, but they can be made ahead, if you wish. Wrap the thin pancakes in foil and reheat them in a moderate oven (350°) for 20 minutes; assemble and serve.

CHARCOAL-ROASTED LOIN OF PORK

PINEAPPLE SAUCE

ROAST CORN　　SUMMER WALDORF SALAD

ICE CREAM PANCAKES, STRAWBERRY SAUCE

CHARCOAL-ROASTED LOIN OF PORK

Rub a 6 or 7-pound pork loin (about half a loin) with salt and pepper. Spit through the center, lengthwise. Cook over low coals for 2 to 2½ hours or until meat thermometer reaches 185°. Makes about 6 servings.

PINEAPPLE SAUCE

Drain 1 large can pineapple (slices, chunks, or crushed), and put in the blender. Blend until it is the consistency of applesauce. Serve hot or cold with a light sprinkling of ginger or cinnamon.

ROAST CORN

Husk corn and remove all silk, using a vegetable brush to expedite the operation. Place each ear on a sheet of aluminum foil and wrap well, using a drugstore wrap. (Or leave husk on, but peel the husk back and remove silk, replace husk, and soak in cold water 1 hour.) Cook on the grill for about 15 minutes, turning a few times. Allow 2 ears per person.

SUMMER WALDORF SALAD

2 cups seedless grapes
1 cup diced celery
½ cup broken walnut meats
Mayonnaise
Lettuce

Combine grapes, celery, and walnut meats. Dress with mayonnaise, and serve in nests of lettuce. Makes 6 servings.

ICE CREAM PANCAKES, STRAWBERRY SAUCE

These may be made in small skillets over the charcoal fire, or cooked on an electric table griddle. Use a pancake mix or your favorite recipe for pancakes or crêpes. (If the latter, they must be made in frying pans.) Make batter thinner than usual and pour into 6-inch cakes. Put a small scoop of ice cream on each hot pancake, fold over, and ladle a spoonful of sliced sugared strawberries over each serving. Serve at once.

A Dinner Featuring Roast Cornish Hens

THIS MENU adapts easily to various numbers of guests. It is simple to figure portions: For each person, plan on ¾ cup consommé, 1 Cornish game hen, and ½ cup of peas. One pint of ice cream serves each 4 persons. You can prepare the relishes early in the day (keep crisp in ice water, and also make the herb dip and the fried rice stuffing, if you wish. Stuff the hens just before you roast them.

ASSORTED RAW VEGETABLES

HERB DIP

CONSOMMÉ WITH AVOCADO

ROAST CORNISH HENS   FRIED RICE

PEAS WITH WATER CHESTNUTS

COFFEE ICE CREAM WITH
GRATED CHOCOLATE

ASSORTED RAW VEGETABLES

Prepare an assortment of any or all of these: carrot sticks, celery hearts, finocchio (fennel), raw asparagus, turnip sticks, green onions, radishes, green pepper strips, sliced cauliflower buds, raw mushrooms, or any other crisp raw vegetables. Serve with Herb Dip.

HERB DIP

1 cup (½ pint) commercial sour cream
1 large package (8 oz.) softened cream cheese
1 tablespoon each minced chives and parsley
1 teaspoon each minced fresh or crumbled dry tarragon, dill weed, soy, and curry powder
Milk

Combine sour cream and cream cheese. Add chives, parsley, tarragon, dill, soy, and curry powder, and enough milk to make the dip soft but not runny. Makes about 1½ cups dip.

CONSOMMÉ WITH AVOCADO

Heat canned consommé. Serve with cubed ripe avocado in each dish.

ROAST CORNISH HENS

These small chickens are now available, frozen, in most large markets. Thaw before cooking. Figure on from ¼ to ½ cup of stuffing for each bird. Stuff with fried rice (see below). Roast in a hot oven (400°) for about 40 minutes, basting with equal parts of soy, sherry, and a bland oil.

FRIED RICE

This may be used as a stuffing for the Cornish hens or served as a separate vegetable.

4 cups cooked rice
3 tablespoons salad oil
1 cup sautéed sliced mushrooms
2 tablespoons minced green onions
1 teaspoon chopped fresh ginger
2 eggs
1 tablespoon soy
Slivered almonds (optional)

Cook the rice in the oil for about 5 minutes, or until lightly browned; stir while cooking. Add the mushrooms, onions, and ginger, and cook for 3 minutes; then break in the eggs and continue to cook and stir until the egg is set. Season with the soy and more salt, if necessary. (Add slivered almonds, if you wish.) Makes enough stuffing for 8 to 10 Cornish hens.

PEAS WITH WATER CHESTNUTS

Cook peas in boiling salted water until tender; drain. Combine with sliced water chestnuts and butter. (Use ¼ cup water chestnuts and 1 tablespoon butter for each 2 cups of peas.)

COFFEE ICE CREAM WITH GRATED CHOCOLATE

Put scoops of coffee ice cream in chilled sherbet glasses. Sprinkle each serving with about 1 tablespoon of shaved chocolate. (You'll find it easy to shave the cake of chocolate with a potato peeler.)

Korean Dinner

THE GENERAL APPROACH of the Korean cook resembles the Chinese and Japanese. She cuts her food in small pieces and cooks her vegetables quickly so they keep their natural color and crispness. Rice is invariably an important part of each meal, and so are mixed meat and vegetable dishes The Korean cook, however, uses hot, spicy seasonings you don't find in many Oriental foods. To add even more zest to the eating, she serves Kim Chee, a peppery pickle of one or more vegetables, with every meal. There are other differences in Korean cookery. Korean cooks generally use a soy that is less salty than that used by the Chinese and Japanese. Korean food is less rich than the Chinese, but not quite so plain and sweet as Japanese. The Koreans do like pork and fish, favorites of the two neighboring countries, but beef is more common These recipes, adaptations of Korean dishes, are easy to prepare for entertaining because they don't require much last-minute cooking. You can partially cook

KOREAN BEEF BARBECUE

MANDOO (HOT SOUP WITH DUMPLINGS)

KOREAN BRAISED CHICKEN

WATER-CRESS NAMUL (SALAD)

SANJUCK (SKEWERED MEAT, ONIONS, AND MUSHROOMS)

KIM CHEE (PICKLED CABBAGE)   RICE

APPLES AND ORANGES

most of the dishes and then reheat or finish cooking them just before you are ready to serve.

In most of these recipes, you use crushed toasted sesame seeds. Prepare them this way: Place sesame seeds in a heavy frying pan. Stirring, cook over medium heat for 10 minutes, or until browned. Turn seeds into a mortar, add 1 teaspoon of salt for each 1 cup of seeds, and crush with a pestle. Store in a tightly covered jar.

KOREAN BEEF BARBECUE

This hot appetizer is easy to prepare when you entertain, for it takes only two minutes to cook, whether you barbecue it over charcoal or cook it in a frying pan. If you barbecue the meat, use a very narrow grill or cake rack over the coals so the meat strips will not fall through.

    1 pound chuck roast, cut 1½ to 2 inches
        thick
    2 tablespoons salad oil
    4 tablespoons soy
    1 teaspoon garlic powder
    ⅛ teaspoon monosodium glutamate
    1½ teaspoons vinegar
        Pepper
    1½ teaspoons crushed toasted sesame seeds
    ¼ teaspoon cayenne (or less if desired)
    1 green onion and top, sliced

Cut meat across the grain in very thin slices. If slices are longer than 3 inches, cut them in half. Place meat in a bowl with the salad oil, soy, garlic powder, monosodium glutamate, vinegar, a sprinkling of pepper, crushed sesame seeds, cayenne, and onion. Mix with your hands until well blended. Cover and chill in refrigerator for at least 4 hours.

To cook, place meat strips on a rack over charcoal and barbecue for 1 minute on each side. Meat should be brown but not crusty. Or, if you wish, heat a large frying pan, toss in meat, and cook over high heat for 2 minutes, stirring occasionally. Spear each piece on a slender skewer. Arrange on platter, and serve at once. Makes 4 to 6 servings.

MANDOO

Korean *Mandoo* (meat-filled dumplings simmered in water or stock) are similar to Chinese *Won Ton*. Generally Korean cooks simmer a chicken in water to obtain the stock. The chicken is then cut into neat sections and seasoned with soy, toasted sesame seeds, garlic, pepper, and onions and is served as a side dish. In this adaptation, canned chicken is used to cook the dumplings, and the seasoned chicken is eliminated.

Many Chinese noodle factories, grocery stores, and restaurants sell the noodle wrappers, or you can make your own by following the recipe given on page 133.

The soy bean cake that binds the meat filling together is available in Oriental grocery stores.

    1 cup bean sprouts
        Boiling water
    ¼ head small cabbage
    1 fresh soy bean cake (2½ inches square)
        or 1 egg
    1 tablespoon salad oil
    ¼ pound chuck roast or round steak,
        chopped
    3 green onions and tops, chopped
    1½ tablespoons soy
    1½ teaspoons crushed toasted sesame seeds
    60 squares (3 inches square) Won Ton
        noodle wrappers
    4 cans (12 oz. each) chicken stock
        Chopped green onions and tops for
        garnish

Cook bean sprouts in boiling water for 3 minutes; drain and chop. Cook cabbage in boiling water for 5 minutes; drain and chop. Cook soy bean cake in boiling water for 3 minutes; drain. Heat salad oil in a frying pan, then brown meat quickly with 1 of the chopped green onions; add soy and simmer for 2 minutes. Place bean sprouts, cabbage, soy bean cake (or slightly beaten egg), meat mixture, and the remainder of the chopped green onion in a bowl; add ½ teaspoon of the crushed sesame seeds. Mash together with your hands until soy bean cake (or egg) loses its identity.

Place 1 teaspoon of the filling in the center of each noodle square; dampen edges slightly, then fold in half diagonally, like a turnover, and pinch edges together to seal. Cover filled dumplings with a damp-dry cloth and refrigerate until ready to use. (Do not fill dumplings more than 4 hours before cooking.)

To cook dumplings, heat chicken stock in a large kettle with the remaining 1 teaspoon crushed sesame seeds; drop dumplings into boiling stock, one at a time. (To keep dumplings from sticking together, cook only 20 at a time.) After they rise to the top of the stock, cook for an additional 4 minutes. For each serving, ladle stock and 5 or 6 of the cooked dumplings into a bowl and sprinkle with chopped green onions. Makes 4 to 6 servings.

Noodle Wrappers:

> 3 *cups flour*
> 1 *egg*
> 1 *cup water*
>   *Pinch of salt*

Combine ingredients, do not add all the water at once, but do mix it all together as quickly as possible. Roll with a forward motion until pastry is very thin, and cut into 3-inch squares. This will make over 100 paper-thin squares.

WATER-CRESS NAMUL

Even in salads you find the typical Korean seasonings — green onion, soy, red chili pepper, and crushed sesame seeds. If you prefer a milder flavored dressing, let the whole chili pepper stand in the dressing for 1 hour, then remove it before dressing the greens.

> 2 *bunches water cress*
> 2 *small green onions and tops, chopped*
> ¼ *teaspoon pepper*
>   *Monosodium glutamate*
> ¾ *teaspoon salt*
> 1½ *teaspoons sugar*
> 2 *tablespoons soy*
> 1½ *tablespoons vinegar*
> 1 *small red chili pepper, crushed*
> 1 *teaspoon crushed toasted sesame seeds*

Wash water cress; drain, then cut in 2-inch lengths. Mix together the green onions and tops, pepper, a dash of monosodium glutamate, salt, sugar, soy, vinegar, and chili pepper. Pour over water cress, then sprinkle with sesame seeds. Chill for 1 hour. Makes 4 servings.

KOREAN BRAISED CHICKEN

The liquid from dried mushrooms, plus soy, gives a rich, dark color to the sauce that goes over this chicken. Korean cooks seldom thicken these juices, but you may wish to thicken them slightly with cornstarch.

> 4 ounces dried mushrooms (preferably Chinese mushrooms)
> 2 tablespoons soy
> 1 tablespoon salad oil
> 2 cloves garlic, mashed or minced
> ½ teaspoon each pepper and monosodium glutamate
> 1 large broiler-fryer (2½ to 3 pounds), cut in small serving-size pieces
> 2 tablespoons salad oil
> 1 large onion, cut in 8 wedges
> 2 stalks celery, cut diagonally in 1-inch lengths
> ⅓ cup slivered toasted almonds
> 4 green onions and tops, cut in 1-inch lengths

Cover mushrooms with cold water and let stand overnight. Combine the soy, the 1 tablespoon salad oil, garlic, pepper, and monosodium glutamate; marinate chicken in sauce for 30 minutes. Heat the 2 tablespoons salad oil in a frying pan; remove chicken from marinade, drain well, and brown slowly in oil. Cut the mushrooms in strips ¼ inch wide, then add to the browned chicken along with ½ cup of the mushroom liquid, onion, celery, and the remaining marinade. Cover and simmer for 40 minutes. Or if you wish, refrigerate chicken, then cover and simmer for 45 minutes before you serve. Garnish with almonds and green onions and tops. Makes 4 servings.

SANJUCK

For this dish you thread beef strips, mushrooms, and green onions on skewers, and then dip them in flour and egg, and fry. Caution: don't place skewers in the frying pan until the oil is quite hot, or the egg coating will come off. Because the shapes of the food are irregular, the meat and mushrooms will take up most of the coating, leaving pieces of green onion showing through.

> ½ pound top round, cut ⅜ inch thick
> 1 can (3 or 4 oz.) sliced mushrooms
> 2 tablespoons each salad oil and soy
> 1 teaspoon crushed toasted sesame seeds
> 1 clove garlic, mashed or minced
> ½ teaspoon sugar
> Pepper and monosodium glutamate
> 2 bunches green onions
> Flour
> 3 eggs, well beaten
> Salad oil for frying

Skewers of meat, onions, and mushrooms for Sanjuck are rolled in flour, then in beaten egg. To "set" coating, let skewered food dry about 5 minutes before frying.

Cut meat across the grain in strips ¼ inch thick, then cut in 2-inch lengths. Toss meat in a bowl with the drained mushrooms, oil, soy, crushed sesame seeds, garlic, sugar, and a dash each of pepper and monosodium glutamate; mix lightly and let stand for at least 15 minutes. Trim and wash onions; cut in 2-inch lengths, cutting only to the place where the tops separate.

On short skewers thread 2 pieces of meat (fold strips in half if they are too long), then 2 pieces of onion (skewer crosswise), and 2 mushroom slices; repeat with another 2 pieces of meat, 2 onions, and 2 mushrooms. Roll skewers in flour, then in beaten eggs; let stand for 5 minutes. Cover bottom of frying pan with salad oil, and heat until medium hot; place skewers in pan and cook until golden brown and crusty, about 10 minutes on each side.

If you want to fry these early in the day, reheat in a moderately hot oven (375°) for 10 minutes before serving. Makes 4 servings.

KIM CHEE

The favorite base of the Korean specialty, *Kim Chee*, is Chinese cabbage, which is seasoned and put down in salt brine to ferment like sauerkraut. The flavor and odor both become stronger as the cabbage ages. You can buy Kim Chee in Oriental grocery stores, but you may prefer to make it yourself so you can obtain a milder flavor.

>   1 *large head Chinese cabbage or 1 small head white cabbage*
>   3 *tablespoons salt*
>   4 *green onions and tops*
>   1 *large clove garlic, minced*
>   1 *red chili pepper, crushed*
>   1 *teaspoon grated fresh ginger or 1½ teaspoons chopped preserved ginger*
>   *Water*

Cut cabbage in pieces 1 inch long and 1 inch wide. Sprinkle 2 tablespoons salt over cabbage, mix well, and let stand for 15 minutes. Cut green onions and tops in 1½-inch lengths, then cut lengthwise in thin slices. Wash salted cabbage three times with cold water; add the sliced onions, garlic, chili pepper, ginger, the remaining 1 tablespoon salt, and enough water to cover; mix well. Cover and let stand at room temperature for several days. Taste mixture every day, and when it is acid enough to suit you, place in a covered container and store in the refrigerator where it will keep for about 2 weeks.

RICE

Though rice is eaten daily in Korea, it is served with many additions: peas, sliced mushrooms, small cubes of sweet potato, and soybeans. One favorite variation is to cook rice with cubes of white potato—1 part potato to 5 parts uncooked rice. Use about 1 cup uncooked rice for 4 servings. To serve rice, pack each portion in a small round-bottom bowl; invert bowl over individual serving bowl and tap lightly so rice comes out in a mound.

Teen-Agers' Buffet

TEEN-AGE GUESTS will enjoy this buffet of lasagne Napoli, salad, and rolls. It's a good choice for an after-the-game supper. The young host or hostess can prepare most of the food, doing a good share of the work the day before the party. (This easy buffet is fine for adults, too.) The lasagne can be assembled the day before, refrigerated, then baked before serving. The dessert should be made ahead and refrigerated overnight. Heat the rolls and toss the salad at serving time.

LASAGNE NAPOLI

TOSSED GREEN SALAD WITH SALTED NUTS

 GARLIC FRENCH DRESSING

HOT BUTTERED CRUSTY ROLLS

CHOCOLATE GRAHAM RIBBON LOAF

HOT APPLE CIDER

LASAGNE NAPOLI

You can assemble this casserole hours ahead—even the night before—and keep it in the refrigerator, ready to bake.

> 1 medium onion, finely chopped
> 1 clove garlic, minced or mashed
> 2 tablespoons olive oil or salad oil
> 1 pound ground chuck
> 1 can (3 or 4 oz.) sliced mushrooms
> 1 can (8 oz.) tomato sauce
> 1 can (6 oz.) tomato paste
> 2 teaspoons salt
> 1 teaspoon dried oregano
> ¾ cup water
> 2 eggs
> 1 package (10 oz.) frozen chopped spinach, thawed
> 1 cup cream-style cottage cheese
> ⅓ cup grated Parmesan cheese
> 1 package (12 oz.) lasagne, cooked and drained
> 1 package (8 oz.) American cheese slices cut in strips

In a medium-sized frying pan, lightly brown onion and garlic in 1 tablespoon of the oil; add ground chuck, and break apart; cook until brown. Blend in mushrooms (including mushroom liquid), tomato sauce, tomato paste, 1 teaspoon of the salt, oregano, and water; simmer 15 minutes. Meanwhile, mix 1 of the eggs with the spinach, cottage cheese, Parmesan cheese, remaining 1 tablespoon oil, and 1 teaspoon salt. Beat the second egg slightly and toss with cooked lasagne. Pour half the meat sauce in an oblong baking pan (about 9 by 13 inches) and cover with a layer of half the lasagne. Spread all the spinach mixture over lasagne. Complete layers with remaining lasagne and meat sauce. Cover and bake in moderate oven (350°) for 45 minutes. Remove cover and arrange strips of American cheese on top; bake for 15 minutes longer. Serve hot. Makes 6 to 8 servings.

TOSSED GREEN SALAD WITH SALTED NUTS

Just before serving, toss crisp salad greens lightly with garlic French dressing and sprinkle with a handful of coarsely chopped salted peanuts or mixed nuts.

CHOCOLATE GRAHAM RIBBON LOAF

> 2 cups heavy cream
> 2 tablespoons sugar
> 2 tablespoons cocoa
> 24 square cocoa graham crackers
> 2 or 3 tablespoons toasted flaked coconut

Whip cream with sugar and cocoa. Spread a layer of cream about ¼ inch thick on one side of each graham cracker. Stand them on edge on a serving plate, with layers of cream between crackers, so that they form a loaf shape—you should use about half of the whipped cream mixture. Coat top and sides of loaf with remaining cream; sprinkle top with toasted coconut. Refrigerate overnight. For ribbon effect, cut slices on a diagonal. Serve with mugs of hot apple cider. Makes 8 servings.

Chocolate graham loaf is sliced on the diagonal to create a ribbon effect. Loaf is topped with toasted coconut.

Thirty-Minute Dinner

IN LESS THAN 30 minutes, the salmon, seasoned delicately with an onion-lemon mixture, bakes under a sour cream mask. The salad is a digression from the usual bacon-and-vinegar dressed version of wilted salad; this one "wilts" from a browned butter and sesame seed dressing. You can make the berry soup and shell the peas early in the day, but otherwise, this dinner should be cooked just before serving.

WILTED LETTUCE AND TOMATOES

SPRING SALMON BAKED WITH
SOUR CREAM MASK

FRESH PEAS   DILL BUTTER SAUCE

CRISPY HASHED BROWNED POTATOES

CHILLED OLALLIEBERRY SOUP

WILTED LETTUCE AND TOMATOES

Break tender lettuce leaves into salad bowl to make about 4 cups. Add 3 peeled tomatoes (not chilled), cut into thin wedges. Sprinkle with salt and freshly ground pepper. Slowly heat ½ cup (¼ pound) butter with 3 tablespoons sesame seeds until butter is lightly browned. Pour hot butter over lettuce and tomatoes and quickly cover. After 2 minutes remove cover, toss, and serve. Makes 6 servings.

SALMON BAKED WITH SOUR CREAM MASK

    2-pound salmon fillet
    1 tablespoon grated onion
      Juice of ½ lemon
    ½ teaspoon salt
    ¼ teaspoon pepper
    ⅛ teaspoon each paprika and Tabasco
    ½ cup commercial sour cream

Place salmon in greased shallow baking dish. Combine onion, lemon juice, salt, pepper, paprika, and Tabasco. Spread over salmon. Spread sour cream on top of onion seasonings to cover surface of fish. Bake in a moderate oven (350°) for 20 to 30 minutes or until fish flakes when tested with a fork. Makes 6 servings.

FRESH PEAS WITH DILL BUTTER SAUCE

Cook 3½ pounds fresh peas, shelled, in boiling salted water for 8 minutes or just until tender; drain. Pour over a sauce made by heating 4 tablespoons finely chopped dill pickle in ⅓ cup melted butter. Season with salt and pepper. Toss lightly and serve immediately. Makes 6 servings.

CRISPY HASHED BROWNED POTATOES

    4 tablespoons shortening
    4 cups grated boiled potatoes
    4 tablespoons flour
    1½ tablespoons finely minced onion
    ⅓ cup light cream
    1½ teaspoons salt
    ¼ teaspoon pepper

Melt shortening in heavy frying pan. Mix potatoes with flour, onion, cream, salt, and pepper. Pack firmly in frying pan. Cook over low heat until brown on underside (about 20 minutes). Fold over onto warm serving platter as you would an omelet. Makes 6 servings.

CHILLED OLALLIEBERRY SOUP

    1⅓ cups water
       Sugar to taste (about ⅔ cup)
    6 cups fresh olallieberries (or any tart berry,
       such as boysenberry, raspberry,
       loganberry)
    2 tablespoons cornstarch
    3 tablespoons water
       Sweet cream

In a saucepan bring to a boil the 1 cup water and sugar. Add berries; bring to a boil again. Cook for 1 or 2 minutes, taking care that berries do not overcook and fall apart. Blend cornstarch with the 3 tablespoons water. Stir into berry mixture. Stirring gently, bring to boil again. Allow to cool; chill. Serve in sherbet glasses. Pass sweet cream. Makes 6 servings.

New Year's Eve Buffet

Hot Foods

GARLIC PORK NUGGETS

FONDUE NEUFCHATELOISE

FONDUE BOURGUIGNONNE

CHINESE MEAT BALLS

Cold Platters

MEAT TRAY   FISH TRAY

CHEESE TRAY   BREAD TRAY

Spreads

CHOPPED CHICKEN LIVERS

BEEF TARTARE LOAF

HERE'S A PARTY that invites you to usher in the New Year in the most festive of all ways: with lots of people, an abundance of good food—and almost no dishes to wash afterward. Finger food is the key to the flexibility and simplicity of the party. You can invite 50 guests "from 7 o'clock to midnight"; whether they arrive for a cocktail party, or for a buffet supper, or for the evening, they'll find refreshments to suit them The buffet is planned for a minimum of preparation as well as for ease of service and clean-up. Included are some delicacies that can be prepared ahead and some "skewer" specialties that can be kept warm (or even cooked) in chafing dishes or electric frying pans. But the backbone of the menu is an array of cold foods that you can purchase ready to serve: a meat tray, a cheese tray, a fish tray, and a bread tray If you serve the food smörgåsbord style—available to the guests throughout the evening—you can manage easily without extra help; all you have to do during the party is to replenish the food supply. Before guests arrive, arrange platters of the cold food on a buffet table, and place the hot foods at strategic spots throughout the party area. (The two fondue dishes should each be centered on a card table or coffee table.) Bowls of relishes such as olives, carrot sticks or French-fried onions will also satisfy nibblers and help to decentralize activities.

A punch bowl and a large electric coffee maker placed in the party area will require little attendance. You might serve the beverages in inexpensive plastic cups that can be discarded. Everything else will be finger food, so that an ample supply of paper napkins is all that's necessary for serving.

GARLIC PORK NUGGETS

Eat these rich, crispy chunks of pork as they are, or dip them in a bowl of taco sauce (the bottled kind is very good). Pork shoulder is an especially good cut to use for this dish.

> 5 *pounds lean pork*
> 1 *tablespoon salt*
>   *Freshly ground pepper*
> 3 *cloves garlic, puréed*

Cut pork into 1-inch cubes; mix thoroughly with salt, pepper, garlic. Spread in layers in shallow baking pans, and bake in a moderate oven (350°)

Cubes of garlic-flavored pork, baked until they are crisp and browned, are reheated at serving time in chafing dish. Guests spear cubes with skewers or toothpicks, then dip in taco sauce.

for 1 hour. Stir occasionally and drain off fat accumulations. When serving, reheat about a pound at a time in the oven (or in the chafing dish if it has a good heating element); serve in chafing dish. Makes enough for about 50 people.

FONDUE NEUFCHATELOISE

Since this classic dish is best if made in fairly small batches, this recipe serves about 20 people when other food is served. If you wish, have on hand additional shredded cheese and extra ingredients in proportional amounts.

> 1 *clove garlic, peeled*
> 5 *cups light white table wine (such as Riesling or Traminer)*
> 2½ *pounds Switzerland Swiss cheese, shredded*
> ½ *tablespoon flour*
>   *Freshly ground pepper*
> 1 *teaspoon salt*
>   *About ¼ teaspoon ground nutmeg*
> ½ *cup kirschwasser, cognac, or light white rum (optional)*
> 2 *large loaves French bread*

Rub a 2-quart (or larger) chafing dish or earthenware casserole with the garlic; add the wine and heat slowly over chafing dish burner. Lightly mix the cheese with the flour; when the bubbles in the wine rise to the surface (do not boil), add cheese mixture a handful at a time, stirring until each handful melts. Continue until all cheese is melted. Add seasonings and kirschwasser, cognac, or rum; stir well. Turn heat low but keep fondue slowly bubbling.

Cut French bread into cubes, leaving one side of crust on each. Provide long-handled fondue forks or sturdy bamboo skewers. Each guest impales a

Swiss fondue is dipped up with French bread cubes speared on fondue forks. Final twist conveys cheese without drip.

bread cube (from soft side to crust) and dunks it into the fondue, stirring it as he does. If the fondue becomes too thick, add a little hot (never cold) wine. Serves 20.

(The crust that eventually forms at the bottom of the casserole is worth scraping up as a very special treat.)

FONDUE BOURGUIGNONNE

This unusual fondue recipe from Burgundy, France, is made with beef and melted butter. Let your guests cook the skewered meat and dip each chunk into the sauce of their choice. Beef tenderloin is a good meat for this dish, but you will also find these delicious: liver, kidney, sweetbreads, chicken breast, lamb, large peeled and cleaned shrimp, and fish cubes. Serve just one or offer a selection, but do not cook meat and fish in the same fat.

> *About 5 pounds meat or fish*
> *Butter*
> *Cooking oil*
> *2 dozen French rolls, sliced like bread*

Cut meat into bite-size chunks and heap, uncooked, into serving bowls. Put 1½ inches of melted butter and cooking oil in equal parts into electric saucepan, frying pan (or chafing dish with good heating element); arrange with meat, skewers or fondue forks, a selection of sauces (recipes follow), and a platter of French roll slices. During party, keep fat hot (about 210°); meat will take only a couple of minutes to cook. Serves 50 along with other food.

Tender morsels of beef, cooked quickly in hot butter and oil, are dipped in a choice of sauces and placed on French roll slices to eat.

Bearnaise Sauce:

Here is a quick way to make Béarnaise Sauce in a blender.

> *6 green onions or shallots, minced*
> *¼ cup wine vinegar*
> *4 egg yolks*
> *2 teaspoons dried tarragon*
> *¼ teaspoon each salt and dry mustard*
> *Dash Tabasco*
> *1 cup (½ pound) melted butter*

Cook onions in wine vinegar until liquid is absorbed and onion tender. Put in electric blender with egg yolks, dried tarragon, salt, dry mustard, and Tabasco. Turn on blender for 5 seconds; gradually add melted butter. (If your blender does not have a small opening in the lid, cover the blender container with heavy foil, make a hole in it, and insert a funnel. Fasten foil down with a heavy rubber band.) The sauce will thicken at once. If too thick, add a small amount of hot water.

Mock Bearnaise:

This recipe is even simpler than the one above.

> *2 teaspoons dried tarragon*
> *2 tablespoons tarragon vinegar*
> *2 cups mayonnaise*
> *¼ teaspoon dry mustard*
> *6 peeled shallots or green onions*

Soak dried tarragon in tarragon vinegar. Add mayonnaise, dry mustard, and shallots or green onions. Whirl in blender.

Anchovy Sauce:

Add 2 tablespoons (or more, to taste) anchovy paste to 2 cups mayonnaise; mix well.

Garlic Sauce:

Cream 1 pound soft butter with 2 puréed cloves garlic; add cayenne or Worcestershire to taste.

Sour Cream Sauce:

Add 2 tablespoons paprika and ¼ cup very finely minced onion to 2 cups commercial sour cream. Add salt to taste. Dill weed may be used instead of paprika.

Mustard Sauce:

Combine 2 cups mayonnaise, 2 tablespoons tarragon vinegar, and 3 tablespoons dry mustard. Mix well and add salt to taste.

Curry Sauce:

> 2 tablespoons curry powder
> 1 puréed clove garlic
> 1 tablespoon lemon juice
> 2 cans (10½ oz. each) beef gravy

Combine curry powder, garlic, lemon juice, and gravy. Correct seasoning, adding salt if needed. Heat; serve over a candle warmer.

CHINESE MEAT BALLS

These tiny meat balls, fried in deep fat before the party, simmer in a flavorful glaze in a chafing dish.

> 2 cans (20 oz. each) water chestnuts
> 3 bunches green onions
> 5 pounds lean pork, ground
> ¼ cup soy
> 6 eggs, slightly beaten
> 1 tablespoon salt
> 2½ cups fine dry bread crumbs
> Cornstarch

Sauce:

> 1 cup vinegar
> 2 cups pineapple juice
> ¾ cup sugar
> 2 cups canned consommé
> 2 tablespoons soy
> 3 tablespoons grated fresh green ginger (or
>   5 tablespoons chopped crystallized
>   ginger)
> ½ cup cornstarch
> 1 cup cold water

Drain and chop water chestnuts; chop green onions, tops and all; mix both with meat. Add soy, eggs, salt, and bread crumbs; mix thoroughly with your hands. Chill. Form into balls, using a rounded teaspoon for each; roll lightly in cornstarch. Fry in deep fat at 370° until well browned.

To make sauce, heat together vinegar, pineapple juice, sugar, consommé, soy, and ginger. Gradually stir in cornstarch mixed with cold water. Cook, stirring, until clear and thickened. Keep meat balls hot in chafing dish with just enough sauce to form a slight glaze.

MEAT TRAY

You can prepare some of the meats at home, or buy them all at a good delicatessen. Since most people will be temporarily tired of turkey, roast beef and ham are good choices for the main meats. Smoked tongue and corned beef are also popular. Choose good sausages such as salami, cervelat, and Braunschweiger. Head cheese and blood sausage are better liked than you may realize.

If you prepare your own corned beef, press it with a weight before it cools so it will slice easily. Boneless rump of beef, roasted rare, is fine for slicing. A meat loaf and a liver pâté, served chilled and sliced, are also fine additions to a cold meat tray.

For 50 people, count on a total of about 5 pounds of meat. Serve with a bowl of mustard and one of horseradish sauce (1 part freshly grated horseradish or prepared horseradish to 3 or 4 parts sour cream).

FISH TRAY

A good selection is smoked salmon, kippered sturgeon, smoked Alaska cod (sablefish), smoked whitefish, sardines. If you prefer (this may be less expensive in the long run), serve a whole half smoked salmon with a very sharp slicing knife. Decorate the fish tray with lemon wedges, or place a bowl nearby. To serve 50 guests, you will need about 5 pounds of smoked fish.

CHEESE TRAY

Include mild cheese such as Jack, Teleme, Swiss, or mild Cheddar, and sharp ones such as aged Cheddar and Port-Salut. (Usually it is wise to by-pass Limburger or Liederkranz, as their fragrance is not always appreciated and they are difficult to handle.) Serve at least one veined cheese, such as Roquefort, Gorgonzola, or blue cheese; you can make a spread by mashing the cheese with butter (3 parts cheese to 1 part butter) or with cream cheese.

An Edam, Gouda, or pineapple cheese makes an attractive centerpiece for a cheese tray. With these, it is best to scoop out the insides, cream them, and return to the shell; arrange other cheeses on large leaves laid around it.

You will need a total of about 3 pounds of cheese. Arrange some in slices, some in cubes on picks, and provide spreaders for the soft cheese.

BREAD TRAY

Provide one loaf each of three or four kinds of bread; a good rye, a dark pumpernickel, a crusty French bread, and a whole wheat are good choices. Arrange bread, sliced and buttered, in overlapping layers on a large tray, leaving some slices unbuttered for those who prefer it.

CHOPPED CHICKEN LIVERS

This creamy pâté is especially delicious on rye bread. Most meat markets sell chicken fat; use it if possible, since it affects the flavor; however, if you can't obtain it, substitute butter.

> 8 large onions
> 1 cup chicken fat
> 3 pounds chicken livers
> 8 hard-cooked eggs, chopped
>   Salt and pepper

Peel and mince onions, and cook them until brown in the chicken fat. Add chicken livers; cook until they have lost most of their pinkness. (If some of the onions become black, that's to the good; they give a desired flavor.) Cool slightly and chop rather fine. Add chopped hard-cooked eggs and salt and pepper to taste. If the mixture is not moist enough, add more chicken fat or butter. Serves 50.

BEEF TARTARE LOAF

To be authentic, the raw beef should be scraped for this spread; if you don't have that kind of patience, trim off fat and grind the beef, using the fine blade of your food chopper.

> 5 pounds sirloin or other tender beef,
>   trimmed and ground
> 4 or 5 egg yolks, slightly beaten
> 3 medium-sized onions, finely minced
> 5 teaspoons salt
> 1 teaspoon freshly ground pepper
> ½ cup minced parsley
>   Chives
>   Capers

Mix beef with egg yolks, onions, salt, pepper, and parsley. When thoroughly blended, form in a loaf or long roll and sprinkle with minced chives. Stud with whole capers. Makes about 50 servings when accompanied by other foods.

New Year's Eve Supper Party

New Year's Eve provides one of the best excuses for a party. This supper is planned for five or six couples. The entrée is corned beef brisket, presliced, then heated and glazed in a cranberry-wine sauce. You'll find it very simple to serve. Fan-shaped romaine leaves are beds for individual salads of tiny Brussels sprouts with a vinaigrette dressing. Oven-crisped sweet potatoes, rolls and butter, and lemon tarts complete the meal.

CHILLED BRUSSELS SPROUTS VINAIGRETTE

SPICED CORNED BEEF SLICES GLAZED

IN CRANBERRY-WINE SAUCE

SWEET POTATO CRISP

HOT ROLLS   LEMON TARTS

CHILLED BRUSSELS SPROUTS VINAIGRETTE

    3 pounds small Brussels sprouts
   12 crisp romaine leaves
      Pimiento strips
    2 cups tart French dressing
    2 tablespoons each minced green onions
       with tops, green pepper, parsley
       and capers
    2 tablespoons lemon juice
    ½ teaspoon (or more) Tabasco
    ¼ teaspoon pepper

Cook Brussels sprouts until tender; drain and chill. (To help retain bright green color, immerse in ice water immediately after cooking.) On a large platter, arrange chilled, drained sprouts on romaine leaves; garnish each with a few thin strips of pimiento. Sprinkle with vinaigrette dressing made by combining the remaining ingredients. Makes 12 servings.

SPICED CORNED BEEF GLAZED IN CRANBERRY-WINE SAUCE

   10 to 12 pounds corned beef brisket
    2 medium-sized onions, quartered
    2 carrots, sliced
    4 bay leaves
    2 teaspoons each whole black peppers and
       whole allspice
    1 teaspoon whole cloves
      Water

Place corned beef in large kettle; add onions, carrots, and seasonings. Cover meat with water, cover kettle, and simmer meat for 3 hours or until tender. Remove from broth and allow to cool for about 15 minutes or until easy to slice. Cut thin slices and place, overlapping, in a shallow baking pan; pour Cranberry-Wine Sauce (see below) over meat, and bake in a moderate oven (350°) for about 40 minutes to glaze meat and heat it through. Baste frequently. Arrange slices on heated platter, and over them pour remaining sauce. Makes 12 servings.

Cranberry-Wine Sauce:

    1 can (1 lb.) whole cranberry sauce
    2 cups red wine
    4 teaspoons prepared hot mustard
    2 teaspoons prepared horseradish
      Grated peel and juice of 2 oranges

Heat together cranberry sauce, wine, mustard, horseradish, grated orange peel, and orange juice. Pour over corned beef slices.

SWEET POTATO CRISP

   12 sweet potatoes
    ¾ cup butter
    ¼ cup flour
    ½ cup brown sugar
    1½ teaspoons freshly ground black pepper
    ¼ cup heavy cream
    ¼ cup finely chopped nuts

Cook sweet potatoes, peel, and slice crosswise about ⅜ inch thick. Spread in a buttered, large but shallow baking-serving dish. Cut butter into flour and brown sugar. Add pepper, cream, and nuts. Mix well. Sprinkle over potato slices. Broil about 6 inches from heat, checking every few minutes until bubbly and caramelized (about 15 minutes).

LEMON TARTS

    1⅓ cups sugar
    6 tablespoons cornstarch
    ½ teaspoon salt
    1½ cups boiling water
    2 egg yolks, beaten
    2 tablespoons butter
    1 teaspoon grated lemon peel
    ⅓ cup lemon juice
    1 teaspoon vanilla
    1 envelope (1 tablespoon)
       unflavored gelatin
    ¼ cup water
    1 cup whipping cream
    2 egg whites
   12 baked 4-inch tart shells
      Mint sprigs

Mix together sugar, cornstarch, and salt; stir slowly into boiling water. Cook and stir until thick. Place over boiling water; cook for 15 minutes longer. Blend egg yolks with some of the hot mixture, and then add to rest of hot mixture along with butter; cook 2 minutes more. Remove from heat. Stir in lemon peel, lemon juice, and vanilla. Set aside 1 cup of this filling.

Soften gelatin in water; blend into hot mixture to dissolve. Add whipping cream. Cool until mixture begins to set.

Beat egg whites until stiff and fold into gelatin mixture. Spoon into 12 baked 4-inch tart shells; let stand until partially set. Top with reserved 1 cup filling. Chill until set. Serve tarts with a mint sprig in the center of each. Makes 12 small tarts.

Late-Evening Supper Party

A LATE, INFORMAL SUPPER party is a pleasant way to entertain a small group of friends. For such a party, this entrée of Shrimp Custard Tarts is ideal. It requires just a few choice accompaniments, and it can be served easily from the fireplace hearth, coffee table, or a small side table. Early in the day, make the tart shells and cool, cook bacon and drain, make the molded salad, prepare the relishes and crisp them in ice water, make the dessert and chill. Just before serving, complete the tarts and heat and butter the rolls.

INDIVIDUAL SHRIMP CUSTARD TARTS

GRAPEFRUIT-LIME MOLDED SALAD

HOT BUTTERED ROLLS

CRISP RELISHES

CHOCOLATE TOFFEE ANGEL CAKE

SHRIMP CUSTARD TARTS

Pastry based on 3 cups flour
1 pound cleaned, cooked shrimp
4 slices bacon, cooked until crisp
¼ cup grated or shredded Parmesan cheese
4 eggs
2 cups milk
1½ teaspoons minced fresh or crumbled dried thyme or chervil
¾ teaspoon Tabasco
Salt and pepper

Line 8 individual foil pie or tart pans with pastry. Arrange shrimp on bottom of each pan. Crumble bacon over the shrimp. Sprinkle a layer of cheese over the bacon. Beat eggs slightly; add milk, thyme, Tabasco, salt, and pepper. Pour into pastry-lined pans. Bake in a very hot oven (450°) for 10 minutes; reduce heat to 350°, and bake 20 minutes, or until filling is set.

GRAPEFRUIT-LIME MOLDED SALAD

2 packages (3 oz. each) lime-flavored gelatin
2 cups hot water
1½ cups ginger ale
½ teaspoon salt
1 teaspoon grated onion
2 grapefruit
Crisp greens
Mayonnaise
Grated lemon peel

Empty lime-flavored gelatin into a large bowl; add hot water, and stir until dissolved. Add ginger ale, salt, and grated onion. Chill until syrupy. Meanwhile, peel grapefruit, remove all white membrane, cut into sections, and arrange in the bottom of a 2-quart shallow square or rectangular pan. Carefully spoon over enough gelatin to cover grapefruit. Pour in remaining gelatin; chill until firm. Cut into squares and serve on a bed of crisp greens. Serve plain, or with mayonnaise dressing sprinkled with lemon peel. Makes 8 servings.

CHOCOLATE TOFFEE ANGEL CAKE

2 cups (1 pint) whipping cream
1 can (5½ oz.) chocolate syrup
½ teaspoon vanilla
1 angel food loaf cake (about 12 oz.)
1 pound English toffee, crushed

Whip cream until it starts to thicken; gradually pour in chocolate syrup and vanilla, and beat until thick. Cut angel food loaf cake into 4 crosswise layers. Spread whipped chocolate cream on each layer; sprinkle crushed English toffee over the cream (use about half the chocolate cream and crushed candy for filling). Frost top and sides of cake with the rest of the chocolate cream, and sprinkle with remaining toffee. Refrigerate at least 2 hours before serving. Makes 8 servings.

149

Barbecue Buffet

THIS GUEST MEAL makes a striking buffet display, centered by a glamorous fresh fruit curry. The special method of cooking chicken breasts results in tender meat that's juicy and delicious. Success depends on cooking the chicken quickly over hot coals; timing is important ❦ The rest of the menu won't demand such attention. This is one lettuce salad that *should* be made hours ahead. You can spread thick slices of French bread with soft chive butter long before its last-minute toasting under the broiler ❦ Make the simple dessert in the morning, or as close to party time as an hour before—just long enough to let it chill thoroughly.

BARBECUED BREAST OF CHICKEN

MADRAS FRESH FRUIT CURRY

STEAMED WHITE RICE

TOASTED ALMONDS   CHUTNEY

STUFFED HEARTS OF LETTUCE

FRENCH BREAD TOASTED WITH CHIVE BUTTER

CREAM OF MINT PARFAIT

151

BARBECUED BREAST OF CHICKEN

8 *very large split chicken breasts*
  (almost ½ pound each)
¾ *cup melted butter*
1½ *cups flour*
  Salt and pepper
¼ *cup (approximately) melted butter*

Rinse chicken breasts and dry meat thoroughly. Dip pieces, one at a time, into melted butter, then shake in a paper bag with flour, seasoned with salt and pepper, to coat thoroughly. Place pieces on a greased grill 6 to 12 inches above hot coals (grill temperature should be about 375°). Cook 10 to 12 minutes on each side. Baste during cooking with melted butter. Serve immediately. Makes 8 servings.

MADRAS FRESH FRUIT CURRY

To make the most of temperature contrasts, have each guest top hot white rice with cold fresh fruits, then ladle the hot curry sauce from a chafing dish over all. Sprinkle almonds over the fruit and accompany with chutney of your choice.

On a large platter, arrange a selection of these chilled fruits: pineapple, cantaloupe balls, peach and pear slices (dip peach slices in lemon juice), and figs (or bananas, each dipped in lemon juice and cut into 3 pieces). Serve with about 6 cups hot steamed rice.

Curry Sauce:

2 *cups dry white table wine*
1½ *cups chicken broth*
2 *tablespoons curry powder*
1½ *tablespoons arrowroot*
  (or 2 tablespoons cornstarch)
  Cold water

Combine wine and broth in a saucepan. Heat to simmering. Mix curry powder and arrowroot with enough cold water to moisten. Add to liquid and simmer 5 minutes, stirring. Makes 8 servings.

STUFFED HEARTS OF LETTUCE

2 *medium-sized, well-formed heads iceberg lettuce (they should be green and rather loose)*
1 *cup each commercial sour cream and mayonnaise*
4 *ounces crumbled blue cheese*

Remove loose outer leaves from lettuce; core. Run cold water into core to loosen head; drain very thoroughly. Make dressing by whirling in a blender or electric mixer until smooth the sour cream, mayonnaise, and blue cheese. Slowly pour dressing into cored part and between leaves of lettuce heads, so lettuce absorbs as much dressing as possible. Wrap heads in waxed paper or clean, damp towels. Chill in vegetable compartment of refrigerator for 6 hours or until dressing is firm. Cut heads in quarter wedges. Serve immediately. Makes 8 servings.

CREAM OF MINT PARFAIT

1 cup hot water
1 package (3 oz.) lime-flavored gelatin
1 pint softened mint ice cream
½ teaspoon mint extract
1 cup crumbs made by crushing
  chocolate wafers
  Whipped cream
8 mint sprigs dipped in powdered sugar

Pour hot water over flavored gelatin; stir to dissolve. Chill until syrupy. With electric mixer, quickly beat ice cream and mint extract into gelatin. Sprinkle about two-thirds of the chocolate wafer crumbs in bottoms of 8 parfait glasses. Spoon in ice cream mixture. Top with remaining cooky crumbs. Refrigerate until serving time. Top each serving with a spoonful of whipped cream and a sprig of mint dipped in powdered sugar. Makes 8 servings.

Greek Dinner

GREEK DISHES are superbly seasoned—with mint leaves, oregano, bay leaf, and such spices as cinnamon, allspice, and nutmeg. Lemons might be called a staple of Greek cooking. Lemon juice is freely squeezed over vegetables, meats, and poultry for added tang ⚜ The dinner entrée often features chicken or lamb, or perhaps a white fish. In addition, four or five vegetable dishes grace the table, along with a paste or rice. Salad is a "must" in Greece. Raw chopped vegetables and assorted greens, such as endive, chicory, fennel, and lettuce, often go into a large bowl on the table. Everyone takes what he wants and seasons it with olive oil, vinegar or lemon juice, salt and pepper, and oregano ⚜ *Feta*, a white cheese made from goat's milk is usually on the table with bread. If feta is not available, you may substitute ricotta or jack cheese ⚜ The more complicated of these recipes, such as the meat balls, soup, *pita*, and stuffing, can be prepared a day ahead and then reheated. The others are easy to put together the day of the dinner.

LEMON SOUP

GREEN SALAD WITH FETA AND ANCHOVIES

PITA (GREENS PIE)   PARSLEY MEAT BALLS

LEMON-BASTED ROAST CHICKEN

VEGETABLE STUFFING   ARTICHOKES WITH PEAS

    OLIVES

KOURABIEDES (SUGAR-COATED BUTTER CAKES)

155

LEMON SOUP

4 cans (12 oz. each) chicken broth
   (6 cups broth)
3 tablespoons uncooked rice
3 eggs, beaten
3 tablespoons lemon juice

Cook broth and rice until rice is tender, about 20 minutes. Beat eggs until light, and gradually add lemon juice, beating until blended. Pour part of the hot soup slowly, while beating, into the egg mixture; then return to the remainder of the soup. Do not heat further; if it should curdle, beat with a rotary beater. Serve at once. Makes 6 servings.

GREEN SALAD WITH FETA AND ANCHOVIES

Top these individual mixed green salads with a square of feta or jack cheese, crossed by an anchovy fillet.

1 head lettuce
1 head curly endive
2 tomatoes
16 pitted ripe olives
2 green onions, sliced
⅔ cup olive oil
⅓ cup red wine vinegar
   Salt and pepper
   Oregano
6 pieces (1 inch square) feta or
   jack cheese
6 anchovy fillets

Chop greens and tomatoes. Toss together with the olives and onions. Pour over the oil and vinegar and season to taste with salt, pepper, and oregano. Arrange on salad plates, and top each salad with a square of cheese and an anchovy fillet. Makes 6 servings.

PITA

You need tissue-paper-thin dough, called *fila* or leaves, for this flaky, layered pie of mixed greens and cheese. Fila sheets are available, packaged in 1-pound boxes, at Greek shops, or make your own fila sheets, following the directions given at the end of this recipe.

1 bunch Swiss chard
1 bunch spinach
1 bunch curly endive (chicory)
1 bunch parsley
1 bunch green onions
10 leaves mint
½ pound fila (8 sheets)
¾ cup olive oil
1 tablespoon salt
1 teaspoon pepper
1½ teaspoons uncooked rice
¾ pound feta, crumbled, or ½ pound
   Romano or Swiss cheese, grated
   Cinnamon

Wash greens and drain well. Finely chop the Swiss chard, spinach, endive, parsley, green onions, and mint. Spread the greens out on a clean cloth and let stand at room temperature for several hours to dry.

Unfold and spread out fila sheets separately to dry slightly. Spread 2 tablespoons olive oil in the bottom of a 10-by-16-inch baking pan. Place 1 sheet of fila in the pan. Brush lightly with olive oil. Arrange 3 more layers of fila on top (each spread with oil) so that they hang over the top edges of the pan. Toss together the chopped greens, salt, pepper, rice, feta, and ¼ cup of the olive oil, and pile the greens mixture into the dough-lined pan. Sprinkle lightly with cinnamon.

Now fold over edges of first sheet, spread lightly with olive oil, place another sheet of fila on top, and spread it lightly with oil. Continue to fold down the other 3 sheets of dough, oiling edges and inserting a sheet of fila between each.

With a sharp knife, mark fila into squares, cutting just through top sheet of fila. Bake in a hot oven (400°) for 1¼ hours, or until crust is golden brown and the greens are tender. Finish cutting into squares and serve hot or cold. Makes 24 pieces.

Fila:

If you cannot buy the fila, you may make it this way: Sift 2 cups flour with ½ teaspoon salt and mix in enough water to make a soft ball (approximately ½ cup water); knead in 3 tablespoons olive oil and knead until smooth. Let sit 30 minutes. Using an extra long rolling pin or broomstick, roll out one-eighth of dough on a floured board until it is paper thin and approximately 16 by 24 inches. Continue to roll out pieces of dough until you have 8 sheets of the thin fila dough.

Arrange fila in pan so it hangs over the sides. Spread each layer of dough with olive oil.

Heap the greens mixture in dough-lined pan to allow for shrinkage that will occur during the baking.

PARSLEY MEAT BALLS

You can shape this parsley and onion-seasoned meat in small balls for hors d'oeuvres, as in this menu, or in larger balls if you wish to serve them as an entrée.

> ¾ *cup dry bread crumbs*
> ½ *cup milk*
> 2 *onions, chopped*
> ½ *cup water*
> 2 *pounds ground lean beef*
> ½ *bunch parsley, finely chopped (¾ cup)*
> 3 *leaves mint, chopped*
> 2 *egg yolks*
> 3 *small cloves garlic, minced or mashed*
> 1½ *teaspoons salt*
> ¼ *teaspoon pepper*
> 1½ *tablespoons each olive oil and butter*
> ¼ *cup red wine vinegar or lemon juice*
> ½ *teaspoon crumbled dried oregano*

Soak bread crumbs in milk; then beat up until mushy. Cook onions, covered, in the water until the water has boiled away. Mix together thoroughly the meat, soaked bread crumbs, cooked onions, parsley, mint, egg yolks, garlic, salt, and pepper. With wet hands, form into walnut-shaped balls. Heat the oil and butter in a frying pan, and brown meat on all sides, slowly and well. Transfer meat balls to a serving dish. Pour wine vinegar into the pan, heat, and scrape up the drippings; pour over the meat balls. Sprinkle with oregano. Makes 3 dozen small meat balls.

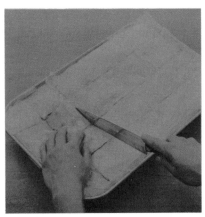

Use a sharp knife to cut 1½-inch squares in the top layer of fila before baking. Finish cutting into squares after baking.

157

LEMON-BASTED ROAST CHICKEN

This roast chicken is extremely moist and tender. The lemon is refreshing on the rich, buttery skin.

> 3-pound (or larger) whole broiler-fryer
> ½ teaspoon crumbled dried oregano
> 2 cloves garlic
> 4 tablespoons (¼ cup) butter or margarine
> Salt and pepper
> Juice of 2 lemons
> ½ teaspoon crumbled, dried oregano
> ½ cup water

Wash chicken and drain. Sprinkle ½ teaspoon oregano inside chicken, and put the 2 cloves peeled garlic inside. Melt butter in the roasting pan and roll chicken in it; sprinkle with salt and pepper. Place chicken, breast side down, in a pan and roast, uncovered, in a hot oven (400°) for 45 minutes, or until golden brown. Turn chicken, breast side up, and continue roasting for 30 to 45 minutes longer, or until golden brown on top. Reduce heat to slow (300°) and continue roasting for 1 hour longer.

Squeeze lemon juice over all, put on the cover, and let stand in the oven for 15 minutes longer. Remove to a platter, sprinkle with remaining ½ teaspoon oregano, and carve. Stir water into the drippings, heat, and pour over the chicken as a sauce. Makes 6 servings.

VEGETABLE STUFFING

The carrots and raisins give this stuffing a pleasing sweetness; walnuts add a crunchy texture. For this menu, the stuffing is baked in a separate pan to serve separately, but it can also be spooned inside a chicken or turkey before roasting.

> 1 pound chestnuts (optional)
> 3 medium-sized onions
> ½ cup water
> ½ pound ground beef
> 1 package (8 oz.) frozen chicken livers, thawed and chopped
> ½ cup (¼ pound) butter or margarine
> ½ cup raisins, chopped
> 3 carrots, peeled and chopped
> 2 stalks celery, sliced
> ½ cup walnuts, chopped
> 1½ teaspoons each poultry seasoning and cinnamon
> 2 teaspoons nutmeg
> ½ teaspoon ground cloves
> 1 package (6 oz.) zwieback
> 6 eggs

Cut a ½-inch slit in the side of each chestnut, cover with boiling water, cook for 10 minutes, and drain; then peel and chop. Peel and chop onions; boil in the ½ cup water just until the water boils away. Brown the ground meat, chopped livers, and cooked onions in butter until meat is browned. Add the chopped chestnuts, raisins, carrots, celery, and walnuts; simmer for 3 to 4 hours, or until very mushy. (If necessary, add more water.)

Add the poultry seasoning, cinnamon, nutmeg, and cloves the last half hour of cooking. Mash well with a potato masher. Crush zwieback finely and mix in. Beat eggs until light, and stir into the slightly cooled stuffing. Turn into a greased 9-inch-square baking pan, cover pan with foil, and bake in a moderate oven (350°) for 1 hour. Makes 8 generous servings.

ARTICHOKES WITH PEAS

Slivers of red pimiento across artichoke halves filled with peas make this a colorful vegetable dish.

> 4 medium-sized artichokes
> Boiling salted water
> Juice of 1 lemon
> 1 can (1 lb.) peas (2 cups cooked peas)
> 1 canned pimiento, sliced

Cut off the tips of the artichokes, and cut in half lengthwise; scoop out the choke with a spoon. Cook in boiling salted water with the lemon juice until tender, about 45 minutes. Heat peas, drain. Arrange cooked artichoke halves on a platter, cavity side up. Spoon peas on top, filling the cavities, and arrange a strip of pimiento over the top of each. Makes 8 servings.

KOURABIEDES

You generously sift powdered sugar over these buttery, almond-filled crescents while they're still warm so a sugar frost blankets each one. These tender, almost fragile cookies are quite similar to the round and rich Mexican Tea (or Wedding) Cakes.

> 1½ cups (¾ pound) *butter*
> 2 tablespoons *powdered sugar*
> 1 *egg yolk*
> ½ cup coarsely grated or finely
>   chopped *almonds*
> 3½ cups *flour (approximately)*
> 2 pounds *powdered sugar (approximately)*

Cream butter until light and fluffy. Mix in the 2 tablespoons sugar and egg yolk, creaming well. Beat in almonds. Gradually add the flour, adding just enough to make a soft dough that you can shape with your hands. Pinch off pieces of dough the size of a large walnut and roll between your hands, shaping into half-moon or stylized "S" shapes. Place on an ungreased baking sheet and bake in a slow oven (275°) for 45 minutes, or until very lightly browned.

Remove from oven and let cool in pan until lukewarm. Sift powdered sugar over butcher paper, arranged in a shallow pan, and carefully transfer cookies from baking sheet to sugared paper. Sift more powdered sugar over the top, coating them at least ¼ inch thick with sugar. Let stand until cool, then store in a crock. Makes about 30.

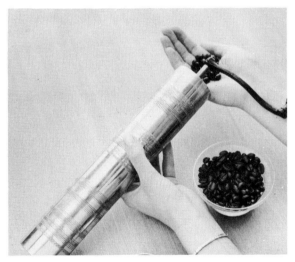

Tall brass coffee mill may be used to grind highly roasted coffee beans, known as French roast, into a fine powder for demitasses of Turkish coffee.

To make Turkish coffee, heat 1 teaspoon each coffee and sugar and 1 demitasse of cold water per serving; boil. Remove, shake; reboil, shake 3 times.

Dinner for Ten

SARDINE PÂTÉ WITH ITALIAN BREAD STICKS

VEAL BIRDS WITH HERB SAUCE

CALABRIAN NOODLES

ASPARAGUS SALAD

BABA AU RHUM WITH STRAWBERRIES

THIS DINNER FOR TEN, served buffet style, starts with sardine pâté, radishes, and thin crisp bread sticks. Veal birds in a full-flavored herb sauce are served with mild cheese-blended Calabrian noodles. Fresh asparagus is a delicious addition to the meal, but if it isn't in season, substitute any green vegetable of your choice. Serve the Baba au Rhum with either fresh or frozen strawberries ⚘ Every item on the menu, except the noodles, can be made ahead of time. The pâté can be made the day before the party and chilled. You can prepare the veal rolls up to the point of baking early in the day; cool and chill, then bake them just before serving. (Add 15 minutes to baking time if chilled.) The dessert can be made a day ahead.

SARDINE PÂTÉ

2 large packages (8 oz. each) cream cheese
3 tablespoons lemon juice
2 tablespoons scraped onion
2 tablespoons minced parsley
3 cans (4 oz. each) boneless sardines
  Minced parsley for garnish
  Radishes

Mash cream cheese with lemon juice, onion, parsley, and sardines. When well blended, form into a mound and sprinkle with minced parsley. Surround with radishes. Serves 10.

VEAL BIRDS WITH HERB SAUCE

4 pounds veal cutlet
1 small onion
¼ pound cooked ham
1½ cups soft bread crumbs
2 tablespoons melted butter
1 teaspoon lemon juice
1 small clove garlic, pressed
¼ teaspoon thyme
2 tablespoons minced parsley
1 teaspoon salt
¼ teaspoon pepper
  Flour
  Shortening
2 tablespoons butter
2 tablespoons flour
1 cup white wine
1 cup consommé or chicken stock
1 tablespoon each minced parsley, chives,
  and mushrooms
½ teaspoon each tarragon and thyme

Have veal cutlet sliced thin, then flattened further by pounding with a mallet. Cut in pieces about 2 by 3 inches, and save the trimmings. Grind the trimmings, along with onion and ham. Mix with bread crumbs, melted butter, lemon juice, garlic, thyme, parsley, salt, and pepper. Spread the mixture on the pieces of veal; roll and tie. Dust with flour and brown on all sides in shortening. Remove to a flat baking dish. In the skillet in which you've browned the veal rolls, add butter, flour, wine, consommé, parsley, chives, mushrooms, tarragon, and thyme. Simmer until thickened, and pour over the veal rolls. Bake in a moderate oven (350°) until hot and tender—about 25 to 30 minutes. Serves 10.

CALABRIAN NOODLES

1 pound ricotta cheese (or cottage cheese)
¾ cup hot water
2 tablespoons olive oil
3 tablespoons melted butter
1 teaspoon salt
½ teaspoon freshly ground pepper
1 pound egg noodles

Combine cheese, water, oil, and butter, and beat until smooth. Season with salt and pepper. Heat in top of double boiler over hot water. Cook noodles, drain well, and mix with hot sauce. Serve at once. Serves 10.

ASPARAGUS SALAD

4 pounds fresh asparagus
Boiling salted water
Butter lettuce hearts
Oil and vinegar dressing

Cook only the tender parts of asparagus in boiling water just until easily pierced with a fork. Do not allow asparagus to become limp or lose its bright green color. Drain immediately and spread on a pan to cool quickly. If you want the full flavor, do not chill, but serve at room temperature. Arrange on a platter, surround with tender hearts of butter lettuce, and dress with a simple oil and vinegar dressing. Serves 10.

BABA AU RHUM

¼ cup currants
¾ cup scalded milk
1 package yeast, active dry or compressed
2 cups flour
4 eggs, well beaten
⅓ cup butter
2 tablespoons sugar
½ teaspoon salt
1 cup strained apricot preserves
1 cup water
½ cup rum or 1 teaspoon rum flavoring
Sliced sugared strawberries
Whipped cream (optional)

Put currants in scalded milk to plump. When cooled to lukewarm, sprinkle or crumble in the yeast, stir in the flour and eggs, and beat well for 3 or 4 minutes. (The French use their bare hands; use a wooden spoon or a heavy-duty mixer if you'd rather.) Allow to rise in a warm place until almost doubled in bulk. Cream butter, sugar, and salt together, and beat into batter. Divide among 12 well-greased custard cups (about 8-oz. size). Allow to rise until doubled, then bake in a hot oven (400°) for 15 minutes. Remove babas from cups, turn upside down, and over them pour warm sauce made by heating the strained apricot preserves with water, then adding rum. Let soak at room temperature for several hours. Serve with sliced sugared strawberries and, if you wish, whipped cream. More rum may be poured over the babas before serving. Makes 12 babas.

Holiday Smörgåsbord

Scandinavians who have settled in this country carry on their own American version of old-country smörgåsbord throughout the holiday season. This tradition of setting a well-laden buffet table originated during the time of the Viking feast days. In Scandinavia, the smörgåsbord is considered a gesture of hospitality and a welcome to the meal that follows. Because this spread is bounteous, Scandinavians approach it with caution. Often they

The smörgåsbord

> **BREADS**
> SWEDISH RYE   LUMPA   PUMPERNICKEL   RYE WAFERS
>
> **CHEESES** (Choose 3 or 4)
> EDAM   KUMINOST (CARAWAY SEED)
> PORT DU SALUT   SHARP CHEDDAR   SWISS
> ROQUEFORT   GJETOST (NORWEGIAN GOAT CHEESE)
>
> **FISHES** (Choose 2 or 3)
> HERRING IN SOUR CREAM   ANCHOVIES
> JELLIED SALMON   CAVIAR AND CREAM DIP
> OMELET WITH CREAMED CRAB
>
> **MEATS**
> SWEDISH MEAT BALLS   CALV SYLTA (PRESSED VEAL)
> ASSORTED HOT OR COLD SAUSAGES

Dinner course

> **BAKED HAM WITH GLAZED APPLES, PRUNES, PEARS**
> **CREAMED PEAS AND CARROTS OR BUTTERED BROCCOLI**
> **PICKLED BEETS**

Dessert sideboard

> CREAM WAFERS   DROMMAR (DREAM COOKIES)
> MORKAKOR (BUTTER LEAVES)
> MANDELFORMAR (ALMOND TARTS)
> FRUIT TRAY OF GRAPES, PEARS, APPLES, TANGERINES
> NUTS IN THE SHELL

sample just two or three items from the smörgåsbord of breads, cheeses, fishes, and meats, saving
room for the dinner to follow. Dessert and coffee
often are served an hour or two after dinner.

This menu is ideal for the hostess who plans to
have numerous small parties throughout Christmas week. The cheeses, fishes, meats, and sweets
will keep well between buffets if returned to the
refrigerator or to tightly covered cans. Or if you
hold a single large buffet, your family will relish
any leftovers as snacks or help-yourself lunches
during the active days that follow the party.

Though the buffet includes numerous dishes, you
don't need to prepare all of them yourself. Delicatessens offer a wide selection of breads, cheeses,
fishes, and sausages. You can prepare and freeze
ahead the meat balls and the cookies. Jellied meat
and fish are best made a day or two in advance of
the party. This is a flexible menu. Freely add
dishes to please your family's tastes or subtract to
suit your cooking time.

JELLIED SALMON

If you mold this jellied salmon in a fish shape, you
may wish to decorate it with olive rings and strips
of pimiento or green pepper.

    4 cups coarsely chopped celery stalks
        and tops
    1½ teaspoons dried dill
    1 onion, peeled
    6-pound piece of salmon
    2 quarts water
    1 bay leaf
    ½ teaspoon each whole allspice and
        white pepper
    4 teaspoons salt
    3 envelopes (3 tablespoons) unflavored
        gelatin
    Water cress
    Lemon wedges

Place coarsely chopped celery in a large kettle;
add dill, onion, and fish. Pour in water. Add bay

leaf, allspice, pepper, and salt. Bring to a boil and
simmer just until fish is tender. Cool; remove skin
and bones. Strain court bouillon (you should have
1½ quarts liquid), taste and add salt if needed.

Soften gelatin in ¾ cup of the cool court bouillon;
heat remaining bouillon and stir in softened gelatin. Line a large fish-shaped mold or other desired
mold with the larger pieces of fish, and fill in the
center with the flaked pieces. Pour in bouillon and
chill. Unmold on a large chop plate and garnish
with sprigs of water cress and lemon wedges, arranged spoke fashion. Makes 16 smörgåsbord
servings.

CAVIAR AND CREAM DIP

    ½ cup whipping cream
    2 teaspoons grated onion
    1 small jar (2 oz.) red or black caviar
        Rye wafers

Whip cream until stiff, and fold in grated onion
and caviar. Pile into a serving dish and serve with
crisp rye wafers. Makes 1 cup dip.

SWEDISH MEAT BALLS

    1 medium-sized onion, finely chopped
    4 tablespoons (¼ cup) butter or margarine
    ½ cup fine dry bread crumbs
    1 cup milk
    1 egg
    2 egg yolks
    2 teaspoons salt
    ¼ teaspoon each freshly ground black pepper
        and monosodium glutamate
    1 teaspoon ground allspice
    ½ teaspoon sugar
    2 pounds lean beef, ground twice

Sauté onion in 1 tablespoon of the butter until golden. Soak bread crumbs in milk. Beat together the 1 egg and 2 yolks until light; mix in salt, pepper, monosodium glutamate, allspice, and sugar. Stir in the soaked bread crumbs, sautéed onion, and ground beef, mixing thoroughly. Roll into balls about 1½ inches in diameter. Sauté in the remaining butter, using 1 tablespoon at a time, turning to brown all sides. Makes about 3 dozen.

CALV SYLTA

You serve this spiced, meaty gelatin loaf with a cruet of cider vinegar so each guest can pour a few drops over his thick slice of jellied veal. Occasionally, head cheese replaces this dish.

- 3½ *pounds lean veal leg or shoulder with bones*
- 1 *quart water*
- 12 *whole allspice*
- 1 *bay leaf*
- ¼ *teaspoon peppercorns*
- 1 *small onion, peeled*
- 1 *medium-sized carrot, peeled*
- 1 *tablespoon salt*
- 1 *envelope (1 tablespoon) unflavored gelatin*
- ¼ *cup cold water*
- ¼ *teaspoon finely ground black pepper*
- 16 *whole allspice*

Wash meat and put in a kettle with the 1 quart water, 12 whole allspice, bay leaf, peppercorns, onion, carrot, and salt; cover and simmer slowly for 2 hours, or until the meat falls away from the bones. Strain broth and reserve (you should have 3½ cups broth). Remove meat from bones and chop it finely. Soften gelatin in cold water and stir into hot broth to dissolve. Stir in meat, black pepper, and the 16 whole allspice. Turn into a 9-inch round or square pan or two 9 by 5-inch loaf pans. Chill until set. Unmold and cut in 1-inch-thick slices. Makes 16 servings.

BAKED HAM WITH GLAZED APPLES, PRUNES, PEARS

Bake a 6 to 9-pound canned ham ahead of time and glaze with a mixture of brown sugar and cider. When cool, decorate the top by pressing whipped butter through a forcebag to say "God Jul" (Merry Christmas). If your dinner is held after Christmas Day, omit this and decorate with lines in a diamond pattern.

For the garnish, steam 1 dozen large prunes until plumped. Quarter and core 4 red-skinned cooking apples. Peel, halve, and core 4 winter pears. Cook the apple quarters and pear halves in a mixture of 3 tablespoons each honey and melted butter or margarine and the juice of ½ lemon. Cook just until fruit is glazed and tender. Place the hot fruits (or they can be cold) around ham arranged on platter.

PICKLED BEETS

It is best to prepare this relish a day or two in advance so the tangy, spicy flavors will have a chance to permeate the sliced beets.

- 2 *cans (1 lb. each) whole beets*
- 1 *cup cider vinegar*
- 4 *tablespoons sugar*
- 1 *teaspoon salt*
- ¼ *teaspoon freshly ground black pepper*
- 18 *whole cloves*

Drain liquid from beets and reserve ½ cup. Slice beets thinly into a bowl. Mix together the reserved beet liquid, vinegar, sugar, salt, and pepper, and pour over the beets. Stir in cloves. Refrigerate. Makes 4 cups.

CREAM WAFERS

You put a cream filling between every pair of these flaky, sugar-coated wafers.

> 1 cup (½ pound) butter or margarine
> 2 cups flour
> ½ cup whipping cream
> Granulated sugar

Filling:

> 4 tablespoons (¼ cup) butter or margarine
> 2 cups sifted powdered sugar
> 1 egg yolk
> 1 teaspoon vanilla

Cream butter until light and fluffy. Sift flour, measure, then add it alternately with the cream to the butter, mixing well. Chill. Roll out a third of the dough at a time on a lightly floured board until ⅛ inch thick. Cut into rounds; lift onto waxed paper that you have heavily covered with granulated sugar, and turn each round with a spatula so both sides are sugar-coated. Place on an ungreased baking sheet and prick each wafer about 4 times with a fork. Bake in a moderately hot oven (375°) for 10 to 12 minutes, or until golden brown. Cool on a rack.

For the filling, cream butter and powdered sugar together thoroughly. Add egg yolk and vanilla, and beat until smooth and creamy. Put 2 wafers together with a thick layer of filling. Makes about 2 dozen cookies.

DROMMAR

It is the ammonium carbonate—available in drugstores—that gives these buttery cookies their interesting light texture and crinkled surface. (If you substitute baking powder, you will not achieve the same result.)

> 1 cup (½ pound) butter or margarine
> ½ cup sugar
> 2 teaspoons vanilla
> 2 cups flour
> 1 teaspoon powdered ammonium carbonate
> 12 whole almonds, blanched and halved

Cream butter and sugar until light. Add vanilla. Sift flour, measure, then sift again with ammonium carbonate, and mix in with the butter and sugar mixture. Form into balls slightly smaller than a walnut, and press down lightly on a greased baking sheet. Press an almond half on top of each. Bake in a slow oven (275°) for 30 minutes. Makes about 2 dozen cookies.

Dessert treat includes a platter of Butter Leaves, Filled Almond Tarts, Dream Cookies, and Cream Wafers, a tray of fruit and nuts, and hot coffee.

MORKAKOR

The sugary, crisp almond topping is very attractive on these thin scalloped wafers. For a variation, bake half the cookies without a topping and put together with currant jelly.

½ cup (¼ pound) butter or margarine
¼ cup sugar
1 cup flour
⅛ teaspoon almond extract

Topping:

1 egg white
18 almonds, finely chopped
⅓ cup sugar

Cream butter and sugar until light. Mix in sifted flour and almond extract. Chill dough. Then roll out dough ⅛ inch thick, and cut out with a scalloped cutter or other desired cutter. Place on a greased baking sheet.

Beat egg white until soft peaks form, and brush over the cut-out cooky dough. Sprinkle with a mixture of almonds and sugar. Bake in a moderate oven (350°) for 10 minutes. Makes about 3½ dozen cookies.

MANDELFORMAR

You need tiny tart pans for this almond-flavored pastry. Most Scandinavian shops stock these fluted pans in round, triangular, and oval shapes.

In Swedish homes, these tarts may be served plain or filled with whipped cream and topped with lingonberries or jelly.

⅔ cup butter or margarine
⅓ cup sugar
1 egg yolk
½ cup ground blanched almonds
1½ cups flour
¼ teaspoon almond extract
  Whipped cream (optional)
  Lingonberries or jelly (optional)

Cream butter and sugar until light. Mix in egg yolk and ground almonds (grind in a nut grinder or blender, or chop very fine). Sift flour, measure, and mix in. Add almond extract. Roll into 2 rolls 1 inch in diameter, wrap in waxed paper, and chill. Cut off ¾-inch-thick pieces and press each into a tiny tart pan, covering the interior ¼ inch thick. Bake in a moderately slow oven (325°) for 12 minutes. When cool, fill with sweetened whipped cream and lingonberries, if desired. Makes 2 dozen tarts.

A Graduation Party for Twelve

A BUFFET SUPPER is a pleasant way to entertain informally for the high school or college graduate. This meal is planned to appeal to young sophisticates with the hearty appetites of youth

Make the melon and ginger cocktail ahead and chill thoroughly—an hour at least, or as long as 6 hours, if you wish. You can cook the stroganoff ahead of time up to the point of adding the sour cream; about 15 minutes before serving, reheat the meat and add the sour cream and seasonings. Prepare the strawberry Alaska early in the day except for making the meringue and baking. The rice, green beans, and herb bread should be prepared just before serving.

MELON AND GINGER COCKTAIL

BEEF STROGANOFF   RICE

HOT HERB BREAD   GREEN BEANS AMANDINE

BAKED STRAWBERRY ALASKA

MELON AND GINGER COCKTAIL

Use 3 or 4 varieties of melons. Cut the melons in balls or—and this is easier—in cylinders. (Use an apple corer and cut the resulting pieces in uniform lengths.)

> 1½ cups sugar
> ¼ cup white corn syrup
> ½ cup water
> 2 tablespoons grated green ginger
> 2 tablespoons lime or lemon juice
> 2 quarts melon balls or cylinders
>   Mint sprigs

Make a ginger sauce of the sugar, corn syrup, water, and ginger; cook sauce for 6 minutes. Cool and add lime or lemon juice. (If desired, the juice from preserved ginger may be used, diluted with lemon juice.) Pour over melon balls and chill thoroughly, at least 1 hour. Serve in sherbet glasses or, if preferred, in halves of small cantaloupes, and garnish with a sprig of mint. Makes 12 servings.

BEEF STROGANOFF

> 4 pounds round steak, sliced ½ inch thick
> 2 cups sliced onions
> ½ cup (¼ pound) butter
> 1 pound mushrooms, sliced
> 1 cup bouillon (may be half dry white table wine)
> 3 cups (1½ pints) commercial sour cream
>   Salt, pepper, and mustard to taste

Pound the steak until very thin, then cut in pieces about 3 inches long and ½ inch wide. Cut the onion slices in half and cook them in the butter until wilted. Then add the mushrooms and the beef, and cook for 5 minutes. Pour in the bouillon and cover. Simmer about 45 minutes or until the meat is tender and the liquid almost evaporated. Stir in the sour cream, season to taste with salt, pepper, and a little prepared mustard, and heat gently but do not boil. Makes 12 servings.

GREEN BEANS AMANDINE

> 3 pounds fresh green beans
> 1 cup slivered almonds
> ½ cup (¼ pound) butter

Slice beans on a long diagonal, and cook until tender but crisp. Dress with slivered almonds cooked golden brown in butter. Makes 12 servings.

HOT HERB BREAD

> 2 large loaves French bread
> 1 cup (½ pound) butter
> ¾ cup each minced chives and parsley
> ¼ cup minced sweet basil

Split bread loaves the long way and toast. Cream together butter, chives, parsley, and sweet basil. Spread bread while it is hot. Cut in 2-inch pieces. Makes 12 servings.

BAKED STRAWBERRY ALASKA

> 2-quart brick vanilla ice cream
> 1 layer (8-inch) sponge or pound cake
> 2 cups sliced sugared strawberries
> 6 egg whites
> ¼ teaspoon cream of tartar
> 1 cup sugar

Put heavy aluminum foil on a board slightly larger than the cake. Put the ice cream on the cake, and hollow out the center enough to pour in the strawberries. Spread surplus ice cream over the opening, and put in the freezer while you make the meringue. Beat the egg whites with the cream of tartar until stiff, then beat in sugar gradually, and continue beating until very stiff. Spread the meringue over the ice cream and cake, covering it completely. Bake in a preheated oven (450°) until nicely browned, about 5 minutes. Serve at once, with more sliced strawberries, if desired. (This Alaska may also be served flaming; pour heated rum or Cognac over it, and light.) Makes 12 servings.

Planked Fish Dinner

FOOD BROILED on a hardwood plank takes on a delicate wood flavor. Serve right from the plank; it not only makes a handsome tray, but also keeps the food warm. Before using a new plank, season it by brushing it generously with salad or olive oil and placing it in a slow oven (250° to 275°) for at least one hour; brush it with more oil when the surface of the wood looks dry. Before you cook on a seasoned plank, always oil it again. Preheat the oiled plank by placing it in a cold oven, turning the heat to 425°, and leaving it for 15 minutes. To simplify preparations for this dinner, make the cornbread ahead of time from a mix; split and toast it at the last minute. Prepare the salad ingredients several hours in advance and chill until serving time. Arrange salad while planked foods broil. Bake the pears ahead, if you wish, then, just before serving, warm them in the oven; or bake them during dinner and serve warm.

PLANKED MACKEREL AND
MUSHROOM CAPS

DILLED GREEN PEA SALAD

TOASTED CORNBREAD SQUARES

BAKED PEARS WITH MAPLE SAUCE

PLANKED MACKEREL AND MUSHROOM CAPS

   3 mackerel (about 1 lb. each)
   6 large (or 12 medium-sized) fresh
       mushrooms, stems removed
     Melted butter
     Salt and pepper
     Lemon wedges

Split mackerel lengthwise. Wash and pat dry. Arrange, cut side down, on a large, oil-seasoned hardwood plank.

Place mushrooms, cap side up, alongside fish. Brush fish and mushrooms with melted butter, and sprinkle with salt and pepper. Broil 6 inches

below heat for about 12 minutes, or until fish flakes when tested with a fork; baste when needed with more butter. Garnish and serve with lemon wedges. Makes 6 servings.

DILLED GREEN PEA SALAD

   2 packages (10 oz. each) frozen peas
   3 tablespoons salad oil
   1 to 2 tablespoons lemon juice
   ¾ teaspoon dill weed
   ¼ teaspoon basil
   1 whole clove garlic
     Salt and pepper to taste
   1 cup thinly sliced celery
     Lettuce
     Hard-cooked eggs

Cook peas as directed on package, reserving ⅓ cup of the cooking water. Combine peas, the reserved cooking water, salad oil, lemon juice, dill weed, basil, garlic, salt, and pepper. Chill thoroughly, at least 2 hours; discard garlic. Toss chilled ingredients with celery. Serve from a lettuce-lined bowl; decorate with hard-cooked eggs. Makes 6 servings.

BAKED PEARS WITH MAPLE NUT SAUCE

   3 medium-sized fresh pears, cut in half
       lengthwise and cored
   ½ cup each water, maple-flavored syrup, and
       firmly packed dark brown sugar
   1 teaspoon maple flavoring
   2 tablespoons melted butter
   ¼ cup chopped pecans

Place pear halves, cut side up, close together in a small, deep casserole. Combine water, syrup, sugar, maple flavoring, and butter; pour over pears. Cover and bake in a hot oven (400°) until pears are tender (about 40 minutes). While still slightly warm, serve in sauce dishes with some of the syrup. Sprinkle each serving with nuts. Makes 6 servings.

Austrian Dinner

THIS PARTY BUFFET begins with apple consommé, proceeds to roll twists, molded fruit salad, meat balls, assorted vegetables, and an elegant six-layer torte ᶄᶄ Practically all of the dishes lend themselves to advance preparation, so you can be quite calm and unhurried as you serve guests a complete Austrian meal ᶄᶄ You can cook the soup, molded salad, and meat balls a day ahead. You'll probably want to buy the *Salztangerl* (long slender rolls sprinkled with coarse salt and caraway seeds); or you can make them using hot roll mix. Assemble the torte a few hours before serving; but you can bake the cake layers a day in advance.

CREAM CONSOMMÉ

STRAWBERRY-BLUEBERRY MOLD

BAKED KOTLETI

CARROTS VICHY

BROWNED NEW POTATOES

BUTTERED BROCCOLI

SALZTANGERL

HIMMEL TORTE

CREAM CONSOMMÉ

You may want to pass small cups of this steaming fruity soup in the living room as a prelude to dinner. A blender is a great time-saver in preparing it.

    1 large onion, parboiled
    1 tart apple, unpeeled
    3 cans (10½ oz. each) consommé
    1½ cups whipping cream
      Salt to taste
      Dash each paprika and curry powder
    1 red-skinned apple
      Juice of ½ lemon

Grate the parboiled onion and the unpeeled apple; add to the consommé and cook until tender, about 10 minutes. Purée in a blender or put through a strainer. Stir in cream, and season with salt, paprika, and curry powder. Reheat slowly, just until hot throughout. Serve in small cups, garnished with chopped apple that you have sprinkled with lemon juice. Makes 10 servings.

STRAWBERRY-BLUEBERRY MOLD

This scarlet salad mold is refreshingly tart as well as brightly colored with jewel-like fruits. When fresh blueberries or huckleberries are in season, substitute them for frozen berries. Make the base of greens, previously tossed in French dressing, generous enough to provide each person with a portion.

    3¾ cups water
    2 packages (3 oz. each) wild cherry or
        cherry-flavored gelatin
    ¼ cup pale dry sherry
    1 basket strawberries (approximately
        1 pint)
    1½ cups fresh blueberries or 1 package
        (10 oz.) frozen blueberries,
        practically thawed
    2 cans (1 lb. each) seedless grapes
      Greens
      French dressing

Heat 2 cups of the water, add flavored gelatin, and stir until dissolved. Stir in the remaining 1¾ cups water and the wine; chill until syrupy. Wash and halve strawberries, and arrange in the bottom of a 3-quart ring mold, or use individual molds. Pour in enough of the chilled gelatin to cover berries; chill. Mix the remaining gelatin with blueberries and grapes, and pour into mold. Chill until firm. When ready to serve, unmold on greens that have been tossed in French dressing. Makes 10 to 12 servings.

BAKED KOTLETI

Austrians have a special way of preparing meat balls. Their trick of folding stiffly beaten egg whites into the meat mixture results in a pleasingly light and tender meat ball. Pass a bowl of sour cream when you serve this savory meat dish.

    3 pounds very lean ground beef
    6 tablespoons butter or margarine
    2 teaspoons salt
    ½ teaspoon freshly ground pepper
    2 tablespoons minced parsley
    6 slices stale bread
    4 eggs, separated
    4 tablespoons flour
    2 cups canned consommé
    6 tablespoons commercial sour cream

Add to the ground meat 2 tablespoons softened butter, salt, pepper, and parsley. Soak bread in water, squeeze nearly dry, and tear up finely; add to the meat mixture, along with egg yolks; mix thoroughly. Whip egg whites until stiff, but not dry, and fold in, stirring with a fork. Form meat mixture into 2 dozen oval-shaped patties. Sauté in the remaining butter until browned on each side. Transfer to a casserole.

Stir flour into the drippings and brown slightly, then stir in consommé; bring to a boil. Stir in sour cream, blending until smooth, and pour over the meat balls. Bake in a moderate oven (350°) for 25 minutes. Makes 10 servings.

CARROTS VICHY

2 *bunches new carrots*
¼ *cup melted butter*
2 *tablespoons sugar*
  Salt and pepper to taste
  Finely chopped parsley

Peel and thinly slice carrots. Place in a saucepan with butter, sugar, salt, and pepper; steam over low heat just until tender, about 7 minutes. Just before serving, sprinkle with finely chopped parsley. Makes 10 servings.

HIMMEL TORTE

Himmel Torte is German for Heavenly Tart, and this dessert deserves the name. It is six layers of crisp butter cooky, spread with a tart jelly and whipped cream (some versions call for sour cream instead).

1½ *cups (¾ pound) butter or margarine*
  ¾ *cup sugar*
  3 *egg yolks*
  1 *whole egg*
2¼ *cups flour*
  ¾ *cup currant jelly*
  1 *cup (½ pint) whipping cream*
    Powdered sugar

Cream the butter and gradually add the sugar, creaming until light and fluffy. Beat in egg yolks, one at a time; add whole egg and beat until smooth. Sift flour, measure, and gradually mix into the creamed mixture. Using a spatula, or rubber scraper, spread dough in a thin layer over the bottom of six 8-inch, round layer pans (you can also use 3 pans and bake 2 batches of cakes). Bake in a moderately hot oven (375°) for 12 to 15 minutes, or until the cakes are golden brown on the edges. Turn out of pans and let cool.

Spread 5 of the cake layers with currant jelly and then with a thin layer of sweetened whipped cream; stack layers and top with the remaining plain cake layer. Sift powdered sugar over it. Chill until ready to serve. Makes 12 servings.

Fritter Buffet

GOLDEN CHICKEN FRITTERS and vegetable fritters, served hot and crisp, make the entrée for this buffet. Start your meal with creamy shrimp bisque (use a favorite recipe or frozen shrimp soup garnished with a few extra shrimp), and crackers with caper butter You can cook the fritters several hours ahead; they are just as good when reheated as when first made. Make the salad at the last minute—your favorite mixed greens tossed with a simple dressing of 3 parts salad oil to 1 part fresh lemon juice, and salt and pepper to taste Let the fig dessert decorate the buffet until time to serve.

SHRIMP BISQUE

CRACKERS WITH CAPERS

CHICKEN FRITTERS

VEGETABLE FRITTERS

SAUCE ROSA

MIXED GREENS WITH LEMON AND OIL DRESSING

HOT BUTTERED RYE BREAD

FIGS IMPERIAL

CRACKERS WITH CAPERS

4 tablespoons (¼ cup) soft butter or
    margarine
1 tablespoon drained, chopped capers
1 tablespoon minced chives
    Unsalted crackers

Blend butter or margarine with capers and chives. Spread on crackers. Makes about 6 servings.

CHICKEN FRITTERS AND VEGETABLE FRITTERS

For an assortment of fritters, you will need 3 whole chicken breasts and a total of 4 or 5 cups of vegetables (eggplant, cauliflower, squash, corn, and peas) cut in various shapes and sizes. Chicken cubes and larger vegetable pieces are dipped into fritter coating before frying, and the corn, peas, and diced vegetables are stirred into batter and fried by spoonfuls.

To prepare the food, skin and bone the chicken breasts and cut meat in two-bite-size chunks; cut eggplant in sticks; break cauliflower into small clusters, then cut clusters in halves or quarters; cut squash (zucchini, patty pan, crookneck) in sticks or slices. Just before cooking the chicken and vegetable chunks, dust them in flour, sprinkle with salt, and dip in beaten egg (allow 1 egg for each cup food).

You may want to dice eggplant, cauliflower, or squash, and prepare in batter as you do corn and peas. To each ¾ cup of vegetables, add these ingredients, beaten together just until blended: 1 egg, 1 tablespoon milk, ¼ teaspoon salt, and 2 tablespoons flour. Cook by spoonfuls as directed below.

To cook fritters, heat fat for deep-frying (at least 1½ inches deep) to 370°; cook coated chicken and vegetable pieces (or spoonfuls of vegetable-batter mixture) until golden brown (about 3 minutes), turning occasionally. Drain on paper toweling. Serve immediately, or place in single layer on trays lined with paper towels and reheat in a moderately hot oven (375°) for 10 to 15 minutes. Serve with Sauce Rosa. Makes 6 to 8 servings.

SAUCE ROSA

1 cup (½ pint) commercial sour cream
2 tablespoons tomato paste
½ teaspoon paprika
¼ teaspoon chili powder
2 teaspoons brown sugar
1 teaspoon lemon juice

Blend sour cream with tomato paste, paprika, chili powder, brown sugar, and lemon juice. Makes about 1 cup.

FIGS IMPERIAL

3 cups white figs or peeled black figs, cut
    in halves
2 tablespoons honey
    Grated peel and juice of 1 medium-sized
    orange
    Juice of 1 lime
    Fig leaves
1 quart vanilla ice cream

Combine figs with honey, orange peel, orange juice, and lime juice. Slowly bring to a boil. Simmer for 2 minutes. Chill fruit in syrup. Drain fruit, saving syrup, and mound in serving dish decorated with fig leaves; put syrup in small pitcher. Serve fruit and syrup over vanilla ice cream. Makes 6 to 8 servings.

Veal Paprika Dinner

This is an undeniably hearty dinner, featuring a bubbling meat dish that is superbly smooth and mellow, yet spicy with bay and caraway. Most of the meal is prepared just before serving, but you can make both the veal dish and fruit compote early in the day and reheat them.

JELLIED MADRILÈNE WITH CHIVES

TART APPLE SLICES ON
SHREDDED WHEAT WAFERS

CARAWAY VEAL PAPRIKA

TOASTED ALMOND-TOPPED NOODLES

PARSLEYED GREEN BEANS

HOT APRICOT-ORANGE COMPOTE

JELLIED MADRILÈNE WITH CHIVES

Chill 2 cans (13 oz. each) consommé Madrilène until jellied; then spoon into chilled small soup cups, break up slightly with fork, sprinkle each serving with finely cut chives. Makes 6 servings.

CARAWAY VEAL PAPRIKA

- ½ pound fresh mushrooms, sliced
- 3 medium-sized onions, sliced
- 3 tablespoons butter
- 2 pounds boneless veal cubes
- 1 can (6 oz.) tomato paste
- ½ cup water
- 1 tablespoon paprika
- 1 bay leaf
- 1 teaspoon salt
- ½ teaspoon caraway seeds
- ¼ teaspoon pepper
- ½ cup commercial sour cream

Sauté mushrooms and onions in butter for 5 minutes. Add veal cubes; brown slowly. Add tomato paste, water, paprika, bay leaf, salt, caraway seeds, and pepper. Cover and simmer for 2 hours or until veal is tender. Just before serving, stir in sour cream. Makes 6 generous servings.

TOASTED ALMOND-TOPPED NOODLES

Cook 8 ounces noodles in boiling salted water until tender; drain. Top with ¼ cup each sliced almonds and fine soft bread crumbs tossed in ¼ cup melted butter. Slip under broiler to brown.

PARSLEYED GREEN BEANS

Cook 2 pounds fresh green beans or 2 packages (10 oz. each) frozen green beans in boiling salted water until tender. Drain and season with melted butter, freshly chopped parsley, salt, and pepper.

HOT APRICOT-ORANGE COMPOTE

- 1 package (11 oz.) dried apricots
- ½ package (1 lb. size) dried prunes
  Brown sugar
- 3 oranges, peeled and sliced
- 1 teaspoon grated orange peel
- ¼ teaspoon ground cloves
- 3 tablespoons each butter, brown sugar, and Ruby Port wine (optional)

Cook apricots and prunes separately according to package directions until almost tender, sweetening to taste with brown sugar. Add prunes with cooking syrup to apricots. Add oranges, orange peel, cloves, butter, the 3 tablespoons brown sugar, and wine. Heat together thoroughly over low heat; do not boil. Ladle while hot into dessert bowls. Serve with additional brown sugar to be sprinkled on. Makes 10 servings.

A Buffet Featuring Curry

THIS CURRY is like that served in the Dutch East Indies; the breads and the *sambals* that accompany it are typical of India itself ⟪ Much of the dinner can be prepared ahead of time. Make the curry early in the day; cool, chill, and reheat at serving time. The curry can even be made a day or two in advance, if desired—it actually improves if allowed to stand. For easiest dinner party organization, make the breads ahead and reheat at serving time as suggested. Prepare the dessert several hours before the party and chill. Toss the salad just before serving.

GREEN SALAD

SEAFOOD CURRY

RICE

CONDIMENTS

CHAPPATIES   PARATHAS

FRESH FRUIT IN PINEAPPLE SHELL

SEAFOOD CURRY

> 3 *large onions, sliced thin*
> 2 *cloves garlic, minced or mashed*
> ¾ *cup butter or margarine*
> 1½ *tablespoons curry powder*
> 5 *medium-sized tomatoes*
> 1 *package (10 oz.) frozen peas, cooked*
> 3½ *cups fish or chicken stock*
> 4 *pounds assorted seafood (crab meat; peeled, cleaned shrimp; baby lobster tails cut in sections; scallops; clams or oysters)*

Cook onions and garlic in half the butter until golden. Add curry powder, and sauté for another 5 minutes. Peel the tomatoes, cut in pieces, and stir into onion mixture. Purée the peas, or whirl them in a blender with 1 cup of the stock. Add the peas, along with the remainder of the stock, to the curry, and simmer for 20 minutes.

Sauté the seafood lightly in the remaining butter, but do not overcook. Combine with the curry sauce; correct seasoning, adding salt to taste and more curry powder, if desired. Before serving, reheat thoroughly.

This curry does not have as much sauce as some, and the peas are its only thickening. If you prefer, thicken it further with a flour paste. Makes 12 to 14 servings.

CONDIMENTS

Let condiments be as many and as varied as you like. An interesting one is egg sambal: Cut 6 hard-cooked eggs in quarters lengthwise, and arrange on a dish. Mix together 4 chopped green onions, 2 peeled green chilies (canned or fresh), ¼ cup salad oil, 2 tablespoons lemon juice, and ½ teaspoon salt. Pour mixture over the quartered eggs, and sprinkle with grated coconut.

In another sambal, made the same way, sliced ripe tomatoes are substituted for the eggs.

To make a coconut sambal, combine 1 cup grated coconut, fresh or dried, with 1 finely chopped onion, 1 tablespoon chili powder, ½ teaspoon salt, and ¼ cup lemon juice.

Here are other condiments to choose from: chutneys; onion rings, raw or French-fried; chopped green onions; crumbled crisp bacon; sliced bananas; shaved or shredded coconut (to shave, use a potato peeler); toasted coconut chips; one or more kinds of nuts; pickles; chopped green pepper; shredded ham; tiny meat balls; grated fresh or candied ginger; raisins plumped in sherry; chopped apple.

CHAPPATIES AND PARATHAS

The dough for these two Indian breads is identical. This recipe will make 12 portions. You can make just one kind, or divide the dough, as described below, and make 6 portions of each. Either of the breads may be rolled, ready to cook, then wrapped (with foil and waxed paper between portions) and frozen. They may also be frozen after cooking, and reheated in a moderate oven (350°) for 10 minutes. The Indians, however, eat them the minute they are baked.

> 2 *cups each unsifted whole wheat flour and sifted all-purpose flour, or 4 cups whole wheat flour*
> 1 *teaspoon salt*
> 2 *tablespoons butter*
> 1½ *cups lukewarm milk*

Combine ingredients and knead very well until the dough is smooth and elastic—this is very important.

To make *chappaties*, which are very much like Mexican flour tortillas, take half the dough and divide it into 6 portions (if you wish to make the chappaties smaller, divide the dough into 8 or 10 portions). Form in balls and roll on a floured board into thin pancakes about 8 inches in diameter. Cook on both sides on an ungreased griddle until lightly browned. Eat at once.

The *parathas*, which most people like even bet-ter, are made this way: Form the remaining dough into a long roll about 1 inch in diameter. Slice in 1-inch pieces. Stack 6 of these pieces carefully one on top of another with dabs of butter (about ¼ teaspoon) between them. Be sure edges are even, then roll out thin just as you would chappaties. Cook either on a greased griddle or in hot deep fat (375°) until golden brown. They will puff and become bubbly during cooking. Serve hot (they may be wrapped in a cloth and kept warm in a 250° oven).

FRESH FRUIT IN PINEAPPLE SHELL

3 medium-sized pineapples or 2
    large pineapples
1 papaya, peeled and diced
1 apple, thinly sliced

Slice each pineapple in half lengthwise, making the cut just off center so the crown is untouched. Use a grapefruit knife to cut the fruit away from the shells. Discard the smaller half shells. Cut off the core, and cut the pineapple into large pieces. Add diced papaya and sliced apple to the cut-up pineapple. Fill pineapple shells with fruit mix-ture. Makes 12 to 14 servings.

Hallowe'en Guest Dinner

STAGE THIS INFORMAL BUFFET for six in the living room or family room, preferably near a fireplace. It's fun to serve on a large, low table (like a coffee table), with your guests sitting on cushions. The pumpkin may be used as a container for the carrot soup ᐸᐸ Start the soup and the sundae the morning or the night before the dinner. If you plan to serve the soup in the pumpkin, cut out the top and clean out the seeds no more than five hours in advance of dinner ᐸᐸ A couple of hours before serving, set the table and prepare the Savory Cheese Pie; pop the pie in the oven about 30 minutes before your guests are due. After assembling the pie, make the salad (reserve dressing) and refrigerate. Cook broccoli and heat the soup just before serving.

CARROT SOUP

GREEN SALAD

SAVORY CHEESE PIE

BUTTERED BROCCOLI

BREAD STICKS

SPICY ORANGE SUNDAE

CARROT SOUP

4 to 6 large carrots, sliced (about 2½ cups)
½ teaspoon salt
1¾ cups water
1 can (13 oz.) undiluted evaporated milk
¼ teaspoon each coarse ground pepper and nutmeg
1 tablespoon minced parsley

Cook carrots in salted water until tender. Put carrots, including water in which they were cooked, in an electric blender and whirl until smooth. (You may have to do half at a time if your blender won't hold this amount.) Return to saucepan and stir in evaporated milk, pepper, nutmeg, and parsley. Return to heat, bring to a boil, and serve (or refrigerate to reheat and serve later). Makes 6 to 8 servings.

Heat pumpkin immediately before serving soup by pouring in boiling water and leaving it for 1 minute.

GREEN SALAD

1 small head each iceberg lettuce and romaine
French dressing

Tear lettuce and romaine into small pieces. Toss with French dressing just before serving. (In the spirit of the occasion, you might serve the salad in an iron pot resembling a witch's caldron, as shown in the photograph.) Makes 6 to 8 servings.

SAVORY CHEESE PIE

Pastry for a double-crust 9-inch pie
½ teaspoon black pepper
¼ teaspoon each dry mustard and paprika
½ pound sharp Cheddar cheese, shredded (about 2½ cups)
2 eggs
⅔ cup milk
¼ teaspoon salt
1½ tablespoons finely chopped onion
2 medium tomatoes, peeled and sliced
Beaten egg

Work pepper, mustard, and paprika into the pastry as you blend it. Divide pastry into 2 balls and roll out one; use to line a 9-inch pie pan. Distribute shredded cheese in pastry-lined pan. Beat eggs with milk, salt, and onion; pour over cheese. Cover with a layer of tomato slices. Top with remaining rolled-out pastry; trim (save trimmings), crimp edges, and make slits in top. Make 2 or 3 pastry leaves from scraps and place on center of pie. Brush top with beaten egg. Bake in a very hot oven (425°) for 10 minutes, reduce heat to 325° and cook 30 minutes longer or until browned. Serve hot. Makes 6 servings.

BUTTERED BROCCOLI

Cook about 2 pounds fresh broccoli or 2 packages (10 oz. each) frozen broccoli in salted water shortly before serving. Drain, butter, and serve.

Spicy orange sauce is spooned over individual servings of ice cream which has been frozen in an orange shell.

SPICY ORANGE SUNDAE

    3 *medium oranges*
    ¾ *cup sugar*
    1 *teaspoon cornstarch*
    ¾ *teaspoon ground ginger*
    ½ *teaspoon cinnamon*
    2 *tablespoons raisins*
       About 1½ pints vanilla ice cream

Halve oranges, making zigzag edges. Cut around orange pulp with a grapefruit knife. Use a spoon to remove any remaining pulp from the scooped-out shells; rinse them out, dry, and put them in the freezing compartment of your refrigerator. Meanwhile, remove the seeds and fibrous material from the orange pulp. Put the remaining pulp in a saucepan with a mixture of sugar, cornstarch, ginger, and cinnamon; bring to a boil. Add raisins and boil gently for about 12 minutes or until it begins to thicken. Chill before serving.

Remove the orange shells from freezer and fill each with a scoop of vanilla ice cream. Cover with foil or plastic wrap and return to freezer until serving time. To serve, put each filled orange in a small dish and pass the spicy syrup in a serving dish or pitcher. Makes 6 sundaes.

189

Hawaiian Party

EVERYONE SEEMS TO RELAX and have fun at a Hawaiian party. The way you dress, the customary sitting on the floor or on the ground, the food and the way it is served, the fragrance of flowers, and the music—all contribute to the warm and friendly mood ❧ Once you've decided where to have your party—in the garden, on the patio, or indoors—start with whatever materials are at hand to create an effect of flowers and greenery in abundance. Ferns, ivy or other vines, potted plants, and flowers can be combined with fruits and vegetables. Now is also the time to bring out any Hawaiian props you have acquired—fish net, hula skirts, coconut hats, tapa cloth, palm fronds. If you are entertaining outside, luau torches provide the most dramatic lighting as well as the most authentic effect ❧ Let your guests know how they should dress. Almost anything comfortable is the thing at a Hawaiian party—including, of course, muumuus and aloha shirts. Greet each guest with a flower lei—make leis of paper flowers, or buy inexpensive paper leis. You might arrange to have Hawaiian music playing on your record player as people arrive—but also suggest that anyone who has a musical instrument bring it ❧ Your guests should sit around a large table—unless you spread your feast on the floor or ground in true Hawaiian style. Provide each guest with a cushion to sit

TROPICAL PUNCH

SALTED NUTS   COCONUT CHIPS

FLAKED SALMON, LOMI STYLE

SPIT-ROASTED BARBECUED PORK

BAKED FISH

CHICKEN AND LONG RICE

SWEET POTATOES IN ORANGE BASKETS

BAKED BANANAS

PINEAPPLE IN RUM CUSTARD

HAUPIA

on. The table might be a ping-pong table top or a large sheet of plywood, set about 1 foot off the ground. In Hawaii, the table would be covered with *ti* leaves. Any large, broad leaves or ferns will work; the idea is to make a solid "tablecloth" of the greenery. Or cover the table with fish net, inexpensive yardage in brown-and-white or green-and-white colors, strips of plain brown wrapping paper, or paper printed in a tapa cloth design (available in some gift shops), or your own tapa design painted on cloth. Your table decorations should be a casual arrangement of fruit and flowers down the center of the table. Use any colorful fruits, but try to include some fresh pineapples and a cluster or two of bananas. Tuck garden flowers here and there among the fruits. Use candles on the table, or hurricane lamps or candles enclosed in glass if your party is out of doors.

Paper plates are most appropriate for setting your table. In addition to a large plate, there should be a salad plate for fish and a punch cup at each place. If you have wooden dishes, or sea shell or coconut dishes, they would be ideal to use. For serving dishes, monkeypod wood bowls, or any wooden trays, baskets, or platters will do. Decorate your punch bowl with flowers—you might even float some flowers on the punch. Coconut shells make good punch cups. To make the cups, hold a fresh coconut in a vise while you saw about a 1½-inch piece from the eye end. Take off another slice about 1 inch wide; this makes the ring to support the cup. Clean out all the meat, then use sandpaper to clean off the outside fuzz.

The food really should be eaten with fingers, but a few utensils can be very helpful. Plastic or wooden spoons and forks are fine. If you decide to go all the way and have your guests use their fingers, it would be well to have some kind of finger bowl at each place. Score a slice of lemon to look like a flower, and float in each bowl. Provide plenty of napkins.

Food in abundance and variety helps set the stage for the party. Much of the food preparation for the following menu can be done in advance of the party. You may decide, of course, to simplify the menu by leaving out a few of the items. It wouldn't be necessary to have both the baked fish and the chicken and long rice, for example, and you could omit either the *haupia* or pineapple for dessert. And you may want to serve coffee with dessert.

TROPICAL PUNCH

> 1 large can (about 6 cups) each passion fruit
>   juice and pineapple-grapefruit juice
> 1 cup lemon juice
> 2 large bottles (26 oz. each) sparkling water

Combine passion fruit juice, pineapple-grapefruit juice, and lemon juice. Chill. Just before serving, add sparkling water. Pour over a block of ice in the punch bowl. Makes 40 small (8 oz.) or 20 large servings.

Tropical fruit punch is served in punch cups made of coconut shells. Waxed flowers float on punch. For accompaniments, serve coconut chips and salted nuts.

SPIT-ROASTED BARBECUED PORK

Order a whole leg of fresh pork, and have your meat man bone and roll it. To serve 12, the net weight should be about 12 pounds.

Prepare the pork marinade (recipe follows) and marinate the pork for at least 1 hour. Place on spit, and roast over medium coals until well done, 6 to 7 hours for the 12-pound roast (internal temperature on the meat thermometer should read 185°). Baste frequently with the marinade as it roasts. When done, remove from spit, slice, and serve on a large platter. For a sauce to go with the meat, add the remaining 1 cup applesauce to the marinade that's left; heat and serve.

Pork Marinade:

- 1 can (1 lb.) applesauce
- ¾ cup dry white table wine
- ½ cup soy
- 2 tablespoons salad oil
- 1 cup chopped onion
- 1 clove garlic, minced or mashed
- 1 teaspoon ground ginger

Combine half of the applesauce (1 cup) with the remaining ingredients; mix well. Use the remaining 1 cup of applesauce for sauce to serve with meat (see above).

CHICKEN AND LONG RICE

- 2 stewing chickens, 4 to 5 pounds each
- 3 quarts water
- 2 medium-sized onions, coarsely chopped
- 2 carrots, coarsely chopped
- 4 celery stalks
- 2 large sprigs parsley
- 1 tablespoon salt
- ½ teaspoon pepper
- ½ pound long rice
- 1 can (1 lb. 4 oz.) tomatoes
- 2 medium-sized fresh tomatoes, peeled and cut in ½-inch squares

In a very large kettle, put the cleaned chickens with water, onion, carrot, celery, parsley, salt, and

pepper. Simmer gently until chickens are tender, about 2 to 2½ hours. Meanwhile, soak long rice in cold water for at least 1 hour. Cool chicken and stock. Discard skin from chicken, and remove the pieces of meat in large pieces. Skim fat from the cooled stock, strain; to the clear stock (should be about 2 quarts), add canned and fresh tomatoes, drained long rice, and the chicken pieces. Cover and simmer slowly for about 1 hour. Serve hot. Makes 12 servings.

BAKED WHOLE FISH

A whole ling cod, sea bass, or rock cod (about 8 pounds) will serve a party of 12. Scale, clean, and sprinkle inside and out with coarse salt. Arrange slices of onion, tomato, and lemon on top. Then wrap very securely in heavy foil, so none of the juices will be lost.

Set the whole fish on a rack in a shallow baking dish with a little water in the bottom and bake in a slow oven (300°) for 1 hour; turn fish over, lower oven heat to 250° and continue to bake for another hour. Open up the bundle so the fish shows. Put on a platter or tray to serve.

Spit-roasted, barbecued pork, sliced and ready to serve, is impressive on a large wooden tray surrounded by sweet potatoes in orange baskets, hot from the oven and with a garnish of marguerites.

FLAKED SALMON, LOMI STYLE

Lomi salmon, Hawaiian style, is made of a special salted salmon. This version starts with fresh, poached salmon.

2 quarts water
2 tablespoons salt
2 lemons, sliced
3 tablespoons lemon juice
2 bay leaves
12 each whole peppercorns and
    whole allspice
5½ pounds fresh salmon
3 cups sliced green onions, with tops
8 medium-sized tomatoes, coarsely
    chopped
Salt and pepper to taste

In a court bouillon made by combining the water, salt, lemon, lemon juice, bay leaves, peppers, and allspice, poach salmon about 12 minutes, or until the fish is just tender and flakes easily with a fork. Remove from heat and let fish stand in the liquid until cold. Remove from liquid, flake fish and keep in refrigerator until time to serve. Add onions and tomatoes to salmon and toss together lightly, adding salt and pepper to taste. Makes 12 servings.

SWEET POTATOES IN ORANGE BASKETS

12 oranges
10 medium-sized sweet potatoes
½ cup (¼ pound) butter
½ cup orange juice
2 egg whites

Cut each orange into a basket shape as follows: Cut it in half, but leave strip across top, slightly to one side of center, to form handle. Hollow out inside and save the fruit for later use.

Cook potatoes until tender; peel, and mash. Stir in butter, then orange juice. Beat egg whites until stiff; fold into sweet potato mixture. Heap into orange-peel basket. Just before serving, bake in a moderate oven (350°) for about 10 minutes, until heated through. Makes 12 servings.

Baked bananas have peel rolled into a curlicue. Before baking, bananas were seasoned with butter, brown sugar, and ginger.

BAKED BANANAS

12 ripe bananas
4 tablespoons (¼ cup) butter
½ cup brown sugar, firmly packed
1 teaspoon ground ginger

Peel a strip (about 1 inch wide) down the length of each banana, leaving it attached at one end. Roll this peel into a curlicue, and fasten it with a toothpick. Arrange bananas, open side up, in a buttered shallow baking dish. Heat together the butter, brown sugar, and ginger; brush over exposed part of bananas. Bake in a moderate oven (350°) for about 18 minutes. Makes 12 servings.

PINEAPPLE IN RUM CUSTARD

6 small pineapples, with crowns
4 cups milk
1 cup sugar
1½ tablespoons water
4 tablespoons cornstarch
8 egg yolks
½ teaspoon salt
½ teaspoon vanilla
6 tablespoons rum, or rum flavoring
    to taste

Cut pineapples in half, lengthwise, through crowns. Using a grapefruit knife, remove fruit from shells; cube. Chill. In the top of a double boiler, heat together milk and sugar. Mix cornstarch with water until smooth, and add gradually to milk and sugar. Beat egg yolks with salt. Add to milk mixture gradually, and cook, stirring, until mixture thickens and coats the back of a metal spoon. Remove from heat; add vanilla and rum. Chill. Just before serving, fold pineapple cubes into chilled custard. Spoon into pineapple half-shells. Makes 12 servings.

HAUPIA

The dessert is a simple fresh coconut pudding that is chilled, then cut into squares. Have it on the table all during the meal. You can make it with frozen coconut milk (available in many supermarkets), or make coconut milk from fresh coconut (see below).

> 2 cups coconut milk
> 2 cups regular milk
> ½ cup sugar
> ½ teaspoon salt
> ½ cup cornstarch

In the top of a double boiler, combine the coconut milk, milk, sugar, and salt. Set over boiling water, and when hot, add the cornstarch, which has been blended until smooth with a little of the liquid. Cook, stirring, until thick and smooth. Pour into a 9-inch-square pan and chill until firm. Cut into 12 squares to serve.

To make coconut milk: Pour 2 cups boiling water or scalded milk over 4 cups finely grated fresh coconut; let stand for 20 minutes. Strain through double thickness of cheesecloth, squeezing tightly.

Whole baked fish, seasoned and garnished, is wrapped securely in foil before baking. To serve, pull back foil, and place on leaf-covered, flower-decorated platter or board.

A Venison Dinner for Gourmets

THE VIENNESE are recognized masters of game cookery. If you are fortunate enough to acquire a fine venison roast, this menu, featuring adaptations of Viennese recipes, will really do it justice ⚜ Since the dinner is rather a production, it is especially suited to cooperative preparation. It would be an ideal menu for a cooperative gourmet dinner party given by a group of couples who share an adventurous attitude toward food and enjoy planning and cooking an occasional elegant dinner. The group could meet early in the evening and participate in the preparation, with one member presiding as supervising chef. The ice and the dessert can be prepared by the hostess ahead of time ⚜ If you do not choose to make this

FLAMING SHRIMP

ORANGES WITH AVOCADO DRESSING

SOLE WITH WINE-HOLLANDAISE SAUCE

ROLLED ROAST OF VENISON ANDREAS

RED CABBAGE WITH APPLES

POTATO DUMPLINGS

LEMON ICE

RASPBERRY MOUSSE

197

a cooperative party, you can serve this elaborate menu yourself because much can be done ahead. Make the ice and dessert early in the day, and start appetizers, salad, and vegetables in the afternoon. Prepare the sole while the venison roasts.

FLAMING SHRIMP

- 2 pounds medium-sized shrimp
- ½ cup (¼ pound) butter
- Salt and pepper to taste
- 1 cup rum

Shell and devein shrimp, leaving tails on. Sauté in butter until pink, about 5 minutes. Add salt and pepper. Turn into chafing dish with warm rum in bottom. Ignite rum. Shake pan, and let flame burn down. Serve at once with or without cocktail picks. Makes 8 servings.

Flaming shrimp dramatically introduce this meal. Shelled and deveined shrimp are sautéed first in butter, then flamed with rum.

ORANGES WITH AVOCADO DRESSING

- 8 large oranges
- Lettuce
- 4 small ripe avocados
- Juice of 2 large limes
- 4 tablespoons Dijon-style mustard
- Mayonnaise (about 2 cups)
- Salt
- Parsley sprigs

Cut peel from oranges, removing all white membrane. Place peel of 1 orange in saucepan with cold water to cover. Simmer until peel is soft; drain. With a spoon, scrape loosened white pith off peel; finely shred remaining zest.

Cut each orange into even crosswise slices, keeping slices from each orange together; remove seeds. On lettuce-lined salad plate, arrange each orange to resemble whole orange. Top with this dressing: Peel avocados, mash gently, and blend in lime juice, mustard, enough mayonnaise to make a creamy dressing, and a pinch of salt. Sprinkle salad with shredded orange zest and garnish with parsley sprigs. Makes 8 servings.

SOLE WITH WINE-HOLLANDAISE SAUCE

- 8 medium-sized fillets of sole
- ¾ cup seedless grapes
- 3 small tomatoes, peeled, seeded, and chopped
- 3 shallots, chopped
- 3 sprigs parsley
- Dry white wine (about 1¾ cups)
- 2 cups hollandaise sauce (canned or made from your own recipe)
- Salt and pepper
- Additional seedless grapes and chopped parsley for garnish

Place sole fillets in bottom of a large shallow pan, overlapping as little as possible. Arrange grapes over fish; cover with chopped tomatoes, shallots, and sprigs of parsley. Pour over dry white wine, barely to cover. Simmer very slowly for about 10 minutes, or just until the fish will flake when tested with a fork. Carefully remove sole to a hot, rimmed serving dish; keep it warm in oven.

Strain sauce in which fish was cooked, discarding parsley; press tomatoes, grapes, and shallots through a wire strainer. Blend 1½ cups strained sauce with hollandaise sauce, and season to taste with salt and pepper. Pour sauce over sole. Garnish with more seedless grapes and chopped parsley. Serve immediately. Makes 8 servings.

Sole, poached in wine, is masked with hollandaise sauce blended with some of the wine.

ROLLED ROAST OF VENISON ANDREAS

Boneless, rolled, oven venison roast (about 5 pounds)
1 bottle (4/5 quart) dry red table wine
1 cup apple brandy
¼ cup cognac
3 bay leaves
6 juniper berries
4 whole peppercorns
3 sprigs each fresh tarragon and dill (or a pinch of the dried herbs)
Strips of larding pork
Melted butter
½ cup dry red table wine
2 cups (1 pint) commercial sour cream
1 tablespoon flour
Salt

Marinate roast for 24 hours in a mixture of the 1 bottle red table wine, apple brandy, cognac, bay leaves, juniper berries, peppercorns, tarragon, and dill. Drain meat; strain marinade and reserve.

Lard meat well with strips of larding pork. Roast in a very hot oven (500°) for 5 minutes. Reduce oven heat to moderate (350°), and roast for about 2 hours or until done to your liking (meat thermometer should read 140° when rare). Baste often with pan juices and melted butter. Place roast on hot platter; keep hot.

Make this sauce to serve separately: Pour off all but ½ cup of the pan juices. Place pan over low heat, and add 1 cup of strained marinade, the ½ cup red wine, and sour cream that has been blended with the flour. Stirring constantly, heat sauce slowly until hot. Add salt to taste. Garnish roast with Walnut Mushrooms.

Walnut Mushrooms:

18 to 24 medium-sized mushroom caps
4 tablespoons (¼ cup) butter
2 tablespoons lemon juice
Goose liver pâté
18 to 24 walnut halves

Sauté mushroom caps in butter and lemon juice just until tender. Drain; fill with goose liver pâté. Top each with a walnut half that has been sautéed in butter.

RED CABBAGE WITH APPLES

1 medium-sized head red cabbage
2 teaspoons salt
½ teaspoon pepper
2 tablespoons each shortening and tarragon
    vinegar
3 tablespoons each sugar and water
2 tart apples, peeled, cored, and thinly sliced
½ cup dry red table wine
2 tablespoons red currant jelly
½ teaspoon each caraway seeds and
    powdered cloves

Shred cabbage; sprinkle with salt and pepper. In a heavy pan melt shortening. Add cabbage; sprinkle with tarragon vinegar. Stir and press down cabbage with a wooden spoon. Cook, covered, over low heat until wilted. (If more liquid is needed, add a little dry red table wine.)

Dissolve sugar in water; cook until syrup is brown and caramelized. Add the caramel to cabbage; cover and simmer for 1½ hours. Add sliced apples, wine, currant jelly, caraway seeds, and cloves. Simmer, covered, for 20 minutes more; drain cabbage. Serve immediately. Makes 8 servings.

POTATO DUMPLINGS

8 medium-sized potatoes
¼ cup flour
2 tablespoons melted butter
2 eggs, slightly beaten
1 teaspoon salt
    Few grains pepper
    Boiling salted water
1 cup (½ pound) butter
⅔ cups fine dry bread crumbs

Peel and cook potatoes. Rice potatoes. Mix riced potatoes thoroughly with flour, the 2 tablespoons melted butter, eggs, salt, and pepper. Divide into 24 portions and shape into balls. Chill. Drop balls into large kettle of gently boiling salted water. Cover closely and steam for 12 minutes. Remove from water; drain well.

Split each dumpling in half with 2 forks and arrange on a hot platter. Heat ¾ cup of the butter until browned. Pour over split dumplings. Brown bread crumbs in the remaining ¼ cup butter and sprinkle on dumplings. Makes 8 servings.

LEMON ICE

2 cups water
¾ cup sugar
1 teaspoon grated lemon peel
2 teaspoons unflavored gelatin
¼ cup cold water
⅛ teaspoon salt
⅓ cup lemon juice
    Sugar to taste
1 cup whipping cream

In a saucepan combine water, sugar, and lemon peel. Bring to a boil; reduce heat, and simmer for 10 minutes. Remove from heat; stir in unflavored gelatin that has been softened in the cold water. Stir in salt. Strain through double thickness of cheesecloth. Chill. When cold, stir in lemon juice. Taste, and add sugar if necessary. Pour into freezing tray (about 1 quart) and freeze until almost firm. Turn from tray into chilled bowl; add cream. Blend until mixture is soft, then whip until light. Return to freezing tray and freeze until firm. Serve in chilled glasses. Makes 8 servings.

RASPBERRY MOUSSE

1 cup milk

4 egg yolks, slightly beaten

3 tablespoons sugar

1 tablespoon red maraschino cherry syrup

½ teaspoon vanilla

2 cups fresh red raspberries (or frozen raspberries, thawed and drained)

2 cups heavy cream, whipped

4 egg whites

Whipped cream and raspberries for garnish

Sauce of crushed and sweetened raspberries

In the top of a double boiler combine milk with egg yolks and sugar. Cook over hot water, stirring constantly, until the custard coats a spoon. Remove from heat; blend in maraschino cherry syrup and vanilla. Chill thoroughly.

Rub raspberries through a wire strainer. Fold in whipped cream. Beat egg whites until stiff but not dry, and fold in. Turn into serving bowl; chill at least 4 hours. Serve with a garnish of whipped cream, red raspberries, and an additional sauce of crushed and sweetened raspberries. Makes 10 to 12 servings.

Smooth and light, pink raspberry mousse is a perfect finale for this elegant meal.

Chinese Festival Dinner

JEAT KUAR TONG (HAIRY MELON SOUP)

FUNG GUY YICK (CHINESE CHICKEN WINGS)

GEE BOW (PAPER-WRAPPED CHICKEN)

SAI WOO OP (PARSLEY DUCK)

 BOK CHET GUY (CHINESE BOILED CHICKEN)

GUY CHOY YUKE (CHINESE MUSTARD GREENS WITH BEEF)

RICE

GREEN TEA

A CHINESE MEAL is like a bag of assorted penny candy—it contains many small surprises. In fact, when a guest list is increased, the Chinese add more dishes rather than cook more of those already on the menu ⟿ The festival dishes described here are not difficult to prepare. You can do a lot of the chopping and slicing ahead of time, but you must give last-minute attention to most of these dishes if they are to have that freshness typical of Chinese cookery. At first, better not try more than one or two for the same meal. If you wish to serve Parsley Duck, for example, you might like to start the meal with hot chicken broth with a beaten egg whisked in at the last minute. Buttered green beans with almonds is a good choice for a vegetable. A fruit salad containing some mandarin orange segments would be appropriate. Rice and tea are staples at every Chinese meal ⟿ You can increase the Oriental character of a dinner featuring one Chinese specialty by including one or two of the sweet-sour or hot and savory sauces available at many grocery stores. You can cut any vegetable Chinese style and serve with chopsticks ⟿ When you cook the following dishes, you will have to get some of the ingredients in a store that specializes in Oriental foodstuffs.

JEAT KUAR TONG

The rather small, fuzzy-skinned melons in this recipe have a sweet flavor that contrasts well with the spicy pork-and-prawn filling. The skin of the hairy melon is gray-green, but it turns lime green when scraped and cooked. In a Chinese household, the melons are usually placed whole in a serving bowl, broth is poured over, and each person can take as much of the melon as he wishes. An alternative is to cut the melons in ½-inch-thick rings and place one in each soup bowl, along with some broth.

⅓ *pound lean raw pork*
⅓ *pound raw prawns, shucked*
1 *can (2 oz.) sliced mushrooms, drained*
½ *teaspoon salt*
⅛ *teaspoon pepper*
2 *hairy melons*
2 *quarts (8 cups) seasoned chicken stock*
8 *dried mushrooms (optional)*

Grind the pork, prawns, and mushrooms together, using the fine blade of the food chopper; season with salt and pepper and mix well. Wash melons; scrape skin with a cleaver or knife to remove fuzz. Cut the rounded ends off both melons. Working from the large ends, scoop meat from melons; leave a shell ⅜ inch thick; stuff melons with pork mixture.

Heat chicken stock to boiling; place stuffed melons in stock; cover and simmer for 25 minutes, or until melon can be pierced easily with a fork. If desired, let mushrooms stand in warm water for 10 minutes, cut off stems, and cook along with the soup. Makes 8 servings.

Use tablespoon to scoop out melon for Hairy Melon Soup. Leave a ⅜-inch-thick shell; scrape off fuzz.

FUNG GUY YICK

It is easy to bone the chicken wings for Fung Guy Yick after they are cooked just until tender. The *prosciutto* used in the stuffing is usually sold in paper-thin slices, so be sure to specify a thickness of ⅛ inch when you have it cut. You can stuff the chicken wings ahead of time, but the dish should not be assembled until just before you are ready to serve.

12 *chicken wings*
   Hot water
½ *teaspoon salt*
2 *slices prosciutto (Italian ham), cut ⅛ inch thick*
1 *can (1 lb. 1½ oz.) bamboo shoots*
2 *tablespoons peanut oil or salad oil*
1 *clove garlic, mashed or minced*
1 *can (2 oz.) sliced mushrooms*
1 *teaspoon soy*
½ *teaspoon monosodium glutamate*
20 *Chinese peas (melting sugar peas) or ½ cup thinly sliced celery*
1 *tablespoon cornstarch*
¼ *cup water*

Cut parboiled wings between joints; discard tips. Chop bone ends off both center and bottom wing sections and discard.

Wash chicken wings and place in a saucepan; pour in enough hot water to barely cover, and add salt; cover pan and boil for 5 minutes. Remove pan from heat and let wings stand in stock until cool enough to handle. Reserve stock. Bone wings as follows: Cut parboiled wings between joints; discard tips. Chop bone ends off both center and bottom wing sections, and discard. Push small end of bone part way up through wing, then pull out from opposite end, using a gentle twisting action.

Simmer prosciutto in water for 15 minutes; drain. Trim fat and cut ham in strips ⅛ inch wide and 1½ inches long. You will need 24 ham strips. Cut bamboo shoots in slices ⅛ inch thick, then cut in strips ⅛ wide and 1½ inches long. You will need 4 dozen bamboo strips for stuffing. Cut enough additional bamboo strips to make ½ cup.

Lay a ham strip between two bamboo shoots; start from the end with the largest hole, and slide strips into the boned wing.

Heat oil in a large, heavy frying pan or *wok*; sauté garlic just until lightly browned. Drain mush-

rooms and reserve liquid. Add mushrooms to pan and cook and stir over high heat for 2 minutes. Combine mushroom liquid with enough chicken stock to make 1 cup liquid; stir into frying pan, along with soy and monosodium glutamate.

Break off the tips of the Chinese peas and pull off the strings. Add peas (or celery) to pan, along with the ½ cup bamboo shoots; toss lightly. Place stuffed chicken wings over vegetable mixture; cover pan, and shaking occasionally, cook for 3 minutes. Blend cornstarch with the ¼ cup water; stir mixture in at the side of the frying pan. Stirring, cook until sauce is slightly thickened. Remove wings to a serving dish and pour over vegetable mixture and sauce. Makes 6 to 8 servings.

Push small end of bone part way up through wing, then pull out from opposite end, using gentle twisting action.

Lay a ham strip between two bamboo shoots. Starting from end with largest hole, slide strips into the boned wing.

GEE BOW

The paper wrapping keeps the chicken from absorbing fat as it cooks in hot oil. To eat the chicken, tear open the front side of the package with a fork, and spear out the tender meat.

> 3-pound broiler-fryer, cut in pieces
> ⅔ cup soy
> ⅓ cup catsup
> 2 tablespoons sugar
> 1 clove garlic, mashed
> ¼ teaspoon salt

Cut meat from bone. Slice the raw chicken across the grain in strips ¼ inch thick, 1 inch long, and 1½ inches wide. Combine soy, catsup, sugar, garlic, and salt, and let chicken strips stand in this mixture for 10 minutes. Place 2 pieces of chicken in center of a 5-inch parchment paper square; fold and seal as shown in the photographs.

Cook packets in 1½ inches medium hot fat until brown—about 3 minutes. Turn during cooking. Serve at once in the parchment wrapping. Makes 6 servings.

SAI WOO OP

This duck is one of the most elegant of the Chinese festival dishes. It is more time-consuming than difficult, for the duck, marinated and browned first, is steamed until very tender. You serve it with a rich vegetable sauce.

> 4- to 4½-pound duck (ready to cook weight)
> 1 star anise seed
> 1 teaspoon 5-flavor seasoning (see end of recipe)
> 1 cup soy
> Peanut oil or salad oil for frying
> 6 large dried mushrooms
> ½ cup gum choy (optional)
> 2 slices bacon
> ¼ pound lean pork
> ½ teaspoon minced green ginger root or ⅛ teaspoon ground ginger
> 1 tablespoon finely chopped dried tangerine or orange peel
> 1 cup sliced bamboo shoots, cut ⅛ inch thick, ⅛ inch wide, and 2 inches long
> 1 clove garlic, mashed or minced
> 1½ cups chicken stock
> 3 tablespoons cornstarch
> ½ cup cold chicken stock or water
> Chinese parsley or parsley for garnish

Slice raw chicken across the grain in strips. Let strips stand in soy mixture for 10 minutes. Save bones for stock.

Place 2 chicken pieces on parchment square. Fold diagonally to within ½ inch of edge; fold right corner to center.

Fold left corner to center; fold bottom up so packet looks like envelope (bottom line forms one side).

Turn top corner down (as you would to close envelope) and fit into slit made by folds in paper. Packet is sealed.

Cook in 1½ inches medium hot fat for 3 minutes. Turn during cooking. Serve in wrapping.

Cut the duck down the back; leave it attached at the breast bone. Crush the star anise; mix with 5-flavor seasoning and soy in a shallow pan. Marinate duck in soy mixture for 20 minutes, turning several times. Drain very well.

Pour 1 inch of oil in a large, deep kettle, and heat until moderately hot. Place well-drained duck in fat and cook for 5 minutes; turn duck over and cook on other side for 5 minutes, or until well browned. Carefully lift the browned duck into a shallow pan that will fit inside a steamer; pour over pan drippings. Place pan on a steamer rack and set in steamer with 1 inch water in the bottom.

While duck is browning, cover mushrooms with warm water and let stand for 10 minutes; drain; cut in slices ¼ inch wide and sprinkle over duck. Cover steamer and steam for 2½ to 3 hours, or until duck is tender. As water evaporates, add more to bottom of steamer.

To prepare sauce, pour warm water over gum choy and let soak for 20 minutes. Cut bacon crosswise in strips ¼ inch thick. Cut pork in small strips the same size. Quickly fry bacon and pork until meat is brown; add ginger root, tangerine peel, gum choy, bamboo shoots, garlic, and the 1½ cups chicken stock. Blend cornstarch with the ½ cup stock stirring, pour into meat mixture. Stir and cook until sauce is thickened.

To serve, carefully lift duck into a large, shallow serving bowl; pour over sauce; garnish with parsley. The Chinese people cut or pick the meat from the bones after the duck is brought to the table. You might find it easier to serve if you cut the meat into serving-size pieces before pouring over the sauce. Makes 6 servings.

To make the 5-flavor seasoning called for in the recipe, combine equal parts of ground cloves, anise, fennel, licorice root, and cinnamon. Blend to form a smooth powder, then measure out the desired amount.

BOK CHET GUY

For this recipe the Chinese boil the chicken only 25 minutes—total cooking time (though you may prefer to cook it slightly longer). Serve the chicken hot or cold with a hot mustard sauce (blend dry mustard with chicken broth to make a smooth paste) or deep brown oyster sauce made from the pulp of crushed oysters—it is available in Chinese grocery stores.

The Chinese cook and serve the whole chicken (you may, of course, prefer to remove the head). The wing tips are folded back so they lie flat against the body. The ends of the legs are folded back under and up into the chicken. A stuffed kumquat is often placed in the chicken's mouth. It is considered proper etiquette to point the chicken's head toward the guest of honor.

> 1 onion, cut in eighths
> 3 stalks celery and leaves, cut in 2-inch lengths
> 1 carrot, cut in 1-inch lengths
> 2 teaspoons salt
> 2 tablespoons chicken base or 4 chicken bouillon cubes
> 1 teaspoon monosodium glutamate
> 2 quarts (8 cups) hot water
> 1 large broiler-fryer (3 to 3½ pounds)
>   Mustard sauce or oyster sauce

Place onion, celery, carrot, salt, chicken base or the chicken bouillon cubes, and monosodium glutamate in a large kettle; pour in hot water; boil, uncovered, for 20 minutes. Skim off foam several times during cooking. Place whole cleaned chicken in stock; cover and boil hard for 10 minutes; reduce heat to low and simmer for 10 to 15 minutes, or until chicken is just tender. Serve hot or cold with mustard sauce or oyster sauce. Makes 8 servings.

GUY CHOY YUKE

Strips of browned meat give additional flavor to this vegetable dish. The Chinese greens have a flavor that is slightly bitter to many tastes, so several alternates are given in this recipe.

> 1½ pounds Chinese mustard greens, Chinese cabbage, spinach, or Swiss chard
> 2 tablespoons peanut oil or salad oil
> ½ pound flank steak or round steak, cut 1 inch thick, then cut in strips ⅛ inch thick
> Sesame seed oil (optional)
> ½ teaspoon salt
> Pepper
> ½ teaspoon monosodium glutamate
> 2 teaspoons soy
> 1 cup chicken stock
> 1 tablespoon cornstarch
> ¼ cup water

Separate greens. If using mustard greens, peel stalks; cut greens in 2½-inch-wide pieces. If stalks are thick, slash crosswise in 4 sections, cutting to within ½ inch of end of stalk; let stand in cold water until ready to use.

Heat oil in a wide frying pan; add beef strips and toss and cook over high heat until meat is browned. Add 2 or 3 drops sesame seed oil, if desired, and sprinkle with half the salt, pepper, monosodium glutamate, soy; stir, remove meat.

Add enough additional oil to make 2 tablespoons in pan; add well-drained greens, stir and cook for 5 minutes, or until greens are crisp-tender. Season with the remainder of the salt, pepper, monosodium glutamate, and soy. Add stock. Blend cornstarch with the water; pour into pan and cook and stir until slightly thickened. Turn off heat and return meat to pan; toss lightly; place in a serving bowl and serve at once. Makes 4 to 6 servings.

Easy Summer Dinner

THIS IS a refreshing dinner to serve when the weather is warm. The roast of beef marinates in a wine mixture for 24 hours before it is cooked. It is served chilled, so it can be cooked ahead during the cool of the day. Other items on the menu require an absolute minimum of preparation time just before serving.

HOT CLAM AND TOMATO
BROTH TARRAGON

SESAME FINGERS

COLD BEEF A LA MODE

HOMINY PAPRIKA

WATERCRESS SALAD

PEARS WITH CAMEMBERT CHEESE

HOT CLAM AND TOMATO BROTH TARRAGON

Heat 2 cups each clam nectar and tomato juice with 2 teaspoons fresh tarragon for 10 minutes. Strain into cups. You might top each serving with lightly salted whipped cream. Makes 6 servings.

SESAME FINGERS

Brush hot toast with melted butter, sprinkle with toasted sesame seeds, and cut in finger lengths.

BEEF A LA MODE

5 or 6-pound rump roast
2 cups dry red table wine
1 onion, sliced
½ teaspoon thyme
¼ teaspoon crushed whole black peppers
1 bay leaf
  Flour seasoned with salt and pepper
¼ cup rendered beef fat or shortening
1 cup tomato purée
½ cup each sour cream and mayonnaise
¼ cup grated horseradish

Lard the meat (or ask your meat man to do it for you). Place in a large bowl and cover with a mixture of the wine, onion, thyme, black peppers, and bay leaf. Let stand in marinade for 24 hours, turning a few times.

Drain meat, pat dry with paper towels, and dust with seasoned flour. In a Dutch oven, brown meat on all sides in the rendered beef fat. Pour in the marinade and the tomato purée; cover and bake in a moderate oven (350°) for 3 to 4 hours, or until fork-tender; or simmer over very low heat. Add water if necessary; add any additional seasonings you wish. Allow to cool and chill meat thoroughly.

Thinly slice cold roast and arrange on a garnished platter. Serve with a sauce made by combining the sour cream, mayonnaise, and horseradish. Makes 12 to 18 servings.

HOMINY PAPRIKA

Sauté 1 large onion, sliced, in butter until golden. Heat 2 cans (1 lb. 4 oz.) hominy; drain. Combine hominy and onions with 2 cups commercial sour cream, 2 tablespoons paprika, and salt to taste. Reheat and serve. Makes 6 servings.

WATERCRESS SALAD

Remove large stems, wash leaves of cress, and chill. Dress simply with olive oil and wine vinegar.

CHEESE-STUFFED FRESH PINEAPPLE

MELBA TOAST ROUNDS

SESAME SHRIMP

HOT BACON AND CHUTNEY APPETIZERS

HALVED AVOCADOS WITH HOT COCKTAIL SAUCE

HAWAIIAN CHICKEN WITH
RICE, DATES, ALMONDS

SAUTEED PINEAPPLE RINGS

COCONUT ICE CREAM

210

Tropical
Buffet

THIS COLORFUL BUFFET carries out a tropical theme in both decoration and food. Straw mats and *ti* leaves furnish the background. Pineapple crowns, from which the center leaves have been pulled out, are candle holders. Papaya, coconuts, and a straw hat complete the center-piece  Prepare the pineapple ahead and chill; set out at room temperature 30 minutes before serving. You can make the avocado sauce ahead and keep it warm in the top of a double boiler, but cut the avocados just before serving.

CHEESE-STUFFED FRESH PINEAPPLE

Cut crown off pineapple. (Use it to make candlestick shown in photograph.) Scoop out fruit. Blend cut-up fruit with cream cheese, salt, and powdered or candied ginger to suit taste. Pile back into pineapple shell to serve. Let guests help themselves, heaping mixture on Melba toast rounds.

SESAME SHRIMP

Push cocktail picks through small cooked prawns, then dip first in soy and then in toasted sesame seeds. The soy makes the seeds stick to the prawns.

HOT BACON AND CHUTNEY APPETIZERS

Fry 6 slices of bacon, which have been cut into ½-inch squares, until they are just starting to brown. Pour off most of the drippings and add 1 cup mango chutney (cut the large pieces of mango into about ¼-inch squares). Let this bubble over low heat until you are ready to spread it on crisp toast fingers. Serve hot. (This is enough to cover 4 slices of toast, each cut into 3 fingers.)

HALVED AVOCADOS WITH HOT COCKTAIL SAUCE

6 tablespoons butter or margarine
6 tablespoons catsup
2½ tablespoons each vinegar and water
4 teaspoons sugar
2½ teaspoons Worcestershire
½ teaspoon salt
Dash Tabasco
4 small avocados

In the top of a double boiler, mix together the butter, catsup, vinegar, water, sugar, Worcestershire, salt, and Tabasco to taste. Heat over boiling water until butter has melted and sauce is smooth. Cut avocados in half lengthwise, separate halves, and remove seeds. Spoon hot sauce into avocados and serve as an appetizer. Makes 8 servings.

Spicy mango chutney, heated with cooked bacon pieces, is served on crisp toast fingers.

To make candle holders from pineapple, cut 2-inch-deep crown off pineapple, pull out center leaves to make hole the size of candle. Set holder in wooden bowl.

CHICKEN HAWAIIAN

This is a very colorful chicken dish. Dots of pimiento, dates, almonds, and rings of lightly browned pineapple give it a party look. You can cook the chicken ahead of time and reheat it just before serving while you prepare the rice and pineapple.

8 *chicken pieces (large split breasts, or joined thighs and drumsticks)*
¼ *cup soy*
¼ *cup dry white table wine*
  Juice of 1 lime
1 *clove garlic, mashed*
1 *teaspoon each curry and minced ginger root*
¼ *teaspoon each dried thyme, dried oregano, and freshly ground pepper*
2 *medium-sized onions, thinly sliced*
4 *tablespoons (¼ cup) butter or margarine*
2 *cups uncooked rice*
8 *slices pineapple*
1 *tablespoon butter or margarine*
½ *cup toasted slivered almonds*
16 *dates, seeded and sliced*
1 *pimiento, cut in small pieces*
¼ *cup white table wine*

Cut each chicken breast into 2 pieces. Mix together soy, wine, lime juice, garlic, curry, ginger root, thyme, oregano, and pepper (no salt). Pour over chicken and marinate for several hours, turning chicken occasionally. Fry the onions in 2 tablespoons of the butter (bacon drippings may be substituted for half the butter) until light yellow and remove from pan.

Add the other 2 tablespoons butter to the pan and then fry the chicken pieces (which have been drained and dusted with flour) until brown on all sides. Pour in the marinade and sautéed onions, cover, and steam until tender, about 30 minutes; uncovering pan for the last 15 minutes.

While chicken is steaming, cook rice by your preferred method. Sauté the pineapple slices in the tablespoon of butter until lightly browned. To serve, mix the almonds, dates, and pimiento with the rice and heap on a large chop plate. Arrange chicken and fried pineapple slices around the rice. Stir the other ¼ cup wine into the drippings in the pan and heat through. Serve gravy separately. Makes 8 servings.

Some Suggested Appetizers

CHEESE STRAWS

These crisp little strips of cheese pastry may be frozen unbaked; bake them without thawing.

- 1 cup flour
- ½ teaspoon each salt, monosodium glutamate, and powdered ginger
- ⅓ cup shortening (may be part butter)
- 1 cup (¼ pound) shredded sharp process cheese
- ¼ cup sesame seeds, toasted
- ½ teaspoon Worcestershire
- 2 to 2½ tablespoons cold water

Sift flour, measure, and sift with salt, monosodium glutamate, and ginger. Cut in shortening with a pastry blender as you would for pastry. Lightly stir in cheese and sesame seeds. Add Worcestershire to 1 tablespoon of the water, sprinkle over flour, and toss with a fork. Add remaining water while tossing mixture with a fork until moistened. Gather up with fingers and form into a ball. On a lightly floured board, roll out ⅛ inch thick. Cut with a pastry wheel or knife into strips about 3 inches long and ½ inch wide. Place on ungreased baking sheet and bake in a hot oven (400°) for 10 to 12 minutes, or until lightly browned and crisp. Serve hot or when cooled. Makes 6 to 7 dozen.

PECAN-COATED CHEESE BALL

This nut-covered cheese ball, about the size of a small grapefruit, looks handsome on an hors d'oeuvre tray. Because all of the cheeses used in it are spreads, the mixture is easy to blend. It is excellent on shredded wheat crackers.

- 1 large package (8 oz.) cream cheese
- 1 small jar (5 oz.) processed sharp cheese spread
- 2 jars (5 oz. each) processed Roquefort cheese spread
- 1 small onion, minced
- 1 clove garlic, minced or mashed

Let cheese warm to room temperature, then beat together until light and fluffy and blended. Beat in the onion and garlic. Chill. Roll into a ball, then roll in chopped nut meats until well coated. Chill again. Makes 1 large ball.

SPICED CHEESE ROUNDS

You can season these cheese nut rolls with either curry or chili powder (or one roll with each) and keep them on hand for many of your entertaining occasions. If carefully wrapped, they will keep in the refrigerator for a month, or longer in the freezer.

- 1 large package (8 oz.) cream cheese
- ½ pound sharp Cheddar cheese, shredded
- 2 cloves garlic, minced or mashed
- 1 cup finely chopped pecan or walnut meats
- 2 tablespoons curry powder or chili powder

Cream together the cheese and garlic until blended; mix in nut meats. Shape into 2 rolls, about 1½ inches in diameter. Roll in curry or chili powder, which you've sprinkled on waxed paper. Wrap each roll in waxed paper or in foil and chill. To serve, slice into rounds ⅛ inch thick and pass thin crisp crackers. Makes about 150 appetizers.

GLAZED HAM CUBES

Spread a ½-inch-thick slice of cooked ham (about 1 pound) with a thick layer of chunk style peanut butter (you'll need about ⅓ cup). Put under the broiler for 2 to 3 minutes or until the peanut butter forms a brown crust. Place the ham slice on a cutting board and cut it in bite-size pieces (¾-inch squares). Serve on toothpicks.

HAM-STUFFED MUSHROOMS

You can prepare these the day before the party and store them in the refrigerator until time to bake.

- 2 pounds fresh mushrooms, about 1½ inches in diameter
- 3 tablespoons butter
- 2 cups ground cooked ham
- ½ cup commercial sour cream
- Salt and pepper to taste
- Chopped parsley or buttered crumbs

Remove stems from mushrooms, wash mushrooms, and sauté lightly in butter. Stuff caps with a mixture of the ground ham, sour cream, salt and pepper. Just before the party, arrange in bonbon cases on a large platter, sprinkle with parsley, and serve cold; or arrange in pan, sprinkle with buttered crumbs, heat in a moderate oven (350°) for 10 minutes, and serve in bonbon cases on an electric hot tray. Makes 50.

CURRIED CHICKEN APPETIZERS

2 pounds (about 4 cups) raw chicken meat
1 medium-sized onion
2 egg yolks
2 teaspoons each salt and curry powder

In a food chopper, grind chicken and onion. Mix with egg yolks, salt, and curry powder. Form into marble-sized balls, flatten slightly, and fry in deep fat at 370° until lightly browned. Serve promptly on toothpicks. Makes about 6 dozen appetizers.

STUFFED CUCUMBER CANAPES

4 medium-sized cucumbers
1 large package (8 oz.) cream cheese
1 tablespoon Worcestershire
¼ teaspoon each garlic salt and mixed herbs
Cheese-flavored crackers

Cut the ends off cucumbers and run fork tines down sides to make a scalloped edge when cut. Use an apple corer to remove core and seeds from cucumbers. Blend cream cheese with Worcestershire, garlic salt, and mixed herbs; pack into the cucumber hollow. Chill well; then slice thinly and arrange on cheese-flavored crackers. Makes about 7 dozen canapés.

HOT MUSHROOM BOUCHEES

These colorful little snacks can be made 4 or 5 hours ahead, stored on cooky sheets in the refrigerator, and then broiled as needed.

2 tablespoons minced onion
1 cup sliced fresh mushrooms or canned mushroom crowns
4 tablespoons (¼ cup) butter or margarine
4 hard-cooked eggs, sieved
2 tablespoons minced parsley
1 teaspoon salt
⅛ teaspoon pepper
1 egg
32 small rounds of bread, toasted
½ cup grated American cheese

Sauté onion and mushrooms in butter for about 5 minutes. Add sieved hard-cooked eggs, parsley, salt, and pepper. Beat egg slightly, stir in, and cook just long enough to thicken. Spread on the small toast rounds and sprinkle each one with grated cheese. Broil until cheese melts and serve hot. Makes 32 canapés.

TOASTED CHEESE AND NUT SQUARES

Just before serving, heat these crunchy appetizers enough to melt the cheese.

4 slices pumpernickel bread (the heavy, thin-sliced kind)
About ¼ cup sharp Cheddar-flavored cheese spread
1½ tablespoons chopped Brazil nuts or almonds
2 teaspoons butter or margarine

Cut bread slices in quarters. Spread each quarter evenly with cheese. Sauté nuts in butter until golden; spoon an equal amount on each section of bread and cheese. Broil until bubbling. Makes 16.

PICKLED ONION APPETIZERS

This appetizer is easy to make up ahead of time. The onion filling provides ample seasoning.

2 small packages (3 oz. each) cream cheese
24 pickled onions
Finely chopped water cress, chopped parsley, or ground dried beef

Cut each cake of cream cheese into 12 squares (easy to do with a piece of string or a butter wrapper over a knife); let stand at room temperature until soft. Roll each square of cheese into a ball; press a hole in the center, and stuff with a well-drained pickled onion; close hole and reshape cheese into a ball. Roll stuffed balls in water cress, parsley, or dried beef until well coated. Chill in refrigerator for at least 1 hour. Provide toothpicks to spear the balls. Makes 24 appetizers.

GARLIC GARBANZOS

1 can (1 lb.) garbanzos, well drained
3 tablespoons olive oil
1 clove garlic, pressed
Salt

Put drained garbanzos in a skillet with olive oil and garlic, and sauté until nicely browned. Shake the pan occasionally so that they won't stick, but don't stir to mushiness. Drain on paper towels and sprinkle with salt. Serve in place of popcorn or salted nuts.

BEEF AND MUSHROOM APPETIZER

1 box (5 oz.) fresh mushrooms
1 pound lean ground beef
   Tops of 6 green onions, sliced
   Salt and pepper to taste
   Crisp Scandinavian bread or crisp toast

Chop mushrooms into chunks and add to raw beef. Mash together lightly with a fork. Add onion, salt, and pepper. Pile on crisp bread. Makes 12 to 16 appetizers.

FILBERT BUTTER CRISPS

½ cup (¼ pound) butter or margarine
1 cup finely chopped toasted filberts
2 teaspoons Worcestershire
   Dash Tabasco
   Potato crackers or whole wheat crackers

Cream butter until light and fluffy. Add filberts, Worcestershire, and Tabasco, and mix well. Spread thinly on crackers. Makes about 1½ cups.

TINY CHEESE BISCUITS

You can make these, except for baking, as much as a day before the party. Place cut-out biscuits on baking sheet, cover, and refrigerate.

Make a batch of baking powder biscuits based on 3 cups flour, and add 1 cup shredded sharp Cheddar cheese and ½ cup minced chives. Roll dough ⅜ inch thick and cut in 1½-inch circles; arrange in baking pan. Just before the party, bake in a hot oven (450°), for 10 minutes, or until brown. Split and butter. Serve on a hot tray. Makes about 50.

CHUTNEY-PEANUT BUTTER CANAPES

1 jar (5½ oz.) chutney (¾ cup)
1 cup chunk-style peanut butter
1 small package (3 oz.) cream cheese
¼ teaspoon seasoned salt
¼ cup dry red table wine
¼ teaspoon Worcestershire
   Buttered toasted pumpernickel bread
      fingers

Cut large pieces of chutney into small pieces. Cream together the peanut butter, softened cream cheese, seasoned salt, wine, and Worcestershire until blended. Add chutney and mix well. Spread on buttered toasted pumpernickel bread fingers or toast rounds, or spoon inside packaged canapé cuplets. Makes about 2 cups spread.

CHICKEN LIVER-BACON PÂTÉ

1 pound chicken livers
1 to 1½ cups chicken broth (or use part
      white table wine)
¼ cup chopped onion
⅛ teaspoon rosemary
6 to 8 slices bacon, cooked crisp
⅓ cup soft butter or margarine
½ teaspoon dry mustard
¼ teaspoon salt
   Finely chopped green onions or parsley
   Crisp toast or crackers

Simmer chicken livers in the chicken broth with onion and rosemary until they are tender. Cool in the cooking broth that remains. Drain, saving the broth. Put livers and bacon through the food chopper, using the fine blade. (Or press livers through wire strainer and mash smooth; crumble bacon fine.) Blend with butter, mustard, and salt. Add a small amount of the cooking liquid if a softer pâté is desired. Refrigerate in a covered container at least 24 hours to blend flavors. Pile into serving dish and sprinkle top generously with finely chopped green onions or parsley. (To mold this pâté, pack into a small bowl or ring mold that has been lightly oiled. Chill. Unmold and garnish as above.) Serve with toast or crackers. Makes 1½ to 2 cups.

COTTAGE CHEESE ROUNDS

These pale gold flaky rounds have a surprise ingredient: cottage cheese. You can make them ahead, and bake just before serving.

1 cup flour
½ cup soft butter or margarine
1 cup small curd cottage cheese
1 teaspoon salt
1 egg yolk, beaten

Sift and measure flour, combine in a bowl with butter, cottage cheese, and salt. Mix thoroughly with a spoon until well blended. Shape into a ball, place on a lightly floured board, and knead about 10 times. Roll ½-inch thick and cut in rounds 2 inches in diameter (or smaller, if you like). Brush tops with egg yolk. Place on a greased baking sheet and bake in a very hot oven (450°) for 12 to 15 minutes or until lightly browned. Serve hot. Makes about 18.

SHERRIED SHRIMP WITH TANGY SAUCE

    1½ pounds raw shrimp or prawns
    ¼ cup dry sherry
    4 tablespoons (¼ cup) butter
    ½ teaspoon garlic salt
    ¼ cup grated Parmesan cheese

Peel and devein raw shrimp. Place in a bowl and pour sherry over them. Let marinate for several hours. Melt butter in frying pan over low heat. Add shrimp and sherry. Sprinkle with garlic salt and simmer for 10 to 15 minutes. Just before serving, sprinkle cheese over shrimp and place under broiler for 2 to 3 minutes until cheese is lightly browned. Serve hot with sauce. Makes appetizers for 6 to 8 people.

Sauce:

Combine ½ cup of prepared mayonnaise type sauce (for meat, fish, and cheese dishes), 1 tablespoon tomato paste, 1 teaspoon Worcestershire, and 1 teaspoon prepared mustard. Refrigerate until ready to use.

CLAM AND OYSTER ROUNDS

    1 small package (3 oz.) cream cheese
    1 clove garlic, mashed or minced
    1 tablespoon grated onion
    ¼ teaspoon Worcestershire
    ½ teaspoon salt
    ¼ teaspoon pepper
    1 can (7 oz.) minced clams, drained
       Sour cream (approximately 1 tablespoon)
    12 thin slices buffet rye bread or 24 small
       rye cracker rounds
    2 jars (3¼ oz. each) smoked oysters
       Paprika

Mash cream cheese; season with garlic, onion, Worcestershire, salt, and pepper. Add drained clams and mix well; stir in enough sour cream to make mixture spreadable but not thin. Cover each slice of bread or rye cracker with clam mixture. If using bread, cut each slice in half. Drain oysters, and if large, cut into bite-size pieces. Put 1 or 2 pieces of oyster on top of each canapé. Sprinkle with paprika, if desired. Makes 24 canapés.

BROILED MANGO CHEESE ROUNDS

    ½ cup mango chutney
    2 jars (5 oz. each) blue cheese spread
    4 tablespoons finely chopped chives
    1 teaspoon powdered cumin
       Rye or pumpernickel toast rounds
          or fingers

If pieces of chutney are large, chop into smaller bits. Mix together the chutney, blue cheese (warmed to room temperature), chives, and cumin. Spread thinly on toast rounds. When ready to serve, broil for 2 minutes, or just until bubbly. Makes about 30.

RUM CHEESE SPREAD

You might add chopped walnuts, chopped green or ripe olives, chopped green onions, or dill or caraway seeds to part of this snappy cheese spread.

    1 pound (4 cups) grated sharp Cheddar
          cheese
    ½ cup (¼ pound) butter or margarine
    2 tablespoons Jamaica rum
    ⅛ teaspoon cayenne
       Crisp toast or crackers

Blend together thoroughly the grated cheese, butter, rum, and cayenne. Pack into 1 large or several small cheese pots and refrigerate until ready to use. Serve with crisp toast or crackers. Makes about 4½ cups.

CURRIED CRAB MEAT CANAPÉS

    ½ teaspoon minced onion
    2 tablespoons butter or margarine
    1½ teaspoons flour
    ½ teaspoon curry powder
    ⅛ teaspoon salt
    ¼ cup light cream
    ½ cup well-flaked crab meat
    4 thin slices toasted bread
    3 tablespoons grated Parmesan cheese

Sauté onion in butter until lightly browned. Combine flour, curry powder, and salt, and stir into onion. Slowly pour in cream, stirring constantly. Mix in crab meat. Remove crusts and quarter toast. Spread crab meat mixture on toast squares and sprinkle with cheese. Place on a cooky sheet and broil until cheese melts. Serve hot. Makes 16 canapés.

JUMBO BROILED SHRIMP

Peel and devein 25 good-sized raw shrimp (about 2½ pounds). Marinate, refrigerated in French dressing, or in a mixture of 1 cup oil, ½ cup lemon juice, and ¼ cup soy sauce, flavored with 1 clove crushed garlic or about 1 teaspoon slivered fresh ginger for 24 hours. At serving time, drain shrimp and broil for 3 minutes on each side. Serve on picks from a chafing dish or a hot tray. Makes 25 appetizers.

SMOKED OYSTER AND CHEESE SPREAD

Crisp toast rounds are a good base for this smoked oyster cheese. Let guests spread their own so appetizers are crisp.

- 1 small package (3 oz.) cream cheese
- 1 small jar (4 oz.) smoked oysters, chopped
- 1 tablespoon each mayonnaise and sherry or milk
- 1 teaspoon onion juice
- ½ teaspoon paprika
- Finely minced chives

Mix the cheese, oysters, mayonnaise, sherry, onion juice, and paprika. Pile into a serving dish. Chill. Serve sprinkled with chives. Makes 1 cup.

HERB CHEESE SPREAD

- 2 pounds sharp Cheddar cheese, shredded
- 2 tablespoons each minced parsley and chives
- 2 tablespoons each dry thyme, sage, and savory
- ½ cup whipping cream
- 1 cup sherry
- Crisp toast or crackers

Blend well by hand, or with an electric mixer, the cheese, parsley, chives, thyme, sage, savory, cream, and sherry. Refrigerate for 3 days; force through strainer or whirl in blender. Pack into jars or pots, cover tightly, and refrigerate until ready to serve as a spread for toast or crackers. Makes about 5 cups.

POTTED BEEF AND CHEESE SPREAD

- ½ cup (¼ pound) butter
- 1 clove garlic, sliced in half
- 1 pound chipped beef
- 4 large packages (8 oz. each) cream cheese
- ½ cup prepared horseradish
- Rye toast rounds or crackers

In a large frying pan, melt butter with garlic. Add chipped beef and sauté until crisp. Remove garlic and combine beef mixture with cream cheese and horseradish. Pack into jars or pots, cover tightly, and refrigerate until ready to serve as a spread for toast or crackers. Makes about 5 cups.

RAW MUSHROOM DIP

The distinctive essence of fresh mushrooms is shown off to excellent advantage in this simple creamy mixture. Serve it as a dip or spread for canapés.

- 2 small packages (3 oz. each) cream cheese
- 1 tablespoon minced onion
- 1 cup finely chopped raw mushrooms
- ½ teaspoon salt
- Dash monosodium glutamate (optional)
- Minced parsley
- Crisp crackers

Whip cream cheese and onion until light and fluffy. Stir in mushrooms, salt, and monosodium glutamate. Sprinkle with parsley. Serve as a dip for crisp crackers. (Or use as a spread for tiny open-faced wheat bread sandwiches, garnished with parsley.) Makes about 2 cups.

CRAB DIP

- 1 small package (3 oz.) cream cheese
- ½ cup mayonnaise
- ⅔ cup (half of 10½-oz. can) tomato soup
- ½ pound or 1 can (6½ oz.) crab meat
- 1 clove garlic, minced or mashed
- Dash each salt and pepper
- 6 drops Tabasco
- Potato chips for dipping

Soften cheese and add mayonnaise and tomato soup; mix until smooth. Stir in crab meat, garlic, salt, pepper, and Tabasco. Serve with potato chips. Makes about 2 cups.

How to Serve and Stage a Dinner

Serving a Party Dinner is a challenge to any hostess. The final result may be as casual, friendly, and easy-going as can be, yet it is necessarily prefaced with painstaking attention to many details that assure excellent food and perfect service. It is only through experience that expert hostesses have arrived at their smooth, apparently effortless approach to the dinner party.

The simplest way to appear an unharried hostess is simply to *be* unharried. It is not sleight of hand, but an attitude born of very thorough and very careful planning, with no course, no ingredient left to chance. There are various ways of doing this, including the almost classic expedient of serving a casserole dish, a green salad, bread, and fruit. Yet it is safe, with forethought, to serve a full dinner, stripped only of superfluities, without betraying a last-minute flurry of nerves. It can be done. And guests are invariably pleased that you have made no compromise with taste in planning a menu that you can serve adroitly.

The first rule of a successful dinner party is to invite only as many guests as can comfortably be served. Invitation may be by telephone or by means of an informal little note. In either case, be sure to give specific information as to date, time, and the type of party. It is advisable to send written invitations about two weeks before the party so there will be plenty of time for replies to reach you—and don't forget to include RSVP on the invitations. If time is short, telephone invitations will give you immediate knowledge of who is coming.

Hostesses who entertain frequently find a social diary helpful. This can be a card file or a notebook which lists names of guests, dates when they were entertained, menus, and other helpful notes. It provides a reminder of what was served to friends last and of the things they especially liked, or perhaps disliked.

A written schedule is almost always an important aid to the successful hostess. It helps to keep preparations running smoothly and to ensure that nothing will be forgotten. Start by writing down the menu and the order list. Check off those things on hand and make a detailed shopping list for the rest. Then make a time schedule of the work you have to do.

In planning your dinner menu, keep in mind that a good menu is built around foods that balance one another and also look and taste good together. Avoid, for example, a menu that contains several dishes highly seasoned with garlic and herbs, a meal with too many starchy foods, or a grouping of foods in tones of brown, unrelieved by any bright-colored vegetables or fruits.

The clever hostess plans her menu to require only a few last-minute tasks. Certain inevitable chores like tossing the salad, and getting dishes to buffet or table, take one away from company long enough.

The best food loses its appeal if it isn't attractively served. A pretty table, set with good china, silver, and glassware, adds to the festivity. A decoration or two in the living room and on the buffet will make your home seem "dressed up" for a party. Simple arrangements of flowers, fruits, shells, or other ornaments are often sufficient. Many hostesses say candlelight is a must in their homes, and many like soft background music.

The centerpiece itself is a challenge that can be met in varied and imaginative ways. A large pink shell with a single full-blown garden rose is a striking example. A purple glass bird looks very elegant surrounded by a few bunches of violets. A golden casaba melon and clusters of pale green grapes are handsome in a low, black, free-form bowl. Flowers that float—begonias, camellias, dahlias, roses, or rhododendrons—are good choices because the bouquet can be kept low.

The candles used on the dining table should be tall enough so that the flame does not flicker in the eyes of guests.

SETTING THE TABLE

The rules for correct table setting are simple and few, and familiar to nearly every hostess.

Place settings should be far enough apart for comfort, but not so far apart that conversation becomes difficult. Silver should be placed in a straight line about 1 inch in from the edge of the table, with the pieces to be used first placed at the outside or farthest from the plate. Spoons and knives go to the right of the plate. The cocktail fork goes to the right of the spoons, all other forks to the left of the plate. Dessert forks and spoons may be brought in on the dessert plates.

Service plates are optional for informal occasions, though they are always used for formal dinners. If they are used, they should be on the table when the guests are seated. The first course, on its own plate, is placed on the service plate. Service plates are removed when the main course is served.

Glasses go above the knives, with the water glass above the tip of the dinner knife, and wine glasses go to the right of water glasses.

Butter plates should be placed just above the forks, with the butter knife laid across the top edge of the plate. If salad is served with the entrée, the salad plate goes at the left of the forks.

Napkins may be placed at the left of the forks or between the silverware, or on the service plate if one is used.

If you are serving buffet style, arrange the dishes so they will balance in size and height. Usually the two largest and most important-looking serving pieces are at each end of the table, but that depends on what you have. A coffee service at one end, cups and spoons around it, and a big, covered, hot serving dish at the other balance each other. The plates should be stacked on the table with rows of forks and overlapping rows of folded napkins near them. If you are having a big crowd, don't have one towering stack of plates. Divide them into two piles, or replenish the supply from the kitchen or sideboard after some of the guests have served themselves. Arrange the serving dishes, roll tray, relish dishes, etc., around the table with the serving spoon or fork for each beside it.

It's a good idea to preview the table the day before the party. Plan your centerpiece. Get out dishes and silverware, arrange them on the table or buffet, and then juggle them around until you have an attractive—and dramatic—setting. If you find you have too many round dishes on the table, substitute some oval or rectangular ones for better balance. After visualizing the food which will go on the dishes, you may want to make some changes in your color scheme to heighten the effectiveness of the whole scene. If you are serving buffet style, some rearrangement of the dishes may make it easier for guests to serve themselves quickly and easily. This dress rehearsal the day before the party guarantees a well-designed table. You avoid having a table with an "empty" look, and there is no last-minute indecision over which dish to use for the olives and pickles or which serving pieces to put on the table.

If cocktails are served, the host passes them in the living room before dinner, along with the appetizers. Limit the appetizers to one or two really tempting ones. Don't offer your guests so many "nibblies" that they will not enjoy the dinner that is to follow. Appetizers are not given with each dinner in this book, but we have included a few carefully selected ones in a special chapter at the end of the book.

You will naturally want the living room to be reasonably tidy when the guests return to it after dinner. In the maidless household, it simplifies clean-up if a tray is left handy so that the host may gather up glasses quickly and unobtrusively and take them to the kitchen while the hostess is starting the guests in to dinner.

AT-TABLE SERVICE

The hostess without help can usually manage a sit-down dinner for a small group with no trouble. Let the host carve the meat or poultry at the table. The hostess can then serve the vegetables to speed up serving and keep the food from getting cold.

If there is serving help, food is served from the kitchen, and the host and hostess take no part in the service. The food may be served in individual portions or may be placed on platters or in serving dishes from which each guest helps himself as they are offered to him. All food is served from the left, and plates are removed from the right. Water and wine are poured from the right for convenience. Every dish of the main course is usually passed a second time. Before dessert is served, the table should be cleared of everything except glasses, ash trays, and cigarettes.

In the seating arrangement, the woman guest of honor, if there is one, sits at the right of the host. The first-ranking man guest is at the hostess' right. Men and women guests then alternate down the table—with husbands and wives usually not seated side by side.

For a large dinner party, you may want place cards. Otherwise, carefully memorize your seating plan so that you can tell each guest where to sit as he enters the dining room.

Who is served first? It was once customary to serve the hostess first and in some homes this is still the custom, but it is now considered more courteous to serve first the lady on the right of the host. Service then continues counterclockwise around the table.

BUFFET SERVICE

Buffet service, easy on the hostess and pleasant for the guests, is adaptable to many occasions. At this type of dinner party, guests serve themselves from the buffet table, which is set with everything they'll need for the meal—plates, napkins, silver, and food. Then they return to the living room or wander outside to the patio or garden to enjoy their dinner.

A buffet dinner calls for a special menu of foods that are easy to dish up, easy to carry, and easy to eat. For your main dishes, serve one good hot dish that isn't spoiled by standing, and one cold one. Choose foods that will hold up for more than 20 minutes. If you decide on something like a soufflé as part of your menu, plan to make up two of them and give one a 10- or 15-minute head start in the oven. By doing this, you can whisk off the deflated soufflé and substitute a new one in time for "seconds." However, it's much simpler to select a casserole that will stand up through second servings.

Split and butter rolls before you put them on the buffet table—and cut French bread all the way through so guests can help themselves easily while holding a plate in one hand.

Remember the first rule of food for a buffet supper—that it must be easily managed with a fork alone. You'll need only forks on the table and spoons, of course, for the coffee. If there is any reason why knives must be used, your guests will be happier if they can sit at a card table where silver, napkins, and cups have already been placed. Just don't expect any man to be happy about juggling a dinner plate on his knees while he cuts up his meat.

Guests will probably take care of the second-serving situation themselves if they want to, but you can always carry around a tray of buttered rolls or a plate of relishes if they seem shy about it.

Dessert may be served in any one of several ways. You can have the dessert on the table throughout the dinner (especially if it's an elegant one that you want to show off), and let guests help themselves on a return trip to the table when they have finished their main course. Or, after the main course, bring in a large serving dish, plates and forks for the dessert; serve it yourself from a side table, and have someone help you exchange the filled dessert plates for the empty dinner plates. Or ask your guests to bring their empty plates to a side table and then return to the buffet table which has been cleared meanwhile and reset with dessert plates and dessert.

SEATED BUFFET

A combination plan—with guests served at the buffet and then seated at a set table—is probably the most popular type of service. It is easy for the hostess to handle without outside help, and she can relax because the guests are comfortably placed at an attractive table. If the group is a large one, card tables may be set up in the living room and dining room, or, if the weather permits, on the patio or in the garden.

Before the guests are due to arrive, set the tables with small cloths, a small centerpiece for each table, silverware, glasses, and napkins. In this case, only plates and serving dishes will be needed on the buffet table.

Fill the water glasses while the guests are at the buffet table. The host can serve the wine after the guests are seated (or have a bottle of wine at each table and let guests serve themselves).

When it comes to serving the dessert, it is usually simpler to remove the dinner plates and serve the dessert yourself rather than to try to move the guests back to the table again.

WINE SERVICE

Choosing the wine to serve with a particular food is not the problem some people would make of it. The selection of a wine is important, not because one wine will be more "correct" than another, but because some wines better complement the menu and make both food and wine taste better. The oft-repeated rule that white wine *must* be served with fish and poultry and all white meats, while red wine should accompany red meats is a general rule that need not be taken too seriously.

But such well-known preferences do have a solid basis, because they're taste combinations that many people have come to prefer over the years. Red dinner wines seem to go best with red meats because their robust flavors blend better with hearty foods. More delicately flavored fish and chicken take best to the light flavors of white dinner wines. Some hosts offer both a red and white wine. Others prefer to serve a rosé, which is pleasing to most people and which may be served with almost any dish. Desserts and fruits harmonize best with the sweet dessert wines.

On pages 226 and 227 we have suggested some wines that might be served with the dinners in this book. These are intended merely as suggestions, and you should, of course, feel free to substitute any wine of your choice.

At an informal dinner in the maidless home, the host takes charge of serving the wine. He first pours a small amount of wine into his own glass and samples it. There are two good reasons for this ritual. First, some of the cork may have crumbled into the wine, so he pours it out into his own glass. Secondly, he tests the soundness of the wine before pouring it for others. Then he fills the other glasses—a little more than half full—and then pours his own glass. Wine is poured from the right of each guest at the table. A napkin should be wrapped around the bottle to avoid dripping.

While it is very nice to have glasses in all the traditional shapes and sizes, it is not at all necessary. The shape is largely a matter of personal taste; it is the size of the glass that is important.

For most ordinary home occasions, one all-purpose glass will take care of all needs. One or two other special glasses (for sherry and champagne) are useful but not essential.

An *aperitif* (appetizer wine) is a moderately alcoholic and relatively inexpensive beverage to serve before meals or between meals. Dry sherry, vermouth, or one of the many flavored wines now being produced, is usually served in a small (3 to 4-ounce) stemmed glass. However, more and more people are serving these wines over ice cubes, so larger stemmed glasses (as for a dinner wine) or a flat-bottomed glass (similar to an Old-Fashioned glass) are often used.

For dinner wines, red, white, or pink, served with the main course, provide a deep-bowled, tulip-shaped stemmed glass with about an 8-ounce capacity. (The glass should be filled to just over the halfway point, making each service actually about 4 ounces.) The sparkling wines (cham-

pagne, sparkling Burgundy, or sparkling rosé) can be served in the same type of all-purpose glass as a dinner wine, but for the traditionalists there are special glasses to show off the bubbles in these effervescent wines. The hollow-stemmed glass, long associated with champagne, has lost some of its popularity because it is practically impossible to clean and dry the tube of the stem after using the glass. In its place, there is a saucer champagne glass—a shallow, flaring bowl on a long, slender stem of solid glass. Also popular is the tulip champagne glass—a long-stemmed glass with tulip-shaped bowl.

Wines that are corked should always be stored lying on their sides. If they stand upright, the cork dries out, shrinks, and allows air to enter the bottle, spoiling the wine. Wines with metal screw caps or with plastic closures can be stored in any convenient position. It is important to keep all wines in a place where the temperature will be fairly uniform throughout the year. (Fifty to 60 degrees is ideal.) Traditionally, red wines are served at cool room temperature; white and pink dinner wines (rosés) are chilled. To chill a wine, put the bottle in the refrigerator two or three hours before serving. It's a thoughtful gesture to chill the glasses, too.

Dessert wines are usually served at room temperature or chilled only slightly. If an all-purpose glass is used, pour in only about 1½ or 2 ounces of dessert wine. The usual dessert wine glass has a 4-ounce capacity, but is filled only half full. Cordials or liqueurs are stronger both in alcoholic content and in flavor than dessert wines and are therefore served in smaller amounts. Cordial glasses usually hold about an ounce. The cordial is poured directly from its own bottle, or from a small decanter. Sometimes the cordial is frappéd —poured over finely crushed ice. In such a case, a glass with a wide shallow bowl, like the saucer champagne glass, is most suitable.

AFTER-DINNER COFFEE

After-dinner coffee in the living room is a pleasant custom that lends grace to the simplest company dinner. As soon as you lead your guests back to the living room, bring in a large tray with the coffee service and small coffee cups and spoons on it, set it down on any low table and pour the coffee yourself. Pass the filled cups to those within reach and let the host take them to those sitting farther away. Or bring in and pass a tray of filled cups. After-dinner coffee is supposed to be served black, but most modern hostesses provide cream and sugar for those who like it.

IF YOU SERVE OUT-OF-DOORS

The staging of an outdoor dinner party involves a few problems that are not common to indoor entertaining, but an outdoor party can be the easiest kind of dinner party you can give.

The very informality of the garden room allows you to break a few rules. Why shouldn't you stage-manage furniture, cushions, tablecloths, and cut flowers to give color and interest to any corner where it is needed? Try to look at your patio or garden in the same questioning way you look at your living room before guests arrive. Would you like just a dash of yellow against all that green? A mellow glow of copper to prolong the mood of a fire? Some softly shrouded white to take eyes to that far corner? Just a sparkle of light to make shadows move?

A heap of canvas cushions in an outsize basket isn't a perennial border, but it's dependable, gay color. If you need a center of interest for close-up viewing, a big pewter bowl filled with colored pebbles and glass bubbles might do. A yellow tablecloth centered with a bouquet of greenery will provide the color that you can't grow in a shaded corner. A big tree branch "growing" in a copper bucket, becomes by night a decorative miniature tree for the patio.

Wherever you live, it's usually possible to do a little nighttime climate correcting. On chilly nights, you can set up a flaring log fire in a firepit or bucket; supplement it with the glow of charcoal in braziers. Your portable barbecue, minus its grill, will make an efficient patio heater-brazier. Try also to stop the cool wind with a temporary windbreak. If your problem is heat, you can work wonders with ice and dry ice. Ice sculpture isn't really easy, but it's fun and the results are often surprising. Get 150-pound cakes from an ice company. Use an ice pick (cautiously), a wood rasp, or a light hatchet. Try stringing ice cubes with holes to make an ice screen (the cubes are available by the sack from some ice companies and liquor stores). Cubes last longer if deep frozen at 0° for

a few hours before they are used. A lawn sprinkler tape on a roof edge or fence top can be used to set up a cooling "rain."

If you keep the menu, recipes, and serving of your garden meal simple, you won't have to wear a path to the kitchen. Large, lightweight metal or wood trays save you many steps, especially if the kitchen is quite far from the outdoor serving area. Smaller trays are good for guests to use in transporting their meal from the serving table to their chair or cushions.

Electrical outlets near the serving area for various cooking appliances can be used for on-the-spot cooking or for keeping cooked food warm. A portable ice chest is handy for keeping beverages and foods cold for several hours.

PARTY EQUIPMENT YOU CAN RENT

Hosting a large party in your home usually means you'll need at least some extra tableware and chairs to accommodate your guests. If the group isn't too large, you might be able to borrow enough equipment from your neighbors, but for more extensive gatherings, you may want help from a party rental service.

Though a rental service does its biggest business in folding chairs, card tables, and glassware, there's practically no limit to the items and services it offers. You can get a variety of plates, glassware, silverware, and linen. Food storage and dispensing equipment is available. You can rent vacuum-type containers that keep food hot for several hours, chafing dishes, punchbowls and cups, large cooking pots, coffee urns, bars, barbecue equipment, luau mats and tables.

Spotlights, floodlights, and special extension cords are available. You can rent the lights and set them up yourself or have a person on the staff of the rental service plan the lighting for you.

Canvas items range from simple canopies to tents of the circus variety.

Portable dance floors are available in sections from some rental services and can be installed either indoors or over a lawn or patio.

For information on the party equipment and services available in your area, consult the firms listed in the classified telephone directory under *Catering Equipment* or *Party Favors and Supplies.*

Wine List

Below are some suggested wines that might be served with the dinners in this book. The selection of a wine is a matter of personal preference, and we do not intend to imply that these are the only "correct" wines to serve, but we hope that the list will be a helpful guide to selecting the type of wine that is the best complement to a particular menu. We have offered a choice of several wines for each of the dinners. For some of the more elaborate buffets and holiday meals, we have indicated that more than one wine may be served, if desired, and in some cases where it seems especially suitable, we have also suggested a dessert wine.

A SPRINGTIME BUFFET
Rosé, Cabernet Sauvignon, Vino Rosso

CANDLELIGHT DINNER
Brut Champagne, Dry Sauterne, Dry Semillon

A SOUTH AMERICAN SOUP PARTY
Chablis, Riesling, Dry Semillon, Rosé

FOUR-COURSE STEAK DINNER
Burgundy, Red Pinot, Zinfandel, Grignolino

CASSEROLE DINNER FOR A CROWD
Pinot Chardonnay, Dry Sauterne, Chablis

A ROMAN DINNER
Vino Rosso, Zinfandel, Chianti, Rosé

A SALMON DINNER
Dry Sauterne, Riesling, Chablis, Rosé

PATIO DINNER PARTY
Dry Sauterne, Sauvignon Blanc, Traminer, Rosé

GUEST PARTICIPATION DINNER
Claret, Cabernet Sauvignon, Burgundy, Rosé

ST. VALENTINE'S DAY DINNER
Rosé, Dry Semillon, Pinot Chardonnay, Sauterne

CORNED BEEF DINNER, COMPANY STYLE
Zinfandel, Grignolino, Gamay, Claret, Rosé

A SOUP AND SALAD DINNER
Rosé, Vino Rosso, Chenin Blanc, Claret

ECONOMICAL PARTY DINNER
Burgundy, Claret, Rosé, Grignolino, Gamay

A DUCK DINNER
Burgundy, Pinot Noir, Claret, Zinfandel

LABOR DAY DINNER
Rosé, Grignolino, Vino Rosso, Zinfandel

VEAL DINNER FOR EIGHTEEN
Dry Sauterne, Chablis, Rosé, Riesling

DINNER FOR IMPORTANT GUESTS
Claret, Cabernet, Zinfandel, Grignolino, Rosé

SPRING LAMB DINNER
Cabernet Sauvignon, Claret, Red Pinot, Rosé

SEAFOOD SUPPER
Riesling, Chablis, Dry Sauterne, Pinot Blanc

TRADITIONAL THANKSGIVING DINNER
(Serve both a red and a white wine)
Burgundy, Pinot Noir; Dry Sauterne, Pinot Chardonnay; Sparkling Burgundy, Champagne

SIT-DOWN DINNER FOR EIGHT
Cabernet Sauvignon, Gamay, Zinfandel, Claret

TWO-BIRD THANKSGIVING DINNER
(Serve both a red and a white wine)
Burgundy, Pinot Noir; Dry Sauterne, Pinot Chardonnay; Sparkling Burgundy, Champagne
With dessert: Muscat de Frontignan

PICNIC DINNER PARTY
Vino Rosso, Claret, Cabernet Sauvignon

POLYNESIAN BUFFET
Sauterne, Chenin Blanc, Chateau Sauterne

A SIMPLE DINNER FOR GUESTS
Riesling, Dry Semillon, Dry Sauterne, Chablis

FILLET OF SOLE DINNER
Dry Semillon, Chablis, Pinot Blanc, Rhine Wine

A MEXICAN MENU FOR CHRISTMAS EVE
Claret, Cabernet Sauvignon, Rosé, Grignolino

AN AUTUMN DINNER
Sauterne, Pinot Blanc, Dry Semillon, Riesling, Rosé. With dessert: Muscat de Frontignan or Sweet (Cream) Sherry

ELEGANT ROAST CHICKEN DINNER
Pinot Chardonnay, Sauvignon Blanc, Brut Champagne, Dry Sauterne

SUKIYAKI SUPPER
Sauterne, Riesling, Chablis (or serve sake)

EASTER DINNER
Rosé, Sparkling Rosé, Claret, Cabernet

A GUEST DINNER LOW IN CALORIES
Chablis, Riesling, Dry Semillon, Dry Sauterne

A DINNER FOR DECEMBER
Cabernet Sauvignon, Pinot Chardonnay, Claret

A CHRISTMAS DINNER FEATURING ROAST BEEF
Claret, Cabernet Sauvignon, Burgundy

INDIAN DINNER
Sauterne, Chenin Blanc, Chateau Sauterne, Rosé

CRACKED CRAB PARTY
Rhine Wine, Riesling, Chablis

EARLY SPRING DINNER
Rosé, Claret, Zinfandel

INTERNATIONAL DINNER
Cabernet Sauvignon, Zinfandel, Claret, Rosé

BARBECUED PORK DINNER
Cabernet Sauvignon, Claret, Burgundy, Gamay

A DINNER FEATURING CORNISH HENS
Brut Champagne, Sauvignon Blanc, Chablis

KOREAN DINNER
Chablis, Pinot Chardonnay, Sauterne, Traminer

THIRTY-MINUTE DINNER
Dry Semillon, Chablis, Riesling, Dry Sauterne

NEW YEAR'S EVE BUFFET
(Serve all three)
Brut Champagne, Riesling, Cabernet Sauvignon

NEW YEAR'S EVE SUPPER PARTY
Burgundy, Red Pinot, Claret, Zinfandel

LATE-EVENING SUPPER PARTY
Riesling, Chablis, Dry Sauterne, Rosé

BARBECUE BUFFET
Chenin Blanc, Sauterne

GREEK DINNER
Dry Sauterne, Sauvignon Blanc, Riesling, Chablis

DINNER FOR TEN
Dry Sauterne, Pinot Blanc, White Chianti, Rosé

HOLIDAY SMORGASBORD
(Serve both a red and a white wine)
Burgundy, Claret or varietals; Dry Sauterne, Chablis, Riesling

PLANKED FISH DINNER
Chablis, Rhine Wine, Dry Sauterne, Rosé

AUSTRIAN DINNER
Burgundy, Pinot Noir, Zinfandel, Cabernet Sauvignon

FRITTER BUFFET
Dry Sauterne, Chablis, Rosé

VEAL PAPRIKA DINNER
Gewürztraminer, Chenin Blanc, Rhine Wine, Rosé

A BUFFET FEATURING CURRY
Sauterne, Chenin Blanc, Sweet Semillon

HALLOWE'EN GUEST DINNER
Burgundy, Zinfandel, Vino Rosso

HAWAIIAN PARTY
Rosé, Vino Rosso, Chenin Blanc

A VENISON DINNER FOR GOURMETS
With the sole: Chablis, Sauvignon Blanc
With the venison: Burgundy, Pinot Noir, Claret

CHINESE FESTIVAL DINNER
Chablis, Chenin Blanc, Sauterne

EASY SUMMER DINNER
Zinfandel, Claret, Gamay, Rosé

TROPICAL BUFFET
Chenin Blanc, Sauterne, Rosé

SPARKLING WINES

Saucer champagne has shallow, flaring bowl on long, slender stem. Tulip shape is also popular.

DESSERT WINES

Glass has 4-ounce capacity, but is usually filled only about half-way.

RED OR WHITE DINNER WINES

Deep-bowled, tulip-shaped stemmed glass has about an 8-ounce capacity.

APPETIZER WINES

Usually served in 3 to 4-ounce stemmed glass, but may be served in larger glass over ice cubes.

Index

PHOTOGRAPHS IN THIS BOOK ARE BY ERNEST BRAUN, CLYDE CHILDRESS, GLENN CHRISTIANSON, ROBERT COX, BLAIR STAPP, AND DARROW WATT.

THIS BOOK WAS CREATED IN SAN FRANCISCO, CALIFORNIA, USING TYPES COMPOSED BY GRIFFIN TYPOGRAPHERS, LITHOGRAPH FILM PREPARED BY BALZER-SHOPES, PRINTING BY STECHER-TRAUNG LITHOGRAPH CORPORATION AND BINDING BY CARDOZA BOOKBINDING COMPANY. COVER AND DUST JACKET WERE LITHOGRAPHED BY NEAL, STRATFORD & KERR. THE PAPER WAS MADE BY S. D. WARREN COMPANY, CUMBERLAND MILLS, MAINE. THE COVER MATERIAL WAS SUPPLIED BY DUROID PRODUCTS, INC., NEW YORK